THOSE POWERFUL YEARS

The South Coast and Los Angeles
1887-1917

Joseph S. O'Flaherty

ILLUSTRATED

An Exposition-Lochinvar Book

Exposition Press   *Hicksville, New York*

First Edition

© 1978 by Joseph S. O'Flaherty

All rights reserved, including the right of reproduction in whole
or in part, in any form or by any means, electronic or mechanical,
including photocopying, recording, or by any information storage
and retrieval system. No part of this book may be reproduced
without permission in writing from the publisher. Inquiries should
be addressed to Exposition Press, Inc., 900 South Oyster Bay
Road, Hicksville, N.Y. 11801

Library of Congress Cataloging in Publication Data

O'Flaherty, Joseph S.   Those Powerful Years.

1. California, Southern—History.   2. Los Angeles—History.
I. Title.

ISBN 0-682-49103-9   979.4′9′04   78-53590

ISBN 0-682-49103-9

Printed in the United States of America

For my father and grandfather,
JOSEPH AND DANIEL—
engineers and builders
during those powerful years

Contents

Acknowledgments

The writer is grateful to the Henry E. Huntington Library and its staff for the opportunity to examine the daily journals of Henry W. O'Melveny and the papers of Jackson A. Graves. The source notes on quotations in this book reference these data as O'Melveny MSS or Graves MSS.

John O'Melveny, managing partner for many years of his father's law firm, O'Melveny & Meyers, was certainly correct when he indicated to the writer that this reservoir of excellent source material at the Huntington Library had been too long neglected.

Foreword

Occasionally a generation seems twice blessed. Certainly those involved in the decade or so on each side of the turn of the last century in the United States knew that their glass of life was half-full and far indeed from being half-empty. More important they believed that with just an additional effort they could markedly improve the affairs of their world. And why not? The previous half-century had demonstrated an explosive chain reaction of new inventions and social concepts, obviously far exceeding any comparable period which had gone before.

In one seven-league step the nation had moved from a muddy morass of impassable trails to a network of railroads whose steel tracks effectively bound together a country of vast distances and formidable terrain. It was evident that steam, electricity and then oil would provide the energy to move the derricks to move the world. Disease would crumble; look at the astounding public health results with the spread of comprehension of the germ theory of illness. Terrible and distressing things like drunkenness, sweatshops, wretched slums and boodling in the cities could all be cured. The exhausting economic depression of the 1890s could be taken in stride and prosperity would surely follow. The idle, arid lands of the West would now bloom because of irrigation; the miraculous change in the forbidding Colorado Desert was proof enough. Manifest Destiny meant much more to that generation than merely some jingo rationalization for taking over the remote islands of the Philippines halfway around the world.

It was a grand time to live, and possibly the best place to be was southern California and Los Angeles. This book deals with those powerful years on the South Coast.

11

THOSE POWERFUL YEARS

CHAPTER 1

"Hell! We're giving away the land. We're selling the climate."

For two decades after the Civil War, southern California had been systematically publicized in Europe and the United States as the magic land of climate and opportunity. Yet when the Santa Fe drove the last spike of its new railroad line through Cajon Pass in late 1885, the vacant plains of the South Coast and Los Angeles actually had less population than ten years earlier. The most stouthearted land boomer there could visualize no more than the most gradual growth.

The lethargy and lack of interest suddenly changed when a massive rate war flared up between the Southern Pacific and the Santa Fe. A long-smoldering public interest throughout the United States became a crown fire of family council and action. In tens of thousands of homes, the decision was reached to buy the bargain railroad tickets and visit or make a move to southern California, for many a sort of an Avalon at the distant end of a flimsy railroad track through a savage land.

Even husky, brawling Chicago was amazed at the hundreds of emigrant train sections bound for California and the tremendous land boom. The imminent departure of one of them created a minor traffic jam. Islands of baskets, bedrolls and corded bundles expanded almost by the minute in a widening and discommoding semicircle around the train gate. The bellowing of the gateman over the noise of locomotive whistles, escaping steam and the clangor of bells brought the passengers and their visitors in a jostling, arguing snarl through the gate to one of the sixteen or so emigrant coaches hauled by the two locomotives.

Car windows were thrown open and belongings handed up. Leaning over the windowsills the passengers had to shout their leave-taking remarks. Then the conductor looked at his watch and signaled for the preliminary departure whistle. Abruptly, there was a kind of a silence in the surrounding din. Now solemn brothers shook hands, a spare old woman reached up to kiss her son and a harried mother in the coach commenced a frantic search, the first of many, for her subteenage boys. The emigrant train moved and then, almost as if held back by the passengers and relatives who now had grave doubts, it hesitated. Again the coaches jerked forward while the old-fashioned couplings clanked heavily. The destination was Los Angeles, more than 2500 track miles away. The time was any day in 1887 and early 1888.

The driving of a spike at a temporary village called Promontory in Utah meant the completion of a transcontinental railroad in 1869, and the Southern Pacific finally came into Los Angeles from the north seven years later. The railroad continued east out of Los Angeles, meeting a Texas railhead in 1883, and two years later Santa Fe trains reached San Diego from Missouri. Until 1886 passenger fares had held at $118 for a first-class ticket and $85 for second class from Chicago, a very high figure for the day.

The Southern Pacific first cut passenger and freight rates several months after the Santa Fe began through service to San Diego. While the South Coast watched with almost disbelief at what appeared to be a disastrous and futile rate war, the highest fare for a railroad ticket between Pacific Coast and Missouri points was fifteen dollars near the end of 1886. Finally the Santa Fe reduced it to ten dollars and, for a few hours, one dollar per head. With the low passenger fares the people came—first by the hundreds and then by the scores of thousands.

And a good many of them were foreign emigrants, part of the high waves of European migration after the Civil War. The Southern Pacific deposited 120,000 passengers in the small town of Los Angeles within a year's time, and the Santa Fe had three or four trains a day arriving at the foot of Second Street near the Los Angeles River.

While the emigrant train slowly clacked across the frogs and switches of the sprawling railroad yards of Chicago, the passengers watched the sun gleaming from the innumerable wavery glass windows of the fresh stone and brick office buildings and factories constructed since the city's devastating 1871 fire. Shortly the suburbs were dropping away as the train picked up speed. Then the travelers turned away from the passing landscape to examine each other and settle down for a week of communal and highly uncomfortable living. Their creaking wooden car, a long open box inside, was badly lit by several coal oil (kerosene) lamps which fluctuated from pale flickering lights to moribund glimmers. The folding seats flattened into beds of sorts, and straw cushions could be rented. Each end of the coach had a primitive toilet and a coal stove with one of the stoves designed for cooking. *Harper's Weekly* of the period was particularly impressed with the variety and strength of the odors in the coach during the progress of the journey:

"At the start the cars are rude but cleanly. Plenty of water is provided. Some effort is made, too, to keep the air fresh and the car decent, but this is very difficult. Most of the passengers are little accustomed to ventilation or to cleanly habits. Pipes are lighted, meals are spread in which sausage, cheese, garlic and sauerkraut form prominent elements, and their mingled odors combine with the smoke of cheap tobacco to render the cars insupportable. Then there are children, and sometimes sick ones; there are men and women who regard dirt as part of natural protection against cold; there are still other sources of malodorous emanations which would make a resident of ancient Cologne hold his experienced nose."

Most of the occupants of an emigrant coach had a life-long immunity to strong smells and the rest of the inmates endured. The knifing cold of the winter storms was another matter entirely. The passengers ringing the stoves would be sweating in what seemed to be desert heat. Fifteen feet away, other passengers would be convinced they were freezing to death as wind eddies swirled down the aisle from the non-vestibuled doorways and through the warped window frames. When the emigrant train repeatedly creaked on to a sidetrack to allow a regular passenger or fast freight train through, the summer flies swarmed aboard, attracted by the food particles dispersed about the cars. Coming into the deserts of the West where the summer peak temperatures could easily be 120 degrees or more, the passengers braced themselves for the heat while sucking on carefully hoarded lemon drops or drinking a concoction of concentrated lemonade to relieve parched mouths. With the oppressive dead air in the coach, the windows were thrown wide open which meant that sandy dust-devils, liberally intermixed with cinders and occasional live coals from the locomotives' stacks, swirled inside.

This was the kind of weather when one worried even more about one's husband, brother or son riding in a "Zulu" freight car loaded with the family's possessions and livestock. If there was enough traffic the railroad would organize a Zulu train, otherwise the cars would be included in a regular freight. Weather and lack of water were constant hazards. Plain assault and sometimes murder by tramps and hoboes was more than a remote possibility.

Under the best of circumstances whether it was an emigrant train, Zulu car or Pullman, the poorly ballasted track and the excessive number of curves in hilly and mountain regions, made train sickness common. The creaking and pounding of the older hard-springed equipment was obnoxious and tiring, particularly accentuated by car wheels thudding across excessive rail gaps. It still was a long way to California.

Day after day of peering through a grimy window at an empty expanse of land was certain to make many a tired or train-sick passenger discouraged, if not frightened of the West. The sight of bleached bones of buffalo, cattle and horses strewn beside the track and the limitless horizon of lonesome plains, deserts or mountains relieved only by an occasional sod hut in the intermediate distance began to cast a pall over even the most exuberant spirits. The passenger's reassurance, as he told himself constantly, was that with all of the delays he was traveling in an hour the distance which would require a long and exhausting day by prairie schooner, less than a generation earlier.

A sure sign of the cars' rapid progress west and an important novelty of the trip was when the conductor ceremoniously announced that all watches were to be set back an hour because the train had progressed into what was just being called the next "standard time zone." It was only several years before that the nation's railroads had finally adopted Prof. Charles F. Dowd's invention of the time-zone system, ending a welter of sometimes deadly railroad confusion because of local time.

Passengers were sternly warned by guidebooks that the trains were often late arriving at planned stops for meals, and the publicized diners for the Pullman people were often not available when scheduled. Breakfast might be late in the morning and supper near midnight if at all. Large and well-provisioned lunch baskets were recommended for both Pullman and second-class passengers. Many a youngster's principal recollection of the long trip was hungrily watching his mother go through the ceremony of pulling the basket from underneath the seat and carefully opening the packages, boxes and bottles of olives and pickles. Whereupon she would unfeelingly ration delectable portions of fried chicken, ham, hard-boiled eggs, cakes, bread with jam and hard candy.

But carry-on food supplies diminished or spoiled during the passing days. To his dismay the average traveler learned about the privately owned eating houses along the railroad lines with their atrocious food and sharp practices. Often their owners "were in cahoots with train crews. The charge was four bits [fifty cents] in advance. No sooner had the customer paid and started to eat, than the bell rang, the whistle blew and the passenger had to dash back aboard the train, most of his meal uneaten [and uncooked]. The beanery then paid off the train crew at a dime a passenger and waited for the next victims."

Only the Santa Fe with its Harvey Houses offered to all passengers food outstanding both for quality and price. The Fred Harvey restaurants, usually located in Santa Fe train depots, were arranged so that while the passengers ate, the locomotive and the rolling stock could be watered, fueled and checked. The dining room meals with standard entrees were fifty cents, and cost still less at the lunch counters. Even at Holbrook, Arizona, where the first Harvey House consisted of five battered boxcars, the interior was furnished in the Harvey tradition of English silverplate, Irish linen, crystal and bouquets of fresh flowers—all of this in a howling wilderness. A mile from the Holbrook depot the engineer on an arriving train blew his whistle. This was the signal for the waitresses, or the Harvey Girls as they were known all along the route of the Santa Fe, to place the first course on the table while thick and tender steaks from Chicago were put on to fry.

The guidebooks had advice for the train passenger on a great many subjects. Constipation was to be cured by taking Seidlitz powders or a teaspoon of Rochelle salt. The kit of a traveler should have a bottle of paregoric to relieve diarrhea and pain, and a flask of aromatic spirits of ammonia for fainting spells. A bottle of good whiskey, presumably for medical use, was considered essential. Conviviality and becoming "one of the family" was strongly recommended to the travelers. It was pointed out that "elderly ladies and children are the earliest passengers to start the social ball rolling while . . . a young man with a violin, or a young lady with a sweet voice is a great acquisition to any party." The method suggested for insuring group participation from the last holdouts in the Pullman was to have a child stand on a vacant seat and throw a string around the neck of an unsuspecting passenger in front of him while "crying in childish glee, 'Get up, horsey!'" Even if such extensive conviviality did not result in charges of mayhem, the four-day trip from Kansas City must have been nerve-racking to many passengers who were neither elderly ladies nor children.

It made little difference whether it was the few nabobs riding in the luxury cars, the large number of Pullman and coach passengers or the thousands in the emigrant trains. All knew when the beginning of the end of their wearily protracted trip had arrived. This was when the trains added locomotives for the passage from the choking alkali of the desert through the passes of the bristling mountains cupping the plains and rolling hills of the South Coast. Almost on signal, the dog-eared volumes which dealt with the wonders of southern California were brought out and read once again. The passengers commenced to gossip about powerful Western personalities like railroad czar Collis P. Huntington and the notorious Lucky Baldwin, his current amorous affair and his rumored tens of thousands of acres of rich South Coast holdings. Through all the talk there was a common question—what really was this distant land they were about to enter?

The sally points of the railroads into the South Coast were the 7000-foot tunnel through San Fernando Mountain to the northwest, Cajon Pass from the high desert to the northeast, and San Gorgonio Pass from the lower deserts to the east. After hundreds of miles of dry, forbidding terrain, it was the same fresh miracle for the train passengers, just as for the wagon trains a generation ahead of them, to sense the distant ocean sea breezes vaguely touching the flanks of the brush-wooded mountains. A number of the passengers were already prospects for the first echelon of real estate salesmen or land boomers who boarded the trains at San Fernando, San Bernardino or Colton, where bundles of the three daily Los Angeles newspapers were put on the cars. This was the earliest real sense of the heady boom excitement taking place in Los Angeles, the little town of a dozen or so thousand people only a score of months before. While the trains passed by the young orange groves in the bright sun, and through showplaces like Lucky Baldwin's Santa Anita ranch, it was increasingly easy to accept the fact that some of these groves were actually selling for more than a thousand dollars an acre, an unheard-of figure for land in the East or Midwest. Even so, none of the outlanders was prepared for what they found in this frontier region when the coaches pulled into the Santa Fe depot, or when they craned out the windows while their Southern Pacific train creaked down Alameda Street into the cavernous and still incomplete Arcade Station between Fourth and Sixth streets.

The Arcade Station was the result of a recent decision of the Southern Pacific to build "a magnificent railroad station . . . a splendid arcade" in an attempt to counteract the South Coast popularity of the Santa Fe and to handle the astounding influx of passengers. A huge thing for a Western depot, it readily swallowed a number of trains inside its massive shed. A ninety-foot roof arch, supported by an iron network of beams and struts, echoed and reechoed the frenetic train noises of a pulsing station. When the passengers straggled up from the trains through the exit areas into the arcade, they were enveloped by a swirling throng. The crowd brought with it another assortment of sound and the waving of name signs and placards carried by farm colony groups, back-home country societies and friends of friends meeting the newcomers. Intermixed with these were the home-based echelon of land boomers along with touts from rooming houses, saloons and questionable hotels; all handing out cards while a pickpocket continued his usual work in the milling crowd. On the outskirts were the ice-cream vendors and the tamale-enchilada carts, the latter a curiosity and one of the few visible vestiges of the Californio period.

Finding a baggage porter or hackman who was not on a commission basis for a tout or a land boomer was almost impossible. During the hack ride of the well-to-do to the Nadeau or Westminster hotels, the driver would spend the trip describing the tremendous opportunities offered by several of the innumerable land tracts being subdivided. Any sensible traveler by this time must have reached the conclusion that he had arrived in a considerably overrated earthly paradise. Nevertheless, while wary, he would naturally be alert for a substantial opportunity.

To the Boom incomers there were two diametrically opposing views of the prospects for the South Coast and Los Angeles. Perhaps the Los Angeles *City Directory* of the time best represented one of them. It had to be the least popular. The directory showed only a minuscule amount of manufacturing and a minimum number of service firms in a small regional trading center of a huge semiarid tributary area. And this region was in an isolated corner pocket of the United States rimmed by mountains and deserts to the north and east, a rock-ribbed Mexican territory to the south and a vacant ocean to the west. Any logical person could have asked of the land promoters like the well-known Nathaniel C. Carter, the flamboyant Lucky Baldwin or the horde of other speculators why property in this empty region of casual rainfall was appreciating in value so rapidly. When one prospect told Baldwin that $200 an acre for bare land and an uncertain water supply was a very rich price, the promoter's cocky retort was: "Hell! We're giving away the land. We're selling the climate."

This cockiness and enthusiasm of Lucky Baldwin carried a great deal of weight with the prospective buyers. They knew his national reputation for successful Western speculation in mining and his heavy property commitment on the South Coast, made more than a decade earlier. Also in a convoluted way Baldwin's complete indifference to public censure of his personal life seemed somehow to give credence to his evident passion for the lands of southern California.

At least part of the time Elias J. Baldwin detested his "Lucky" nickname. One of an extensive breed of frontier egotists he felt he had an unfailing instinct for the main chance, much as Howard Hughes believed this about himself three-quarters of a century later. According to Baldwin "to be a success you've got to keep your eye on two ends—when to go into a deal and

when to get out—and don't waste any time doing either."
While "E. J.," as he was known to his friends, preached the
foregoing much more than he practiced it in either his business
or personal affairs, Baldwin indeed had pyramided and sold
out his speculative positions in the Comstock bonanzas in Nevada
at the right times.

The mining speculator had fallen in love with the San
Gabriel Valley when he came from San Francisco in 1874 to
look at some gold-mining acreage in Bear Valley on top of the
San Bernardino Mountains. Baldwin paid a high price of
$200,000 for the 6000-acre Rancho Santa Anita a few months
later, and he was quietly determined to acquire additional
acreage. Baldwin saw a probable opportunity when he lent the
Temple & Workman Bank what eventually amounted to $310,000.
In return the speculator received a blanket mortgage on all of
the landholdings of the two bank partners, F. P. F. Temple and
William Workman, plus 2200 acres of prime land adjacent to
his Santa Anita ranch and owned by Juan Matias Sanchez.

The bank partners did not realize that Baldwin may have
cold-bloodedly evaluated their bank's prospects and the strong
likelihood of its failure. The bank did fail a few weeks later.
Baldwin, at his leisure, foreclosed on his blanket mortgage leaving Temple, Workman and Sanchez landless and virtually pen-
niless. William Workman committed suicide; unquestionably
the most brutal blow of all for him was to see an old and
cherished friend, Juan Matias Sanchez, lose his hereditary holdings. F. P. F. Temple was a broken man. Shortly after Workman's death he had a stroke and died several years later.

E. J. Baldwin ignored such matters. He had achieved his
purpose and was absorbed in his own affairs. The speculator
now owned tens of thousands of acres within a day's ride of
Los Angeles—the Ranchos Merced, Potrero Grande, Potrero de
Felipe Lugo, Puente, and the hill portions of the Ciengas along
with key property in Los Angeles. The Santa Anita remained
the heartland of Baldwin's ranching complex and racehorse activities and became a prime land boom attraction.

This unconventional and amoral man was born in 1828 near a crossroads village in Ohio. E. J. Baldwin wandered to the West and ended up in the later stages of the Gold Rush with his first of four (or perhaps five) wives and a six-year-old daughter, Clara. By 1863 he was divorced and Clara, now sixteen, had made the first of her own numerous marriages. Meanwhile Baldwin was in the process of constructing a substantial reputation for being a lone business wolf at the fringes of a speculative mining herd who slashed in and out quickly.

Yet the notoriety of his personal life exceeded his improved business fortunes. Baldwin had, and continued to have, a sustained sexual interest in a succession of very young women, irrespective of the concomitant and perennial heart balm, seduction and paternity suits. His consistent attitude concerning these attractive females seemed to be: "When tempted, succumb at once, and avoid the struggle."

Of somewhat more than medium height, Lucky Baldwin habitually wore high-crowned, broad-brimmed black hats. A long frock coat (in which he usually carried a small pistol or derringer) gave a superficial illusion of slimness. Actually, he was a muscular, well-built man, a brawler at heart, who selectively sought a fight even into his seventies. In his later years Baldwin shaved off his well-trimmed full beard while keeping a drooping mustache, so typical of the period. His numerous marriages had no evident effect in stemming his continued and well-publicized liaisons. Women shot at him at least twice, once "through the left arm at the level of the heart as he was leaving his private dining room on the second floor of [San Francisco's] Baldwin Hotel" and another time in a Los Angeles courtroom where the bullet brushed his hair and buried itself in the ceiling. For years he and his scandals were pure joy to the pretabloid editors as a certified circulation booster, and to the morality forces of the Temperance Movement as a prime example of the basic male iniquity which could and would be overcome.

The financial luck of the libertine and speculator turned for the worse in the early 1880s when he developed a chronic cash problem in his far-flung property involvements. Almost immediately Baldwin demonstrated an ability to make a relatively few dollars go a long way by the simple expedient of not paying his bills until all legal recourse had been taken. Baldwin obstinately refused to sell the bulk of his lands, and the great boom was a blessing for him because it enabled him to offer limited acreage at rich prices. His known reluctance to relinquish his lands helped to give him the reputation of a superb salesman. Unquestionably, he was a key factor in maintaining the Boom's momentum on the South Coast.

In keeping with Baldwin's usual practice, his land promotional moves were planned well ahead. Typical was his handling of the Santa Fe which found his holdings a major barrier to direct and speedy entry into Los Angeles. With the subdivision of Arcadia and the surrounding district in mind, and envisioning the construction of a nearby hotel to be called the Oakwood, Baldwin readily gave the Santa Fe a right-of-way through his land early in the Boom. The only proviso he made was that passenger trains stop at the Santa Anita station on signal.

A long-time ranch manager for the landholder always liked to tell the story, undoubtedly embellished, of the time when he first discovered that *all* Santa Fe trains stopped on signal at the Santa Anita station. One day the manager and Lucky Baldwin were returning to the home ranch from a Santa Fe depot north of San Bernardino. The famous speculator asked at the window for tickets to Santa Anita and was informed by the agent that there was an eight-hour wait because the through train, just coming into the depot, did not stop at the ranch station:

"Baldwin looked the agent over coldly. 'It doesn't, eh?' he said at last. 'Then give me a telegraph blank.' The blank was provided, and Baldwin wrote: 'J. F. Falvey, Superintendent, Santa Anita Ranch. Put 200 men to work at once tearing up Santa Fe tracks through my ranch. E. J. Baldwin.'

"The local station agent, who was also the telegraph operator, read the message and his eyes popped. 'Oh!' he said. 'Oh! You're

Mr. Baldwin . . . certainly, Mr. Baldwin. Here is your ticket. I'll speak to the conductor.' "

After listening to men like Lucky Baldwin and watching train sections arrive by the dozen, even the most skeptical of the newcomers began to consider seriously the land boomers' assertions that 10,000,000 acres of southern California land would easily support an agricultural population of 5,000,000 people and that another 5,000,000 would live in the cities. It was an intoxicating concept. There was 60,000,000 population in the rest of the United States plus all of western Europe to draw on. "After all, the climate was wonderful, and the soil could support a great population; so why should not these predictions come true? The man who came to scoff, remained to speculate."

CHAPTER 2

"To call it a craze or a bubble is the veriest nonsense"

The roll of drums and the blast of trumpets were sure to attract the attention of a newcomer while he strolled out of his Los Angeles hotel or boardinghouse on a spring day in 1887. Coming down the street was a horse-drawn omnibus filled on the inside with a brass band and draped on the outside with cloth banners announcing a grand land auction. The auction sale of lots could well be at any one of a dozen or more subdivisions currently being promoted on the South Coast in this peak year of land sales. The sign on the omnibus of greatest interest to even the most casual visitor was the huge block lettering in red: "A FREE RIDE AND A FREE LUNCH." What better, pleasant and no-cost way was there to see part of the South Coast? Obviously, there was none. The promoters had no difficulty in attracting crowds to their land sales. A typical scene at one of the more splendiferous auctions included:

"A brass band of some thirty pieces . . . the performers resplendent in purple and gold and glittering helmets, with a drum-major lost in swathings and bandings of scarlet and blue, twirling a gilded staff beneath a bale of crimson wool, while a caterer in a dress-suit, with white necktie and diamond pin, was bustling to and fro preparing a sumptuous lunch. Hundreds of people were already on the ground, and barouches and broughams, drawn by sleek horses in silver-plated harness driven by combinations of silk hats, white neckties and dogskin gloves were steadily unloading . . . retired merchants and stock-brokers, grain-dealers, liquor dealers, lawyers and doctors, nearly all of whom . . . had come out for a picnic at the expense of a stranger.

"None of them seemed to think there was anything mean in thus accepting the hospitality of the stranger when they had not the remotest idea of buying anything. And, strangely enough, the owner of the property did not think there was anything mean about it either; for he smiled and rubbed his hands as he looked over this portion of the crowd. These folks seemed to give him far more satisfaction than dozens of others who wore a business air, but little evidence of superfluous wealth. . . . The owner of the property, an old hand from the East who had lately bought it on an option . . . proposed making some money out of it before the time of the next payment came around."

That old hand from the East made money out of the auction. So much so in fact that in his next promotion he actually invested more of his own money. And so it went.

The newspapers and their special supplements were in the forefront of the Boom parade, and printers setting type at the three local newspapers could earn incentive bonuses equal to their daily pay. The copy they set sometimes was bad poetry, like the Vernon promotion:

Sweet Vernon, loveliest village of the plain
Where health and plenty cheers the laboring swain,
Where smiling Spring its earliest visit paid
And parting Summer's lingering blooms delayed

The poster-type copy, the most popular, was in many formats and could occupy a quarter to a full newspaper page:

Boom   **Boom**

Arcadia!

Boom   **Boom**

One full-page advertisement had the caption, "Veni, Vidi, Vici!" while announcing:

Magnificent Monte Vista!

The Gem of the Mountains!

The Queen of the Valley!

Some promoters evidently liked alliteration in their posters, typified by this Santa Ana advertisement:

THIS IS PURE GOLD

SANTA ANA

The Metropolis of Southern California's Fairest Valley!

Chief Among Ten Thousand, or the One

ALTOGETHER LOVELY!

BEAUTIFUL! BUSY! BUSTLING!

IT CAN'T BE BEAT!

The town now has the biggest kind of a
big, big boom. . . . . . .

A Great Big Boom!
And you can accumulate Ducats by Investing!

Pseudo news articles were used extensively to promote subdivision offerings and real estate firms, very often on the front page:

BARGAINS IN REAL ESTATE

Do not fail to read the advertisements of J. C. Bryan in the "wants" column of today's *Times*. This firm is having great success in handling city, suburban, and ranch property. You will make no mistake in placing any kind of real estate in their hands for sale or exchange.

Ben E. Ward's promotions and auction sales of Santa Monica land were equal to the efforts of any widely known real estate boomer. He ran private trains from Los Angeles and sold town lots, acre parcels and five- and ten-acre farms. Ten percent of the price was to be paid "at the fall of the hammer" with the balance of the first quarter of the selling price payable on receipt of the agreement. The remaining three quarterly payments were due in six, twelve and eighteen months. Typical of Ward's advertising in June of 1887 was:

HO, FOR THE BEACH!
Tomorrow   Tomorrow
Grand Auction Sale
at
Santa Monica
350 — Acres — 350

One of the Grandest Panoramic Views the Human Eye ever rested upon, including Ballona, Lake and Harbor, with its out-going and in-coming vessels, the Grand Old Pacific, the handsome new Hotel Arcadia, while in the distance may be seen Los Angeles, the Pride of All, and the coming city of two hundred thousand people.

Nothing appeared to be impossible. Fifteen large wooden hotels were eventually erected on the vacant plains in townsites scattered about the South Coast and any number more were planned or underway. These hotels were supposed to house the expected substantial number of prospective buyers for lots and later serve as bustling centers of their surrounding country-sides. After all, a major Santa Ana subdivision sold $80,000 (a million dollars in mid-1970s' money) of lots in two hours. For people who timed such affairs, and there were many, some miles away the Fullerton auction sale was $90,000 but it required a half-day to reach that total.

After reading the advertisements, making several auction trips and being immersed in the gossip of fortunes quickly made, a curious alchemy of change would occur in a thoughtful new-comer's perspective. Initially he had been cynical of the pyramiding land values. But he also watched the dozens of train sections which deposited succeedingly higher waves of fresh arrivals on the South Coast. About then, the outlander first might quote the views of the local capitalists, initially with elaborate casualness. By mid-1887 the term "capitalist" was used on the South Coast to describe a man who, on paper, was reputed to be worth at least a million dollars. More and more often this solid-sounding appellation appeared in directories and letter-heads of land syndicates and water corporations. The local breed of capitalists went out of its way to stress the underlying dictum of sober investment in land. The capitalist certainly did expect a minimum investment appreciation much above the standards of the staid East, with twenty percent appreciation per year usually mentioned. Of course, with just modest good fortune, much more than that figure could be expected.

The shift to the speculative psychology was complete when the convert could strongly support the view of the Los Angeles *Tribune* in May of 1887, as the newspaper snorted about critical comments on South Coast land speculation: "To call it a craze or a bubble is the veriest nonsense."

When speculation exploded in early 1886, the direction which Los Angeles would grow was of paramount interest to the urban land boomers. Only a very few years earlier Remi Nadeau, ignoring the advice of astute friends like Harris Newmark, had built a four-story hotel, the tallest building in Los Angeles, practically on the outskirts of the downtown area at First and Spring streets. Nadeau was right, and the commercial operations of the town followed him south from the several blocks immediately around the Plaza, the traditional business center. At the height of the Boom speculation, even parcels at Sixth and Main streets on the southern fringe of the new commercial district had increased forty times in value in four years.

Owners of land on the bluffs east of Los Angeles could practically taste the tantalizing odor of sky-high prices being paid for in-town lots, located such a short distance away. The only barrier was a river, nearly bone-dry a good part of the year. Outlanders had difficulty understanding why this joke of a river could be any real obstacle to the expansion of the city to the north and east, particularly when it was crossed by seven bridges by the late 1880s. They learned after the arrival of a series of heavy seasonal rains. Near the end of the dry season in early October, the Los Angeles River was a small stream of water "which a good vaulter could leap over" wandering desultorily over a wide sand bed studded with heavy stones. Two months later the stream could be a raging torrent rolling the same stones along the bottom and crazily spinning tree trunks in its ravenous current. Except in the major flood years some of the bridges remained in commission, but crossing the river was chancy enough that Boyle Heights and the suburbs immediately east remained a residential area.

Western growth of the city was also retarded—in this instance by a series of rolling hills. So the logical expansion of Los Angeles was to be on the plains south and southwest from the Plaza. Figueroa Street (earlier Grasshopper and then Pearl) and Grand Avenue (earlier Charity), subdivided south of Ninth Street, quickly became a prime residential district and brought additional subdivisions.

Because of the high ground to the west of the Plaza, the original center of El Pueblo de Nuestra Senora, la Reina de Los Angeles, de Porciuncula (speedily abbreviated to Los Angeles), the trails coming in from San Pedro and the southern ranchos during Spanish and Mexican days stayed on the plains at the base of the hills. This meant they were cocked in a northeasterly direction as they tracked toward the Plaza. After Alta California was ceded to the United States in 1848, American surveyors laid out standard grid or township lines on cardinal compass points outside the original pueblo limits. These lines became the direction of the new roads. So later streets like Adams, with its elegant residential development after the Boom, bent sharply when they changed direction to due west when crossing the old pueblo boundaries at Hoover Street.

The Boom brought a number of subdivisions well south of Adams Street and even west of Rosedale Avenue (later Normandie), undoubtedly influenced by the establishment of the University of Southern California. One of these published a more erudite flyer than most:

"LET US REASON TOGETHER. . . . The people thronging to this beautiful city should not be met by an increase in values that would force them to go elsewhere. . . . Thousands who are coming to see us with their families for shelter from the frightful storms of winter and the biting cold of northern regions, have no money to fill the pockets of hungry speculators. Let us welcome them without fleecing them, and offer them lands without leaving an empty purse to meet future necessities."

It was a foregone conclusion that speculation in countryside land on the South Coast would first take place in the San Gabriel Valley. This beautiful and fertile district with its overhanging mountains to the north and its gigantic sunflowers on the foothill slopes was the route of the Santa Fe and the Southern Pacific from the Cajon and San Gorgonio passes. Shortly the young town of Pasadena in the western part of the valley became the center of its urban development.

For a great many people over the next half-century, Pasadena with its surrounding groves and orchards lapping at the base of the mountains represented all of southern California at its idyllic best. David M. Berry and his San Gabriel Orange Grove Association bought 4000 acres of land west of present-day Fair Oaks Avenue in 1874. This turned out to be the nucleus of Pasadena district development along with adjoining acreage carefully subdivided by J. de Barth Shorb. Pasadena and the Boom became synonymous. Five daily trains arrived from Los

Angeles; land was selling for a thousand dollars an acre and going up. The beating of hammers and the rasping of saws continued to add to the enveloping smell of fresh-cut lumber. And that Boom-time odor was more addictive than alcohol. Within a year Pasadena had a population of 6500, a group of satellite villages like San Marino and an unshakable confidence in its manifest destiny.

The plains and rolling hills stretching eastward from Pasadena to San Bernardino and Riverside were platted with townsite after townsite along and near the lines of the two railroads. San Gabriel Valley speculation reached its peak in late 1887, and Azusa probably exemplified the greed and hysteria excesses of the period. The promotion of this townsite located in a dry and sandy streambed strewn with gravel and boulders was highly successful and equally controversial. Because of extravagant newspaper advertising and word-of-mouth publicity about Azusa ". . . buyers stood in line all night before the sale opened; the person who held second place in line supposedly refused an offer of $1000 to give it up, and the eager investor who held fifth place reluctantly sold his location for $500. . . . Not one in a hundred had seen the townsite. Fewer still expected to live there." The unprepossessing Azusa site selected by the syndicate headed by Jonathan S. Slauson and John D. Bicknell sold a remarkable $280,000 of lots in the first day, and the venture had an estimated profit of $1,175,000 in two months' time. Even in the caveat emptor environment of the times, the syndicate's sales methods were sharply criticized by many including the *Times.* However, Slauson and his partners had a strident defender in the *Tribune* who felt "the *Times* is worse than a mad dog" and was determined "to create bad blood in the community."

The tiny seaside resort of Long Beach was heavily promoted in such rapidly growing inland towns as Pasadena. The touted resort was reached by a miniature steam railroad which traversed Cerritos Slough from the Wilmington station of the Southern Pacific. The usual large wooden hotel with numerous cupolas and spires was built on the low bluff across from today's Lincoln Park with dressing rooms for bathers on ". . . a beach of hard white sand, as level as a floor extending many miles each way. This beach is a perfect racecourse, and during the season spanking teams from the city can always be seen dashing over the superb driveway."

Shortly to become a powerful and balanced prototype of the larger South Coast cities, Long Beach had a dispiriting beginning under the name of Willmore City in the early 1880s. William E. Willmore, a kindly, honest man and an unlucky promoter, organized his American Colony Land, Water and Town Association which acquired from the Cerritos Ranch 4000 acres of oceanfront land on a performance contract basis. He advertised the lands in Eastern newspapers and magazines at prices from twelve to twenty-five dollars an acre. Even at these prices acreage sales were slow although flowing artesian wells were brought in around present-day Lakewood Village. The well water was extremely soft, but it also had a substantial sulphur content and was slightly yellowish in color. Long Beach's distinctive water flavor and color, supplemented by a vague rotten egg odor when lawns were watered in the summer's hot sun, was a subject of bad jokes and caustic tourist comment for a long time.

Willmore, the unlucky promoter, finally defaulted on his performance contract less than two years before the initial Boom surge. One business failure after another dogged him until his death in 1901 at the County Poor Farm in Downey. His oceanfront lands were taken over by a syndicate headed by Robert M. Widney who renamed the development "Long Beach," promoted it successfully as a seaside resort and built a legendary railroad of sorts. Widney constructed a narrow-gauge horsecar line which ran on an undulating, swampy roadbed and across three bridges to the Wilmington depot utilizing three-by-four redwood ties and three-inch pine timbers laid on the ties as rails. The horse-drawn cars soon showed a discouraging propensity for going off the track especially when the wooden rails weathered and cracked under the load. From then on the shaky little line was locally known as the "G.O.P. R.R." or "Get Out and Push Railroad" even after steel rails on a standard-gauge track were laid. A small steam locomotive was a major equipment addition during the Boom which prompted a bit of doggerel about the tiny railroad in the local press:

> *Oh, fireman, fill the teacup,*
> *The water's running low,*
> *And you'd better scratch a parlor match*
> *For fuel as we go;*
> *And scare the squirrels off the track,*
> *Before they wreck the car;*
> *Oh, everybody, get out and push,*
> *On the G.O.P. R.R.*

After the rosy vision of being the seaport of Los Angeles was blasted by the Southern Pacific in the 1870s, Santa Monica stopped calling itself the "Zenith City by the Sunset Sea" and shrewdly publicized itself to be the prime ocean resort for the South Coast. The community was one of the first outlying districts to feel the early effects of land speculation. The town's large hotel of the Boom period was the Arcadia, named after a prominent Californio, Arcadia Bandini de Baker, who had remarried after the death of Abel Stearns, the great landholder of years earlier. Santa Monica and South Santa Monica (later Ocean Park) had a solid growth, certainly due in part to the 300-acre donation made by Mrs. de Baker and Senator John P. Jones to the Federal Government for the establishment of a war veteran facility in southern California.

The National Home for Disabled Volunteer Soldiers was located in 1887 near a crossroads village of Sawtelle in the wheat fields east of Santa Monica. Initial construction of the "Old Soldiers' Home" (as it was popularly called for the next several generations) consisted of a wooden hospital, barracks and chapel for a thousand men. The location of the facility on the South Coast was considered a major coup in the region's drive toward attaining national recognition, and it was also one of the prime reasons for the building of an interurban during the 1890s stretching from the San Fernando Valley to Santa Monica.

The Boom found the fertile eastern end of the San Fernando Valley to be wheat fields from the mountains to the horizon. "Glendale" was selected as the name of a townsite in the early 1880s, but years went by before the post office would accept the name for a mailing address. Both Glendale and Burbank land boomers emphasized the location of the villages on the Southern Pacific main line south to Los Angeles, and the Burbank promoters almost (but not quite) said that the passenger trains stopped there. If a prospective lot buyer drew such an erroneous inference, it was too bad, but the boomers felt he was getting a land bargain under any circumstances.

The Santa Fe completed a loop rail line from Riverside via Orange to Los Angeles and thence to Redondo Beach, reaching tidewater in August of 1888. With the Santa Fe encouraging business in the triangle of Santa Ana, Anaheim and Orange and the Southern Pacific building an extension to Santa Ana, the agricultural development of what was shortly to be Orange County in 1889 had a solid foundation. But it was San Diego which belatedly came to roaring life with the arrival of the transcontinental road of the Santa Fe.

Nothing ever seemed to go right for San Diego which "crawled along for years like a starved dwarf, wandering among trees laden with fruit beyond his reach." It seemed incredible to the little town of 1500 people "living largely on faith, hope and climate" that a shallow, saltwater lagoon in back of San Pedro and more than twenty miles from Los Angeles would first be developed by Federal moneys in the early 1870s while San Diego had a fine natural harbor only a hundred miles away. The little town's railroad experience had been equally disheartening. Time after time San Diego was going to be the ocean terminal of a transcontinental railroad via the southern route, and time after time the railroad planning came to nothing.

Finally, with the Santa Fe's California Southern, the long-sought railroad connection was completed. And then to San Diego's dismay shortly there was evidence that the Santa Fe really intended to have its western terminal in Los Angeles.

In the early months of the land speculation, Los Angeles appeared to have all the action while San Diego watched sourly and dispiritedly on the sidelines. This changed dramatically during the fall of 1886. In a year's time there were optimistic estimates of a town population of 50,000, and one real estate firm was moved to go several steps beyond the estimate when it said in an advertisement: "In fact, we may say that San Diego has a population of 150,000, only they are not all here yet." Shortly San Diego in a thoroughly enjoyable and newfound expansive mood was taking heavy slaps at its sister city in the north: "Los Angeles is part of our back country. Flea-infested in summer, mired in winter, roasted at noon day, chilled at night, unsewered, typhoid-afflicted, pneumoniated Los Angeles . . ." If possible, San Diego copywriters exceeded the lyrical prose and lack of veracity of their Los Angeles peers in the later Boom stages as indicated in the promotion of the arid, sunbaked acres of Tia Juana City on the American side of the border:

"It has oranges of finer flavor than those of Cypress, rustling corn equal to that of Illinois, figs more delicious than those of Smyrna, grapes more luscious than that of Portugal, olives equal to those of Italy, vines like those that creep and trail along the castled Rhine . . ."

Stung by the rapid growth of San Diego and the consequent benefits to the Santa Fe, the Southern Pacific was determined to add another fiefdom. A line would be built north from Saugus through the Santa Clara Valley to San Buenaventura and Santa Barbara. The railroad timetable quickly shortened the name of the mission town to Ventura while the railhead moved beyond and just above the thundering surf of the Pacific. Because the mountain range rose abruptly from the sea there, stagecoaches heading north had found their only passage to be at low tide through the wrack in the surf. The Southern Pacific made a blasted-out shelf in the mountainside, some forty feet above the beach, close enough that the salt spray caked the seaward windows of the coaches on a stormy day while the booming of the pounding surf at high tide made passenger conversation difficult.

The railhead reached Santa Barbara in August of 1887, time enough for the town to savor some of the Boom and to explain the odor of oil oftentimes carried on the afternoon sea breeze. The latter required some interpretation to a world which knew nothing of raw petroleum. David M. Berry, no sailor, had already feelingly commented on the comforting presence of oil slicks observed from his steamer as it churned through the waters off the coast: "Near Santa Barbara vast quantities of petroleum rise to the surface of the sea and overspread and perfume a large area. Our recollections of good Saint Barbara will be that she was a messenger of peace pouring oil upon the troubled waters." If additional reason was needed to wax enthusiastic about the heavy oil seepage from the fissures on the fractured ocean floor, some of the local doctors provided a rationalization when they commented that "the oleaginous fumes wafted ashore by the prevailing winds were an effective panacea for respiratory diseases."

Because or in spite of the oleaginous fumes, Santa Barbara quickly gained a reputation as a superb tourist and health resort, aided by the construction of its Hotel Arlington, rated the equal of the Raymond in Pasadena and the Coronado across the bay from San Diego.

Much like the news of a major gold strike, word of the paper fortunes being made in South Coast land speculation spread throughout the United States. By mid-1887, hard-eyed professionals of sleazy land promotion were arriving in Los Angeles. James M. Guinn, a conscientious reporter of the times, took a dim view of the new arrivals:

"These professionals had learned the tricks of their trade

in the boom cities of the West when that great wave of immigration which began moving after the close of the war was sweeping westward from the Mississippi River to the shores of the Pacific. These came here not to build up the country, but to make money, honestly if they could not make it any other way. It is needless to say they made it the other way."

With the speculative fever mounting to almost a dancing madness in the streets, the professional operators were in their element. Chicago Park was platted in the dry streambed of the San Gabriel River with posters which showed steamers puffing up the San Gabriel. Desert sites such as Border City, Manchester, and Maynard were said to be easily accessible from Los Angeles and with adequate water. In fact they were inaccessible, precipitous lands with no water for a score of miles. Horace Bell asserted that, in one desert subdivision promotion, oranges were thrust on the spikes of large cactus surrounding the lots to be auctioned, and the eager buyers were told that these were the first of a new type of cacitrus orange grove. Certainly Elsinore was advertised to be the center of a coal-mining and manufacturing district with three- to nine-foot coal beds and readily accessible iron ore. One saving grace for many of the buyers caught up in the speculation hysteria was that there was little land sales below the ocean high-tide line. This was only because South Coast beaches shelve downward fairly rapidly and the tides are only five to seven feet. The result is a relatively small amount of exposed sand at low water.

It seemed that anything could be sold and resold while the feverish prosperity spun wildly toward what the local banking community feared was an obvious climax. Yet there was a loud public chorus of agreement with the prestigious Philip D. Armour, head of the national meat packing company. He snapped back when asked about the surging land values and pyramiding speculation: "Boom—will it break soon? There is no boom to break! This is merely the preliminary to a boom which will so outclass the present activities that its sound will be as thunder to the cracking of a hickory nut."

CHAPTER 3

"Excitement intense. Business paralyzed."

The enormous balloon of land speculation on the South Coast did not explode nor was it pricked. Rather the end of the Boom of the eighties was similar to the first hesitant and then full release of a rubberband on the balloon's stem with the resultant sough of escaping air and deflating egos. T. S. Van Dyke's contemporary description of his apocryphal General Applehead was fairly representative of the decline and fall of most of the short-lived millionaires:

"General Applehead, who had some two millions worth of property scattered about in various towns, upon which he owed a little matter of $200,000, awoke one morning soon after the lull and concluded that the little two hundred thousand might not be such a bagatelle as he had so far considered it. . . . He concluded that he would at once sell off enough to pay his debts. . . . Before he realized it, two weeks were lost in discovering that it would not sell for the same price he had been offered for it three weeks before. He at once became alarmed, and said to the agent, 'Sell it for five thousand less.'

"'All right,' said the agent, and lost two weeks more in trying to sell it for the old price so as to pocket the difference. The next month was lost in trying several other agents with about the same results, and the General finally concluded that he would have to take the field himself. . . . He hunted up a rich old chap from St. Paul who a few weeks before had made him a large offer for some of his property. But the old gentleman sucked wisdom from the head of his cane, and stared at him over his glasses with a frosty eye that blighted the General's hopes at once . . .

"The General got a few nibbles at greatly reduced prices, but the fish were so tender in the mouth that it was impossible to land them. After about two months of hard work he found himself in the position of a hunter who was willing to let go of the bear at a very reasonable discount on his expectations . . ."

The windup of the Applehead saga was bankruptcy. The General was not remotely able to pay his debts and he and his recent paper fortune disappeared from the scene. The fictitious Applehead had a great deal of company far beyond the Boom froth of "financiers and capitalists who were worth millions." There were thousands upon thousands who thought they had finally made their financial stakes only to find their townsite lots and their shares in land and water companies of little or no value, yet suddenly they owed more money than they could pay. Retail business too felt the financial collapse almost immediately throughout southern California, and numerous small enterprises such as restaurants were closed or simply abandoned.

And now there was a fairly common new feature of the landscape—a recently completed and yet deserted hotel towering awkwardly in a vacant townsite, much like the carcass of a stranded whale that had been deposited on the beach by an enormous tide. The townsite's sole occupant might be a coyote trotting down the plot's main street as indicated by stakes and signs which were already falling into gopher holes. Most of these boarded-up hotels stood unused over the years until for one reason or another they burnt down.

Concomitant with vacant buildings and lost savings was a widespread psychological trauma similar to that which was experienced by many in the Great Depression of several generations later:

"As the 'Boom' had arisen not so much out of actual advance made by the country in production and population as by the sudden elation that had come into the minds of the people, so now, as the wave receded, the greatest danger did not lie in the veritable loss of inhabitants and the diminution of combined effort so much as discouragement and apathy of those that remained. . . . A panic has been amusingly but truthfully characterized as a national fit of hysterics . . ."

The South Coast would have had a catastrophic financial collapse, not a fit of hysterics, if Isaias W. Hellman and several other bankers like him had not learned from the bitter experiences of only a decade or so earlier. They remembered well the tragedies and business depression connected with the Temple & Workman Bank failure.

Because of pyramiding land values the leading South Coast banks became more and more conservative in their lending policies. In January of 1888 when the local economy was nearing its inflationary peak, the banks had fifty percent of their deposits in cash, a remarkable achievement. It was no accident. The banks of Los Angeles headed by I. W. Hellman's Farmers and Merchants moved into an ultracautious posture by adopting increasingly stringent criteria for local stocks and bonds offered as collateral. Loans were only made on a pre-Boom value for property outside the city. There was also a firm agreement that the banks themselves would not speculate in real estate ventures. With no national banking system and only a loose skein of financial relationships between banks in different parts of the United States, the basic economic stability of an isolated region like the South Coast rested on the acumen of the local financial institutions.

All Los Angeles banks withstood the initial heavy bank runs in the spring of 1888. Concurrently, a bank debtor with sound collateral but caught in a serious liquidity squeeze found his loans extended on a month-to-month basis until he was in a position to pay his debts. Because of these policies the usual domino effect of major financial dislocations, distressed property auctions and deficiency judgments were kept to a minimum. A sophisticated performance indeed for a young banking system on an isolated South Coast. It established Isaias W. Hellman's reputation nationally as a banker and a pervading force in California affairs for the next third of a century.

Whether he wanted to or not, anybody who managed a store which had a safe ran a free safety-deposit-box service for gold dust or money in the halcyon days of the 1850s and the desperate times of the 1860s. One of these unwilling safety-deposit operators was Isaias W. Hellman who was convinced there was a better way of performing the task. After one unpleasant episode with a drunken miner he commented to a friend: "What is to prevent one of those fellows from cracking me over the head, sticking a knife into my ribs or shooting me?" Hellman settled on a different approach. He would buy the gold dust or money of the customer at current rates and set the amount up as a credit balance for the depositor who could check out the money as he pleased. The plan worked satisfactorily, and the more the young merchant thought about the financial field in general the more he was determined to make a career in banking.

Isaias W. Hellman arrived in Los Angeles with his younger brother, Herman, in 1859. Isaias, or I. W. as he was generally called, was sixteen when he left Bavaria to work in his cousin's dry goods store. Six years later he was able to buy out Portugal's clothing store on the southeast corner of Main and Commercial streets and the business flourished. Hellman invested his profits not only in store expansion but also in the careful and selective purchase of both town lots and acreage. His land investments appreciated enormously in value as time went by, but long before this occurred the young merchant changed careers. No doubt stimulated by John G. Downey opening the first bank in southern California a few months earlier, Hellman decided his own future lay in banking. His first such venture, with Francis P. F. Temple and an inactive elderly partner, William Workman, ended two years later after Hellman realized that "Mr. Temple's only qualification for a borrower was that he must be poor. I saw that doing a banking business on that basis would leave me poor also, and I dissolved the partnership."

With the ending of the Temple-Workman relationship, two strong-minded and able men came together in a banking partnership—John G. Downey, who had been governor of California in his early thirties, and Hellman. They formed the Farmers and Merchants Bank which rode through the economic crisis of the 1870s and Downey finally agreed to sell Hellman enough shares to give the younger man control.

For the next forty-four years the Los Angeles bank remained a mirror of Hellman's own financial tenets of huge cash reserves and loan conservatism. From a borrower's viewpoint this policy had an advantage. Hellman was notoriously slow in foreclosing a mortgage until he was absolutely compelled to do so. Jackson A. Graves, a close associate, once remonstrated with the banker for being far too easygoing with a borrower. Hellman's reply was: "Graves, I have to be a better man than you are, because I am a Jew. You can do things that I cannot do. If I did them, I would be criticized, while you will not be." Undoubtedly there was some truth in Hellman's comment to Graves. Much more important, one would suspect, was the banker's feeling that a borrower who met his rigorous criteria for a loan was entitled to forbearance and understanding.

Hellman also kept a close watch on the operating expenses of his enterprises. He had used Jackson A. Graves as an attorney for years yet had no hesitation in complaining to Graves about the size of lawyer's fees in an 1893 letter while saying: "I certainly have no objections for our attorneys to be well paid" and adding an afterthought that "this is written in the most friendly spirit and I hope you will treat it as such."

The brilliant financial handling of the Boom's collapse brought I. W. Hellman the presidency of the powerful Nevada Bank of San Francisco (the present Wells-Fargo is a descendant). His younger brother, Herman, took over the family's flagship bank, the Farmers and Merchants. Three years later the South Coast and Los Angeles received its full regional brunt of a national business panic followed by a disastrous depression.

Not for the last time, the South Coast found that ready transportation had disadvantages. By the early winter of 1893 the region was inundated with "tramps," unemployed men savaged by the national business panic, who rode the freight cars to escape the snow and sometimes plain hunger during the

Eastern winter. Somehow the first multitude of hungry and desperate men were fed. Then the rolling effect of the national depression struck southern California itself. Agricultural prices dropped to less than half their normal level and "crops, which could not be sold to pay the cost of harvesting and transportation, rotted on the ground; and wages fell from 25 to 50 percent below the customary rate."

The wrenching strain on the economic fabric and the nineteen banks in Los Angeles peaked in June of 1893, in much the same way as the California bank panic of nearly twenty years earlier had done. The daily journal entries of Henry W. O'Melveny, a local lawyer, reflected the mounting tension and fear in Los Angeles:

"June 20. The City Bank closed its door, or rather did not open them at 10 o'clock A.M. The same is true of the University Bank. The news produced immense excitement and by 11 o'clock a visible run on the Los Angeles National [had] begun. It kept up with increasing intensity the whole day. The run on the First National was less conspicuous but severer. My Sunday trip to the [Chicago] World's Fair is knocked into a cocked hat. All business was paralyzed. People are out on the streets, and rumors of every character in full circulation . . .

"June 21. The First National, So. Cal. National, East-Side Bank and Broadway closed their doors. The Los Angeles National is paying one person at a time a fractional part of his deposit. Excitement intense. Business paralyzed. I do not feel like doing any work.

"Blue Wednesday for Los Angeles. The news has produced great consternation. My trip to Chicago will go up the flue and I am greatly disappointed . . .

"June 22. Excitement still intense and no telling when things will resume normal position. The run on the Los Angeles National seems to be subsiding. I hope there will be a resumption speedily."

O'Melveny was correct in his June 22 comments on the Los Angeles National which just barely made it through. The First National, one of the older and larger institutions, announced that after paying out $600,000 in customer withdrawals it was forced to close the doors, and the National remained closed for a month. Other banks, like Security Savings headed by Tomas L. Duque, had been able to withstand the pressure. But now the banks' ability to remain open rested upon I. W. Hellman's leadership in quieting the serious apprehension and turmoil. He announced the shipment of $250,000 in gold coin from San Francisco, and the stacks of gold pieces were carefully displayed to maximum advantage at the Farmers and Merchants Bank. He well publicized the fact that another $250,000 shipment could be expected from the north almost immediately and more was forthcoming as required. This was enough. The run on the Farmers and Merchants and the other banks was over and the local financial position soon stabilized.

A major embezzlement provided titillating scandal to the South Coast and a series of ugly blows to a precise Isaias W. Hellman at the apex of his career. Over the objection of his brother, Herman, who was managing the operations of the Farmers and Merchants, Hellman appointed Henry J. Fleishman cashier in 1895, the second-ranking operating officer of the bank. A long-time bank employee, Fleishman had lived with the Isaias Hellmans some years earlier and many believed he was a relative. Early in 1901 the cashier simply disappeared, and all thoughts of an untoward accident were discarded when a review of the bank's books showed embezzled funds variously estimated by outsiders to total from $100,000 to more than $150,000, a huge sum.

For years there were rumors of the absconder being seen in various parts of the United States, Mexico and abroad but he was never arrested. While I. W. Hellman insisted on replacing the missing funds in excess of the $30,000 bond from his personal fortune, the Fleishman episode was the capstone of a series of disagreements between him and his brother. The younger Hellman on his own initiative resigned from the bank in 1903 along with his son, Marco.

The well-known local lawyer, Jackson A. Graves, was named by I. W. Hellman to take over the operations of the Farmers and Merchants. Later Graves indicated his reason for changing careers: "I had considerable money invested in the bank, a crisis had arisen where someone had to take hold of it, and my interest was large enough to justify my doing so."

The bank's crisis in confidence passed shortly. The regional financial and banking system easily rode out the earthquake and fire in San Francisco followed by the short-lived national panic of 1907 and was ready for the major business expansion of the 1910s. An isolated South Coast during its days of being a gangling stripling in economic matters owed a considerable debt to Isaias W. Hellman and his undeviating policy of enlightened self-interest.

The effects of the real estate collapse of 1888 varied in different parts of southern California. The more isolated districts such as Santa Barbara and Ventura counties were only moderately concerned, while the Pasadena area, the center of the greatest Boom speculation, found the drop in property values the most drastic. Practically all of the cities and towns showed a major ebb in population:

Year	Los Angeles	Pasadena	San Bernardino	San Diego	Santa Ana	Santa Barbara	Ventura
1870	5,728	—	—	2,300	—	—	—
1880	11,183	391	1,673	2,637	711	3,460	1,370
1888*	80,000	6,500	8,000	35,000	4,000	8,000	—
1890	50,935	4,882	4,012	16,159	3,628	5,864	2,320

*Glenn S. Dumke's estimates

In Los Angeles population dropped from 80,000 to 51,000 in less than two years' time. Losing nearly forty percent of its people when a good share of the residents had been convinced the population was going to increase by an even larger percentage was certain to cause pocketbook and ego trauma. Not until the spring of 1895 would the bank deposits of Los Angeles equal their level of eight and a half years earlier.

The mid-1890s were depression years throughout the United States and very much so on the South Coast. Houses were vacant, and broken windows were a worry to the owners who could neither sell nor rent the residences. Railroads ran empty passenger cars, a contrast to the crowded train sections of a few years earlier. Good agricultural land was being neglected by bankrupt, apathetic or absent owners. Everywhere around Los Angeles were speculative tracts, ranging from a few lots to hundreds of acres, which had gone to utter ruin; the citrus trees were dried up and covered with cottony scale, and the soil was eroded and tangled with weeds. Along with the abandoned hulks of the hotels of forgotten subdivisions, the neglected land stood out as unsightly, festering wounds discouraging visitors and new investments. It was nearly the turn of the century before all of the forgotten land parcels were sold or leased for farming.

Faced with declining sales, disastrous price-cutting and the gnawing threat of bankruptcy, the commercial firms of Los Angeles in 1893 formed the Merchants' Association in a valiant attempt to hang together rather than separately during the economic depression. When Max Meyberg, one of the organizers of the association, suggested a carnival in the city similar to New Orleans' Mardi Gras, he received strong support for the idea as an inexpensive way of helping to change the pervading sense of business gloom in southern California.

Meyberg was forthwith designated director-general of La Fiesta de Los Angeles. The community and regional support for the fiesta exceeded the association's fondest dreams, and its three days of parades, exhibitions, celebrations, fireworks and balls in April of 1894 was a dazzling success. Henry O'Melveny was most impressed with the large crowds in the street, and he felt that "the Chinese were the great features of the parade." He was writing in his journal about the wondrous dragon, two hundred feet long and carried on the heads of the local Chinese, which serpentined up the street at the end of the parade to the continuous accompaniment of strings of popping firecrackers.

To many, La Fiesta de Los Angeles seemed to be the catalytic agent which brought the beginning of a business revival to the South Coast. Theodore S. Van Dyke reflected the first flush of this new confidence which had been missing for years:

" . . . the best and most rapid growth of the city has been since the [Boom] excitement died away, and during the long process of liquidation so general and so severe it would have made hard times in any other country and in the midst of any prosperity. . . . Every hammer and saw in the city has been busy, and business houses, fine residences and neat cottages are arising as fast as ever."

CHAPTER 4

"The Lord has not given you much to start with, that is certain"

If he thought about an ocean harbor at all, the average Los Angeles citizen of the 1880s still felt that "the government must have a great deal of money to waste, if it could spend so many thousands of dollars on a useless mudhole like the Wilmington Lagoon." All one had to do to share this view was to cross the new Southern Pacific trestle from Wilmington to San Pedro above the tidal swamps stretching for miles from the Los Angeles River to the base of the San Pedro hills.

The mud flats were deserted except perhaps for a pelican perched morosely on the broken stump of a long-dead tree trunk, carried down by a forgotten winter flood and half-buried in the sea of tidal mud. Yet this unprepossessing Wilmington Lagoon along with the adjoining San Pedro Harbor would shortly be known throughout California and a good part of the United States because of the machinations of the railroad magnate, Collis P. Huntington, and his Southern Pacific Railroad.

The astute lobbying of Phineas Banning and Benjamin D. Wilson (after whom Mount Wilson is named) had resulted in the allocation of Federal rivers and harbors money to the initial construction of San Pedro Harbor. The entrance by the late 1880s was formed by a 3000-foot easterly breakwater extending from a skinny Rattlesnake Island (shortly to be called Terminal and widened through harbor dredging) south to a point 400 feet beyond Dead Man's Island in the open sea. Considerably less than two acres in extent, the principal feature on Dead Man's Island was a forty-foot-high eroded rock whose summit covered an area of about fifty by one hundred feet. The islet was situated in the present-day Main Channel opposite San Pedro's Twentieth Street, well over a mile inland from Point Fermin. The other side of the narrow harbor entrance was formed by a curving westerly jetty to the base of the sixty-foot-high bluffs of Timm's Point near today's Signal and Miner streets.

Dead Man's Island was blasted out of the main harbor channel in 1928. Four human skeletons in unknown graves were unearthed while the blasting and excavating progressed. This was a surprise as it had been thought that all the bodies on Isla de Los Muertos (as the islet was called on the old charts) had been removed many years earlier. A burial place of expediency, probably the first known graves were in 1769 which resulted in the macabre name of the rocky islet. Six American sailors and marines off the U.S.S. *Savannah* who had been killed or died of wounds received in the 1846 Dominguez Hill skirmish were interred there. After the U.S. Army Engineers built the easterly breakwater to Rattlesnake Island, current and wave action accelerated Dead Man's Island erosion "and the caskets of some of the buried were exposed to the weather. The remains of the sailors and marines (in 1888) were taken to San Francisco where they were reburied, and the other bodies were taken to San Pedro Cemetery."

Between the tidal scouring action in the central channel past Dead Man's Island and a modest amount of dredging, the depth over the bar at the 400-foot-wide harbor mouth was fourteen feet at low tide in the mid-1880s—a significant engineering achievement when measured against a natural bar of just eighteen inches before the harbor improvement. Vessels with a draft of eighteen feet could be handled in the main channel nearly to Tenth Street in San Pedro and smaller-draft coastal vessels came in to First Street. Further inland, the empty Wilmington Lagoon, sprawling in all directions, consisted of tidal mud flats sectioned by drainage courses feeding into tidal rivers which meandered into the central San Pedro channel of the estuary. One back-bay channel was Dominguez Creek which drained into Wilmington Lagoon from the north-

east, and still another was from a slough variously called Ma-
chado, Oakley and Bixby (now Harbor Park).

Phineas Banning had used another one of these tidal rivers,
Cerritos Creek, supplemented by a little dredging, to establish
his "goose pond" of a landing, as the San Diego *Union* contemptuously referred to it, at the edge of a town he called
Wilmington. Banning's reply to the *Union* canard was ceremoniously to give four bits (fifty cents) to a friend who was
going to San Diego and say: "Here, take this and buy Horton's
Addition [New San Diego] for me. You can keep the change."
This then was the little South Coast harbor of San Pedro, with
its unprepossessing back reaches, when the coastal port became
a shuttlecock of national power politics.

Any major transportation issue in California automatically
involved the Southern Pacific during the last third of the nineteenth century. And the Southern Pacific was synonymous with
an aging Big Four—Mark Hopkins, Charles Crocker, Leland
Stanford and Collis P. Huntington (Hopkins died in 1878 and
Crocker followed him a decade later). The Big Four had
successfully put a hammerlock on the economy of California.
Theirs was a mailed-fist transportation monopoly unabashedly
charging what the traffic would bear as the Big Four's rail
system expanded.

The Southern Pacific line across the Sierras joined the Union
Pacific at Ogden, Utah; its coast lines covered California and
were moving into the Northwest, and the 1883 hookup in Texas
gave the Southern Pacific a southern transcontinental route with
markedly easier grades than other railroads. Collis P. Huntington and Leland Stanford foresaw major trade with the Orient
and the flourishing industrial eastern half of the United States
via their own transcontinental line. Japan was emerging from
its self-imposed chrysalis of centuries and China appeared to
be ripe for further exploitation.

San Francisco was not the logical Southern Pacific terminal
for the Orient traffic via the southern route. The bay city was
450 miles further from Pacific tidewater at San Pedro, and those
additional miles required crossing three summits with heavy

grades. The Southern Pacific controlled the San Pedro water-front in the 1880s except for the apparently worthless sandbar of Rattlesnake Island, probably called that because of snakes riding winter flood debris from the upper reaches of the Los Angeles River and being deposited on the island's beaches. San Pedro Harbor itself was only adequate for the existing coastal traffic. Then Leland Stanford, the president of the railroad at the time of the Boom, let it be known that his powerful transportation company now supported the development of a deep-water harbor at San Pedro, to be built of course with Federal river and harbor funds.

The Southern Pacific, according to Stanford, was planning a trans-Pacific steamship line utilizing big ships of 15,000 to 20,000 tons. Demonstrating tangible evidence of his company's interest in San Pedro, he reported the allocation of funds for the construction of a long Southern Pacific slip near Timm's Point just inside the westerly arm of the harbor breakwater (and where the large fish boats now tie up). The Southern Pacific's announcement was fine news to regional business struggling in the end of the Boom's doldrums on the South Coast.

The fledgling Los Angeles Chamber of Commerce, organized in October of 1888 because of all the district's business problems, needed a cause. A year later it found one with more prickly consequences than it ever anticipated. Members of Congress were invited to visit San Pedro as guests of the Chamber of Commerce to hear the reasons why a deep-water harbor built with Federal funds was needed at that location. Unfortunately, the net of the Chamber, set to draw broad-scale congressional support, caught a very big and dangerous fish. This was Senator William P. Frye of Maine, long-time chairman of the Senate Commerce Committee. While on the South Coast visiting his old senatorial friend and colleague, John P. Jones of Nevada, he accepted the Chamber's invitation to go to San Pedro with Leland Stanford, president of the Southern Pacific. Frye, not the most tactful man, managed to have himself quoted verbatim in the Los Angeles newspapers while he stood on the San Pedro bluffs and told the Chamber representatives clustered around him and anyone else within earshot:

"Rattlesnake Island, Dead Man's Island, I should think it would scare a mariner to death to come into such a place." And a little later: "Well, as near as I can make out, you propose to ask the Government to create a harbor for you almost out of whole cloth. The Lord has not given you much to start with, that is certain; it will cost four or five million to build, you say; well, is your whole country worth that much?"

Never noted for his flexibility in changing his mind under any circumstances, the strongly adverse reaction locally to his remarks hardened Frye's opinion for all time against the San Pedro location. Further, as later events would show, conceivably Senator Jones may have aided the solidification of Frye's prejudice. Jones had a heavy stake in Santa Monica which he had long considered a logical ocean terminal.

The harbor supporters were depressed by Senator Frye's outspoken opinion of San Pedro's potentialities and the high harbor cost estimate of which the senator spoke. At the urging of the Los Angeles Chamber of Commerce the Congress authorized the establishment of a special board of the Army Corps of Engineers to make a survey of the South Coast from Point Dume to San Juan Capistrano for a deep-water harbor location. Of critical importance in later years when the site controversy was at its height, the Mendell Board in late 1891 unequivocally recommended the San Pedro location to the Congress. It also estimated the cost at three million dollars, a number which would not be forgotten when Collis P. Huntington changed his railroad's mind on San Pedro becoming a principal ocean port.

Phineas Banning and his successor, the Southern Pacific, had dominated Los Angeles seaport affairs almost from the time of the Gold Rush. The Boom with its population influx brought solid challenges to this power structure. Both the Santa Fe and a wealthy Oregon lumber group headed by J. C. Ainsworth and R. R. Thompson became interested in the potentialities of Redondo Beach as a regional port.

Most of the freight and passenger business came from north-ern harbors and Redondo was twenty miles and three hours closer to San Francisco than San Pedro. Of much more impor-tance Redondo had the unusual feature of being at the mouth of a submarine canyon whose mouth was near the beach. Com-paratively short wharves from the shore could be built alongside this canyon, and deep-draft vessels could be loaded close inshore. And still another advantage of Redondo was the loom-ing bulk of the Palos Verdes Peninsula adjacent to the port location which gave good protection to the wharves and ships from the violent southeast storms of the winter months.

Santa Fe tracks reached Redondo in 1888 which immediately made the town a significant regional port. The delighted Oregon lumber group shortly established a joint venture with the heirs of Manuel Dominguez (also owners of Rattlesnake Island in San Pedro harbor) to exploit the 400-acre holdings of the Redondo Beach Development Company. The first move of J. C. Ainsworth and R. R. Thompson was to piece together a railroad to Los Angeles. The lumbermen formed the Redondo Railway Company which bought up a moribund narrow-gauge steam line running from its terminal at Jefferson and Grand streets at the outskirts of Los Angeles to the fading real estate promotion of Rosecrans. By 1890 a 1200-foot wharf (the first of three) had been constructed and the narrow-gauge road completed from there to Los Angeles. The Oregon partners then built the Re-dondo Hotel overlooking the ocean. The hostelry was imme-diately popular with the Los Angeles people who came down on the steam line for the excellent food, tennis tournaments, bathing parties, dances and even the hotel's own theater.

Almost overnight the port of San Pedro and the Southern Pacific found they had a major competitor for much of the South Coast's ocean traffic. Within three years of the opening of the first wharf 250 vessels annually were making Redondo a port of call including many deep-draft ships who otherwise would have been forced to use expensive lighterage services at San Pedro. Other than lumber and coal, Southern Pacific statistics showed sixty percent of San Pedro traffic being diverted to

Redondo. Shortly the great railroad had an additional insult added to the Redondo injury.

The raised sandbar of San Pedro's Rattlesnake Island—one-half mile wide and four miles long—and Mormon Island, a stretch of mud in Wilmington Lagoon, were in litigation. A court decision in 1891 held that the Phineas Banning/Southern Pacific rights to sixty acres of land for a railroad terminal and spurs on Rattlesnake Island were no longer applicable. The same year the U.S. Supreme Court ruled that both Mormon Island and Dead Man's Island were public domain. The result of these decisions meant the Dominguez heirs suddenly had a valuable and strategic commodity in Rattlesnake Island. There was a financial group at hand ready to buy it and more than willing to tweak the tiger tail of the Southern Pacific.

Yet another financial syndicate had become enamored with the South Coast. This one was a loosely knit St. Louis organization headed by R. C. Kerens and George B. Leighton. The syndicate envisaged a regional network of steam lines with a terminal at tidewater San Pedro and eventually a railroad to Utah and junction with the Union Pacific. The Los Angeles Terminal Railway Company was formed in 1890, and rail lines from Glendale and Pasadena to Los Angeles were acquired. Negotiations were opened with the Dominguez heirs for the purchase of Rattlesnake Island. The syndicate paid $300,000 for the sandbar, a high price considering the prevailing business conditions. Meanwhile standard-gauge construction of the Terminal Railway was underway in Los Angeles east of the river at First Street toward the young town of Long Beach. Thence the line could run to its own docks at East San Pedro on Rattlesnake Island, immediately across the channel from the Southern Pacific facilities at Fifth Street. The Long Beach portion of the line opened in late 1891 and East San Pedro was reached the following spring.

Forthwith, and not surprisingly, the name of the island was changed to Terminal from Rattlesnake. The company's promotional literature told of the "one ocean resort, Terminal Island, which can be reached only by the Terminal road, and it is one of the most popular and most beautifully improved beaches to be found anywhere in California. . . . It enjoys surf bathing on one side and still-water bathing on the other, for the Island lies in the arm of the bay." There was indeed a magnificent ocean beach because of tidal currents depositing sand from the harbor mouth at Dead Man's Island. Almost immediately the renamed island became a fashionable beach resort for those people "who loved the windblown open beaches of San Pedro Bay and the smell of mud flat anchorages at dawn." This was where the prestigious South Coast (Los Angeles) Yacht Club formed in 1901.

It would be an overstatement to say that Collis P. Huntington took any pleasure in the fine Redondo Hotel or the recently popular ocean beach on Terminal Island. He was coldly infuriated with his long-time partner, Leland Stanford, calling him "a damned old fool." The aging curmudgeon felt Stanford had bungled the Southern Pacific's monopoly control of ocean traffic on the South Coast in allowing competing rail entries to Redondo and East San Pedro. The fillip to Huntington, who had just ousted Stanford as president of the Southern Pacific, was the court requirement of giving a quitclaim deed to his company's key Rattlesnake Island holdings. He knew an upstart Terminal Company was seriously planning a railroad to Ogden, Utah, and junction with the Union Pacific.

The word was passed from New York. Huntington wanted a reexamination of San Pedro as a major harbor. In the interim, Southern Pacific work was to be stopped on a long railroad wharf extending out into the ocean from Timm's Point. An answer back to the imperious old man was not long in coming. To his staff, a vastly expanded Redondo concept increasingly appeared to be a neat solution to an array of potentially vexing problems to the railroad. Why not arbitrarily select a new South Coast harbor location which the Southern Pacific would control completely? Whereupon, with the benefit of Collis P. Huntington's massive Washington influence, have the Federal Government build an extensive ocean breakwater to provide a protected deepwater harbor at this location?

The railroad decision was made, the site selected and the first construction quietly initiated. The location was near the mouth of Santa Monica Canyon—at first glance a totally unlikely spot for an expensive harbor development other than being a few miles closer to northern ports than Redondo and San Pedro.

Closer examination would show why the location was selected. Huntington himself was well familiar with Santa Monica. This was the stillborn ocean terminal of the Nevada senator, John P. Jones, who made and lost several fortunes. Jones intended his Los Angeles and Independence Railroad to run from Santa Monica to the silver-lead mines of the Inyo Mountains east of Owens Valley and thence to Salt Lake and a tie-in with the Union Pacific. But the bursting of the Nevada silver bubble had forced the Nevada senator to sell his embryonic railroad venture to the Southern Pacific in 1877. John P. Jones remained a powerful United States senator with long seniority, and after the railroad sale Huntington and he continued to work closely together. Jones' home was at Santa Monica surrounded by much of the land of his Rancho Vicente purchase of years earlier.

The steep bluffs or palisades of Santa Monica were the principal physical advantage to the proposed harbor site. By means of a cut and a tunnel through the bluffs, the Southern Pacific entered the beach near the present pleasure pier. The tracks were laid north at the base of the bluffs along a 300-foot-wide beach to a tiny point one-half mile north of Santa Monica Canyon. Control of the land on the bluffs and the single sally point to the beach insured an impenetrable cul-de-sac for the harbor railroad line. Collis P. Huntington was so impressed with the cleverness of the plan that he bought 200 acres on the bluffs immediately above what would shortly be known as "the Long Wharf" and authorized the planting of trees on the barren acreage. Still known as Huntington Palisades, the land was subdivided in the 1920s.

Construction of the Long Wharf at the Southern Pacific railhead near Santa Monica Canyon was underway in 1891. Made of heavy timbers with creosoted piles it was built straight out to sea for most of the 4300-foot length, beyond the 33-foot depth at low tide. While the months went by and the Long Wharf crawled steadily out beyond the breakers, rumors first spread throughout the South Coast that Collis P. Huntington, the new president, had changed the railroad's position on San Pedro. Yet the Southern Pacific continued to make bland statements reiterating its support of the old location and indicating the Long Wharf at Santa Monica was simply ancillary to the railroad's San Pedro operations.

Still taking the Southern Pacific at its word, the San Pedro deep-water-harbor supporters determined in 1892 to make their first try for an initial governmental appropriation of $250,000 in an appearance before Senator William P. Frye's Commerce Committee. Evidently on cue, the official position of the Southern Pacific on the harbor location changed abruptly.

With evident satisfaction, Senator Frye exhibited at the committee hearing a telegram from William Hood, the chief engineer of the railroad. In it Hood asserted that the sea bottom off San Pedro and inside the proposed breakwater was unsatisfactory both for port construction and as a holding ground for ship anchorage purposes. In support of this contention he stated that the railroad had halted construction on a wharf out to sea from Timm's Point because of the inability to drive piles into the rocky ocean floor. This experience was confirmation of the railroad's engineering worry concerning the feasibility of making San Pedro a principal ocean harbor. Sadly and reluctantly, the decision had been made by the Southern Pacific to construct a long wharf at Santa Monica where the ocean floor conditions were found to be excellent. As intended, all of this left the San Pedro advocates in disorder.

Concurrent with the Hood telegram, Collis P. Huntington's representatives in California intimated to principals of the Los Angeles Chamber of Commerce that the central harbor of the South Coast unquestionably was going to be at Santa Monica Canyon and would be called Port Los Angeles, a compliment to the expanding city. Further, there was a strong likelihood that the Federal Government would pay for a major breakwater at sea there, and, finally, the South Coast people should recognize the facts and the railroad's firm position early in the game. Back in Washington, the significant technical objection raised by William Hood meant that the San Pedro harbor appropriation would be removed from the congressional agenda for that year. As a sop to them, the confused San Pedro proponents accepted with alacrity the establishment of still another board from the Army Corps of Engineers to review the South Coast harbor situation. This board, headed by Colonel William P. Craighill, commenced its coastal survey work in the summer of 1892.

To the surprise of the cynical, the Craighill Board concurred with the earlier technical recommendations and strongly recommended the San Pedro location for the deep-water harbor. The San Pedro proponents were warily delighted. They fished again with another $250,000 appropriation request, placed on the agenda of Senator Frye's committee. The Southern Pacific's reaction to the adverse Craighill report was strangely muted. There were only continued expressions of technical regret to key Santa Monica guests of the railroad. It was a pity that the fine Corps of Engineers was continuing to support and expand the Engineers' original questionable decision on spending funds at San Pedro.

The first real indication of Collis P. Huntington's congressional strength on the harbor subject was when the Chamber's second appropriation request was handily voted down with little discussion in Senator Frye's committee. This prompted the Los Angeles *Times* to take a firm position on the harbor argument. The newspaper asked editorially what in fact was the Southern Pacific's plans and did Collis P. Huntington really believe that the Congress could ignore the favorable San Pedro recommendations of the two review boards of the Corps of Engineers, the trusted technical friend of the Congress for many years.

The railroad baron's answers to both rhetorical questions of the *Times* were not long in coming and became a subject of considerable national interest for a long time. The emerging contest had the appeal of a Goliath and a David. On one side was a huge railroad employing 75,000 people headed by a man known throughout the United States for three decades as a kind of power demigod. The opposition consisted of a few South Coast men and a freshman senator, none of whom had given his opposition much forethought, nor much early commitment for that matter. Events and Huntington crystallized their positions.

Collis P. Huntington was seventy-one when he openly entered the South Coast harbor fray, and his basic method of approach had changed little over the years. All things being equal, he naturally preferred the bludgeon approach, and this was the course of action when he underscored the Southern Pacific's position with key Los Angeles Chamber of Commerce members in early 1894:

"You people are making a big mistake in supporting the San Pedro appropriation. The River and Harbor Committee will never report in favor of that place—not in a thousand years. I know them all, and I have talked with them about the matter. The same is true of the Senate Committee on Commerce . . .

"Now, I propose to be frank with you people. I do not find it to my advantage to have the harbor built at San Pedro . . . on the other hand, the Santa Monica location will suit me perfectly. . . . I don't know for sure I can get the money for Santa Monica; I think I can. But I know damned well that you shall never get a cent for the other place."

With Huntington's personal involvement, it was now clear to the business and agriculture people on the South Coast that sides had to be chosen in the harbor war. The *Herald* and the *Express* supported Port Los Angeles. Harrison G. Otis had placed the *Times* on the San Pedro side. The Board of Directors of the Chamber of Commerce had a serious dilemma, and particularly the Chamber's eager young general manager. Originally sort of a business do-gooder in his harbor advocacy, Charles D. Willard had been ardently supporting the San Pedro location. Matters came to a head when a senior Southern Pacific representative in April of 1894 requested the Chamber's board of directors to instruct its Washington lobbyists to work for a Santa Monica appropriation and jettison completely the Chamber's official support of the San Pedro site. Willard's immediate reaction was to recommend strongly a polite rejection of the railroad's request. He changed his view after sounding out a representative sample of his board and the Chamber membership. To his dismay he found the Southern Pacific had quietly been doing its own grass-roots sales work and arm twisting in the local business community.

Sentiment was building up rapidly for Santa Monica and Port Los Angeles. After a review of the situation with the Chamber's president, Daniel Freeman, and the steering committee of the board of directors, the general manager made a simple and key recommendation which was undoubtedly fulcrum in the eventual harbor location. Willard proposed a formal *secret* ballot of all Chamber members on San Pedro versus Santa Monica with the board action, of course, to reflect the majority vote. There was a week of intensive campaigning. The San Pedro adherents commenced to emerge from the shock of finding the Southern Pacific was the antagonist and coined the catch phrase, "a free harbor fight." A high percentage of the Chamber membership balloted. The results showed more than a two-to-one vote for San Pedro. Because of the historic and actual power of the Southern Pacific and its reputation for punishing those who crossed it, there was considerable speculation as to what the result might have been if the ballot had not been secret.

The Chamber was clearly the voice of the South Coast and San Pedro support would be continued. A Democratic majority in the new Congress replaced the cantankerous Senator Frye with Ransome of North Carolina becoming Commerce Committee chairman. Still the deep-water harbor matter remained quiescent even after the Southern Pacific officially opened its Port Los Angeles. Charles D. Willard and his majority of the Chamber appeared to have won a Pyrrhic victory. They discovered that Collis P. Huntington had chosen to place the ocean harbor subject into his special kind of a congressional committee limbo.

CHAPTER 5

"Viva los Estados Unidos! Viva Mexico! Somos Amigos!"

The heritage and history of southern California had largely been forgotten a decade or so after the Boom of the eighties, and with good reason. Not more than five per cent of the population had lived there before 1886 and a fair portion of those that did were infants and children. Also, most of the landmarks of the earlier culture had been removed or submerged in the waves of building construction during and after the Boom.

The sons of the Californios were surprised to find newcomers showing some interest in the demise of the old family fortunes. More bewildering and confusing to them was the outlanders' evident absorption in the mission period before Mexico's independence from Spain. By the time of the final dissolution of the missions of Alta California in 1833, it is doubtful that most Californios had more than heard of Junipero Serra, the founder of those missions.

While Father Serra was a dim legend, the curious newcomer soon discovered there was one annual event of the past on the South Coast which did bring forth strong memories and vivid stories. This was the always noisy and sometimes lusty Fourth of July celebrations, so dearly loved by the Californios almost from the time Mexico ceded Alta California to the United States in 1848.

Probably the most memorable Fourth of July party occurred in 1853 at the desolate little roadstead port of San Pedro, well over twenty miles from Los Angeles. Phineas Banning and his partner, David W. Alexander, staged a celebration distinguished among other things by monumental hangovers. Two thousand

Californios came from scores of miles around for a solid two days of barbecues, drinking, betting and feats of horsemanship punctuated by appropriate oratory and miscellaneous brawling. This was the occasion when Don Juan Capistrano Sepulveda shouted his toast "Viva los Estados Unidos! Viva Mexico! Somos Amigos!" as an elderly Mexican War cannon was ceremoniously discharged atop Dead Man's Island. The cannon had been loaded on a lighter and taken from San Pedro where it was laboriously hoisted to the rocky crown of the islet. After many liquid toasts, the cannon was fired over the grave boards of the six American sailors and marines who had been killed or died of wounds received in the violent Mexican War skirmish of Dominguez Hill seven years before.

Unquestionably the best Fourth of July parade of the Californios was the gala procession and fiesta of 1876 in Los Angeles which was now speaking English nearly as much as Spanish. Billed as a first centennial celebration, most of Los Angeles County and a good part of the population from Santa Barbara to San Diego were in town by the late morning of the Fourth: "There were crowds of people coming into the city by car [railroad] and carriage, buggy and wagon. They were coming on horseback and a-foot, and they continued to come. . . . The Wilmington train came thundering in with three or four hundred passengers, and the passenger cars and engine most beautifully adorned with flags and garlands of flowers."

Californios continued to have their beloved Fourth of July celebrations into the 1890s. The most well known was at the Camulos Ranch, forty-five miles north of Los Angeles on the Santa Clara River, running through lands still held by the Del Valles. The Del Valle party lasted four days with seventy-five guests arriving the second day including Dr. Walter Lindley who described that day's barbecue:

"A fat young steer was lassoed by a vaquero, the aorta was dexterously severed with a knife, and then began some dissecting that would have surprised the most skillful anatomist. The skin was quickly and neatly taken off and spread out to protect the beef from the earth, the muscles were then, layer after layer, deftly removed, and in an incredibly short time this Mexican butcher had the meat ready for the fire.

"A fire in a pit nearby had been heating stones, which were now red-hot. Iron rods were laid across, and the whole beast put on to roast for dinner.

"The noon train from Los Angeles added materially to the number of guests, and seventy-five as happy people as ever lived sat around the heavily laden table under the grapevines. After the dessert had been enjoyed toasts were in order, and among those to the Del Valle family, the State of Southern California . . . [and] the memory of Mrs. Helen Hunt Jackson, which was drunk standing."

Helen Hunt Jackson unquestionably laid the foundation for the southern California pantheon of the long-forgotten missions and their Indians in her 1884 best-seller *Ramona*. The same year her book was published, the future high priest for all such matters, Charles F. Lummis, arrived on the South Coast. His Association for the Preservation of the Missions in the 1890s, and subsequently the Landmarks Club, became an effective fund-raising mechanism for restoration of the old buildings, neglected for three-quarters of a century. Lummis could report after a few years that two acres or so of new roofs had been laid on the mission structures because of the club's efforts.

The accelerated evolution from a program to preserve historical buildings to the full-blown folktale of a Spanish mission heritage (including a cast of larger-than-life characters such as Junipero Serra) probably first began in the second Los Angeles Fiesta. Charles F. Lummis, a born showman and intelligentsia promoter, decided on an integrated heritage theme for the 1895 event. The romanticized and idyllic theme was quickly picked up and exploited by a gallery of entrepreneurs who knew a good thing when they saw it. Everything from furniture suites and candied fruit to commercial and residential architecture stressed the mission motif. By the turn of the century a fleshed-out and Arcadian view of the times of the Californios, the substantial number of "Spanish" land grants, along with a roseate description of the life of the missions and the converted Indians, was rapidly becoming popular and profitable folklore.

Mission Revival became the architectural rage of the early 1900s. This meant structures with Romanesque arches, stucco facades and towers rising above the rooftrees, ersatz bells inserted in miscellaneous places and at least a token amount of red roofing tile. It made little difference whether the building was to be a fire station, church, railroad depot or jail. However, one cautious architect in Riverside did hedge his bets. The First Church of Christ Scientist there combined tall doric pillars with the usual assortment of Mission Revival features. The split-level Victoria Club building in the same town was a refreshing and almost heretical wooden contrast to the prevailing stucco mode although the club was equipped with the square mission oak furniture including the straight-back chairs with the leather seats.

The South Coast had a fascinating heritage, infinitely more human and tragic than the gauzy, idyllic tableau which had been invented by the turn of the century. Alta California was initially colonized as a base for the Philippine galleons bound to Acapulco and then as a barrier to further Pacific Coast penetration by Russia. Part of the well-burnished colonizing mechanism of Spain for Alta California was a chain of missions, about a day's horseback ride apart, extending from San Diego to San Francisco. Each mission was assigned but did not own an enormous tract of land, in one instance covering an area of 350 square miles.

Under the Spanish colony system the purpose of the missions was threefold—to convert the Indians, to settle them on mission lands as loyal subjects of Spain, and to provide them with food, clothing and shelter. In addition to lands allocated to mission and government use, there were some twenty grants made throughout Alta California to private individuals, most of them former soldiers of New Spain. For better or worse the missions accomplished their purpose. In the process, a great many of the converted Indians died from the diseases of the white man, the change in diet and the inability to adapt to the stern mission discipline.

By the time Mexico won its independence from Spain in 1822 the southern California frontier had been secured, and the missions with their subdued labor force and extensive lands had prospered. This prosperity did not go unnoticed. With the precedent of land reform acts in the young nation of Mexico, a number of Californios launched a systematic campaign to have the mission lands returned to the public domain. In theory, such a program would eliminate the powerful religious influence and ensure a more equitable distribution of the wealth of the province to both white man and Indian alike. In fact, it meant the mission lands would be distributed as political plums to the favorites of the current governor of the province, the herds of mission livestock plundered or killed for hides and tallow, and the surviving mission Indians summarily scattered with the wind after several generations of difficult but orderly mission life.

After five years of turmoil the secularization of the missions was completed in the early 1830s, and the mission lands were distributed by a series of inept Mexican governors as boodle to their deserving supporters. This was the sorry origin of most of the "Spanish" grants on the South Coast.

Some of the displaced mission Indians returned to the remnants of their original villages; some went beyond the southern California frontier to the Owens and Mojave river regions; many became part of the ranchos; and a large remainder drifted into and around Los Angeles and the other small towns. When the Indians near the little towns became increasingly degraded, they were considered scarcely human and a serious nuisance, as the Los Angeles *News* said in a descriptive piece of writing: "Decay and extermination have long since marked them for their certain victims . . . their scanty earnings at the end of the week are spent for rum. . . . They have filled our jails, have contributed largely to the filling of our state prison, and are fast filling our graveyards, where they must be buried at public expense or be permitted to rot in the streets and highways . . ." The *News* was correct in its forecast. The Indian problem around the small

California towns did not last long. In a few years the Indians were all dead.

After the breakup of the missions and the distribution of their land and people, the great days of the ranchos arrived. With ample labor provided by the former mission Indians, a major rancho establishment like Canada de Santa Ana might consist of several hundred people. In addition to the expanding Yorba family, according to Don Meadows, there were " . . . four wool-combers, two tanners, one butter and cheeseman who directed every day the milking of from fifty to sixty cows, one harness maker, two shoemakers, one jeweler, one plasterer, one carpenter, one majordomo, two errand boys, one sheepherder, one cook, one baker, two washerwomen, one woman to iron, four sewing women, one dressmaker, two gardeners, and a man to make the wine. . . . More than a hundred lesser employees were maintained on the ranch. . . . Ten steers a month were slaughtered to supply the hacienda."

The Gold Rush after 1849 made the Californio rich for a while. He had hard money for the first time and he spent the dollars as rapidly as they came in. Little was invested in savings, irrigation or stock improvement. Financial planning was negligible, and the Californio with his large family and numerous relatives quickly adjusted to and speedily exceeded the new cash income. The answer to any cash shortage he might have was to borrow money from the local Americano merchants. Interest rates were enormous in a remote economy having a limited amount of loanable money. Typical was the case of Don Jose Ramon Yorba, who mortgaged 17,000 acres of Rancho Las Bolsas along with his hacienda for a compounded interest rate of 5% a *month*. But to Yorba and the other Californios, there was no problem with cattle prices setting new highs in the Gold Rush atmosphere of San Francisco and Sacramento.

Of course, the lucrative selling prices of the Californio cattle soon brought in competition. Herds made the long trek from the Texas and Missouri frontiers. By 1856 full-grown steers were selling in San Francisco for less than half the price of a year earlier and the Los Angeles *Star* regretfully announced: "The

flush times are passed—the days of large prices and full pockets
are gone." The flush times may have passed, yet the price of a
steer was still three times what it had been before the Gold
Rush. But the Californio refused to tailor his expenses to still
what was more than an adequate income.

The worst was yet to come. First there was a flood, then a
terrible drought which lasted more than two years while the
region was ravaged by smallpox. Finally the normal fall and
winter rains arrived in the 1864-65 season, and the frightful
smallpox epidemic had run its miserable course. Over seventy
per cent of the cattle herds of the South Coast had been
destroyed while thousands of carcasses strewed the plains. Much
of the remaining cattle was sold at tax and foreclosure auctions
and the rancho lands lay deserted.

Even a man like Don Abel Stearns, the largest and most
powerful landholder in southern California, was in desperate
financial difficulties. In sharp contrast to the other Californios,
Stearns had the tremendous advantage of English-language flu-
ency, financial knowledge and widespread business contacts. If
Stearns was in deep difficulties, the plight of the bulk of the
ranchos after the drought was easy to envisage. They disappeared into other hands by foreclosure. "On the assessor's lists
these broad leagues of grazing lands dwindled in size to fifty-
vara lots, planted to tiny milpas of beans, melons and chili
peppers."

To have the unenviable reputation of being the worst hell-
hole of the American West in the 1850s and 1860s was a substantial accomplishment for Los Angeles, particularly as there
was considerable competition from many cow towns and miners'
camps. However, fifteen to thirty murders a month over a
sustained period, and not including lynchings, in a town of
4000 people was a difficult record for any competition to top.
Los Angeles had been building up this sorry reputation for a
long period of years and for a variety of reasons.

With Mexican independence from Spain in 1822 the leaders

of Mexico had more important things to concern them, and there was little interest in the remote province of Alta California. What vague government in the distant province that existed as time went by was almost as bad as none at all. The numerous bloodless coups would have been comical except for the effect on Alta California. Systematic defense of the frontiers and policing of the settled areas disintegrated. Stragglers and drifters, salted with a dribble of foreigners of highly questionable backgrounds, began to accumulate in Los Angeles. About the same time came many of the displaced mission Indians who lived in hovels in and about the town and had taken to cheap aguardiente (grape brandy), once the rigorous and paternalistic mission environment ended.

Los Angeles only needed one more major ingredient to make it a witches' cauldron in the 1850s—the dregs of the American frontier. This was provided after the Gold Rush when vigilante committees in San Francisco swept the backwash of the gold mines out of their city. Los Angeles then became the logical roosting place for a sordid assortment of murderers, thieves, badmen and outlaws.

The flimsy and inadequate law apparatus of the new state of California was no better than the chaotic Mexican rule. Local government was near anarchy. These conditions brought the vigilantes and their lynching bees with the strong support of the public. In one year (1854) there were twenty-two hangings in Los Angeles, most of them outside the law. Organized terrorism reached the point that villages and small towns tensed for outlaw attack. San Juan Capistrano was taken over by the Manilas gang, and for a time San Bernardino believed, with good reason, that an attempt would be made to overrun the town and sack it.

The vigilantes were out in force again in the early 1870s, and Los Angeles was in a "hanging mood." Mob violence was just below the surface veneer of police control. The hated Chinese, congregated in warrens around Calle de Los Negros, the notorious gambling and vice street of the town, were too absorbed in a dispute between their two principal tongs to give a thought to the dangerous threat of mob violence in the town.

There were five to ten thousand Chinese, practically all men, in California in the early 1860s. These Orientals had first been recruited around the swarming ports of Canton and Hong Kong a decade earlier to do pick-and-shovel and coolie work in the gold fields. Charles Crocker of the Central Pacific decided in 1865 to use Chinese to build the railroad across the Sierras, initially because of the impossibility of recruiting satisfactory white labor. At the peak of railroad construction, there were about 14,000 Chinese employed, and arriving ships jammed with Cantonese men were a common sight in San Francisco harbor. Early 1869 found railroad labor requirements tapering off. The Chinese who had been working on the Central Pacific settled around the state, living and encouraged to live as complete aliens in a foreign land.

Around this time serious mutterings of the "Yellow Peril" were first heard while the Cantonese fanned out in increasing numbers running laundries, other tiny shops and truck gardens and demonstrated their willingness to do any kind of manual and field labor. Most of the people of California found themselves irrationally detesting the Chinese as a group while loving many of them individually. The mutterings of hatred against the Orientals became a sullen chorus which could turn into a mob crescendo at any time. This occurred in the late afternoon of October 24, 1871, in front of the dilapidated Coronel Building at the head of Calle de Los Negros in Los Angeles.

A mounted policeman charged into the swirling, brawling group of rival Chinese tong members, then dismounted and chased one of them into the Coronel Building. The main hall of the structure echoed with several shots, and the wounded policeman staggered out of the doorway. A white bystander came up to help the policeman and was shot to death from inside the structure. A little time later a dangerous and heavily armed crowd gathered around the Coronel Building and down Calle de Los Negros. The Chinese finally and too late recognized their deadly peril. The transformation to a bloodthirsty mob indiscriminately maiming and killing the hated Chinese occurred when an Oriental attempted to scurry out. He died bleeding from a half-dozen bullet holes. The mob of screaming, cursing men then moved on its own frenzied and wild course of pillaging, burning and massacre. The next day showed a body count of nineteen Chinese, and scores of others badly beaten or crippled. Los Angeles and the rest of the West Coast displayed a marked lassitude and disinterest in subsequent investigations of the massacre.

Harassed as unwanted aliens, the California Chinese had another burden to carry for three decades commencing in the 1880s. Hatchet men or highbinders, professional Chinese killers armed with hatchets or pistols, systematically terrorized their own people in the Chinatowns of San Francisco, Los Angeles and other settlements. The salaried assassins worked for the semisecret tongs which had similarities to the Mafia of a later generation in large American cities.

In sharp contrast to the Six Companies, which acted and spoke for the welfare of the overseas Chinese in California, the tongs were involved in opium traffic and dens, slave girls and whorehouses, and gambling and business protection assessments while systematically bribing the police and custom officials. The internecine killings, kidnappings and incidental hot-iron tortures by the hatchet men were front-page news in the cities involved, and with considerable justification.

San Francisco's Chinese year-around population in the 1890s was about 30,000, far higher than that reported in the U.S. Census, while Los Angeles' total was perhaps a fifth of that. Because of the major influx from the agricultural areas during the winter months a Chinatown seasonal population would double in what were already crowded, decaying ghettos in the cities' central districts. Always there were few facts and many rumors of bubonic plague, cholera and leprosy in those packed and secretive Oriental warrens. A city like Los Angeles with

75,000 inhabitants took a major interest in a concentrated ghetto which half the year accounted for a fair percentage of the total population, and whose ways and mores were incomprehensible and fearsome to the average citizen under the best of circumstances. The rising terror of the tongs which might spew its special form of violence into the surrounding Caucasian sectors of the cities could only fan the underlying misunderstandings and hatreds toward the Orientals.

From the time they first arrived in California, the Chinese insisted on wearing their traditional long hair queues while padding along in their loose trousers and blue cotton blouses. They considered their stay in California to be temporary and hopefully short term. When a Cantonese (or John Chinaman as he was increasingly being called) earned $500 or so, he fully intended to return to his wife or family in his district of south China. If John Chinaman was unfortunate enough to die in the land of foreign devils his Chinese Benevolent Association (the Six Companies) would go to considerable effort to ship his bones if not his body back to his Cantonese village. Meanwhile John had as little interest in becoming Americanized as he had in learning the absurd and difficult language of his temporarily adopted country. Any sensible Chinese knew in his ancestral bones that his race was by a fair degree the most civilized and intelligent in a world of uncultured devil-persons ("gwai-laus" in Cantonese). John Chinaman could afford to be humble, industrious and passive while he ignored some of the laws of his host country and patronized the illicit operations of the tongs.

The Cantonese, who loved gambling, particularly fan-tan and mah-jongg, found utterly incomprehensible the rise of prohibitions against gaming in California. And beginning in 1862 with the arrival in San Francisco of fifty or so chests of opium on the clipper *Ocean Pearl*, many of the overseas Chinese were using an illegal but welcome drug palliative for the vicissitudes of a difficult world. From that time on, the unlawful opium trade flourished with both reformers and addicts of the time comparing the drug's ravages to that of alcohol.

John Chinaman could have opium but very few women other

than what the state's newspapers properly called "slave girls," although their services were not cheap. These were Chinese prostitutes in bondage and housed in brothels by the tongs. This bondage, similar to some of the practices in his native land, did not unduly bother John. He was assured of his only real opportunity for sexual release during the long years of sojourn in the land of foreign devils.

What was so clear to an overseas Chinese, whether it concerned queues or slave girls, was not remotely understood by the Americans who had always feared John's competition anyway. Punitive and harassment laws were enacted by the Congress including the 1882 Chinese Exclusion Act and later the Chinese Registration Act. The explosive growth of the criminal element of the tongs with their salaried hatchet men was additional rationale for the restrictive legislation.

Authenticated but often highly colored reports of the slave-girl auctions operated by the tongs were Chinatown practices which frightened and fascinated the Caucasian neighbors. One such auction location in San Francisco was underneath a joss house on St. Louis Alley:

"Here the girls were stripped of their clothing and put up for bid. Those who resisted could be identified easily by the black-and-blue marks on their bodies. . . . The most recalcitrant sometimes bore the scars of hot irons. But few were ever killed; they were too valuable for that, being worth up to $3000 each."

Much more notorious than the slave-girl trade was the sharply increased use of opium by the Chinese themselves. Compounding this practice for an easily alarmed Caucasian community were police reports supporting a grand jury statement which somberly warned that "white girls between the ages of thirteen and twenty are enticed into these opium dens, become regular habitues, and finally are subject wholly to the wishes of the Oriental visitors."

While undoubtedly there was limited substance in the grand jury's allegations of white slavery through use of drugs, the opium habit was almost exclusively confined to the Chinese with probably more than 10% of the community being substantial users or addicts at the peak of the traffic. The opium dens, with their stupefying reek of smoke which swirled lazily below the black-encrusted ceiling and above the curled-up figures of the smokers in their wooden bunks, made a profound impression on a visitor venturing into the opium rooms. Mark Twain described how the addict took his dope:

"A lamp sits on the bed, the length of the long pipe stem from the smoker's mouth. He puts a pellet of opium on the end of a wire, sets it on fire and plasters it into the pipe much as a Christian would fill a hole with putty. Then he applies the bowl to the lamp and proceeds to smoke—and the stewing and frying of the drug and the gurgling of the juices in the stem would well-nigh turn the stomach of a statue . . ."

The tongs and their hatchet men seemed all-powerful in the 1900s. Their rackets had expanded to Chinatown business protection, and the leadership of the Six Companies was being systematically taken over. And still the Chinese of California continued to be a withdrawn alien establishment. Any reasonable prediction of their future would surely include more turmoil and killings leading to deadly chaos within and outside their community. This was not to be.

In little more than a decade the winds of change swept away the choking miasma of these things while the overseas Chinese moved toward integration with the host country and its people. No single event accounted for such a massive change although an initial reference point was the 1906 earthquake and subsequent fire which wiped out a good part of San Francisco. Chinatown with its tong headquarters, whorehouses and hundreds of opium dens disappeared in the holocaust. The new Chinatown which rose out of the ashes of the old was willing to bring the tongs under control. The end of the Manchu dynasty in 1913 and the acceptance of Sun Yat-sen and his political philosophy in China gave a reason for cutting off the symbolical queues. Sometime over those years, the bulk of the overseas Chinese community had turned its face and heart toward

America. The term "John Chinaman" with its connotations of conflict and hatred joined the "Know-Nothings" and "Copperheads" in the dustbin of history.

A new generation of Californios after the Boom had difficulty remembering the great ranchos of their fathers and the cattle on a thousand hills. Many of this young generation worked on sheep ranches, became farmers or resettled in the towns. A few turned to crime and some had stature in their communities and throughout the state.

Ygnacio Sepulveda, son of Jose Andres, was one of the latter. While a twenty-nine-year-old judge, it was his resolution and outright courage which forced a series of criminal indictments in the wake of the 1871 Chinese Massacre with its lynchings and brutalities. Reginaldo Del Valle, born in 1864, another heir of a famous name on the South Coast, served as Speaker of the Assembly in the state legislature about the time Romulado Paceco was Governor of California in the 1870s.

In the main, however, the generation of Californios reaching maturity after the loss of the rancho lands in the 1860s became submerged in the advancing emigrant tide of the 1880s. The principal South Coast exception was Rancho San Pedro and the heirs of the long-time head of the Dominguez family.

Don Manuel Dominguez was buried from St. Vibiana Cathedral of Los Angeles in 1882. He was seventy-nine when he died in his hacienda at Rancho San Pedro, still an affluent and a powerful Californio. The old Don had accomplished what no other Californio had been able to do. He had held his ancestral lands intact through the misfortunes and vicissitudes of the 1850s and 1860s. He would have been interested in the eventual land management decisions of his heirs although for a time it seemed inevitable that the rancho lands would shortly disappear into other hands. Manuel Dominguez who yielded to nobody in his brutal determination to hold the family lands at whatever the cost must have thought bitterly of the muddle of estate affairs which would surely occur after his death.

The death of Maria Engracia Cota de Dominguez followed that of her husband, Manuel, by only a few months. The estate was left to the six daughters on a tenant-in-common basis. This was the legal doctrine, used so much by the Californios, which enabled a rancho to be held as an entity even though a substantial number of heirs might be involved. In a club-shaped pattern, Rancho San Pedro stretched from Redondo Beach to the Los Angeles River and from present-day Rosecrans Boulevard to Rattlesnake (Terminal) Island opposite San Pedro. At first there was every indication that Don Manuel's inflexible policy of retaining the land in the family would shortly be shattered on the reefs of the differing drives of his daughters. Since the heirs could not agree as to how portions of the estate were to be allocated to each of them, a petition for partition of the rancho lands was filed in Superior Court, and the partition was completed in 1885. Not surprisingly, none of the sisters was satisfied with the results, but neither was there any wholesale disposal of their holdings. Fifteen years after the court partition only 2300 acres had been sold of the original 28,700 acres held by Manuel Dominguez at the time of his death.

However, by the early 1900s the winds of change were very strong and again it seemed likely that most of the Dominguez landholdings would be blown helter skelter into a number of eager and waiting outlander hands. The oldest of the six sisters, Ana Josefa Juliana Dominguez de Guyer, died in 1907 and her husband was excluded from her inheritance by the terms of their marriage contract. Therefore the terms of her will were of substantial interest because the provisions might provide an indication of the eventual disposition of the rancho lands. The will clearly did just that. Except for relatively minor bequests, the estate of more than a million dollars was willed to her five sisters in equal shares. Guadalupe, an unmarried sister who died six years later, followed the same plan with the bulk of the estate going to the four surviving heirs of Manuel Dominguez.

At the suggestion of the family lawyer, Henry K. O'Melveny,

the Dominguez Estate Company was established to administer the inheritances. O'Melveny's involvement in the Dominguez sisters' affairs was prolonged and intimate. John F. Francis, an old friend and married to Maria Jesus de los Reyes, asked to see the lawyer shortly before Francis' death in 1903. Afterwards, O'Melveny noted the visit in his daily journal: "June 11. I went out to see John F. Francis. He was slightly delirious. He knew me. Desired that I look after the affairs of Mrs. Francis and see that everything was all right."

The Dominguez Estate Company turned out to be an appealing arrangement for a family which had evidently been well indoctrinated in the old Don's determination to hold the land at all costs. Dolores Dominguez de Watson, Victoria Dominguez de Carson and Susana Delfina Dominguez de del Amo y Gonzalez all established similar estate enterprises. At the death of Maria Jesus de los Reyes Dominguez de Francis in 1933, the bulk of her $15,000,000 estate was conveyed to the original Dominguez Estate Company.

Following either of two plans during the decades after 1900 was a sure way to become wealthy on the South Coast. The first was to acquire and hold on to a substantial amount of land long after any reasonable person would have sold the property at fat prices. The second was to have vast amounts of oil discovered on your property. The Dominguez family, long advocates of the first plan, qualified for the second approach because of a 1921 oil strike in west Torrance on Del Amo Estate property and shortly thereafter another strike on the Dominguez Hill portion of the Francis land. From then on, family oil revenues increased rapidly over the years.

Old Don Manuel Dominguez was a difficult man to satisfy at times. But even he would have had to be pleased in the way his daughters and their husbands managed their birthrights, in exactly Don Manuel's iron-fisted tradition.

From the beginning of time, that is since California became a state, there has been limited understanding or simpatico between the state's northern and southern halves. Every generation or so since the 1850s, particularly in the southern portion, has felt there were valid reasons why the two sections of California should go their separate ways. At one time the separation appeared to be an accomplished fact.

Leaders of the Californios like Manuel Dominguez and Andres Pico in the remote and nearly deserted cow counties of southern California disliked and feared the northern part of the young state. The Gold Rush brought clipper ships and steam vessels converging on San Francisco from all parts of the world. Along with mining and commercial enterprises, the range and valley lands of northern California began to fill with settlers. On the other hand, a county like Los Angeles had a population of only 11,000 and covered an enormous 9000-square-mile area, nearly twice its present size. There was a strong feeling by the Californios that their large ranchos in the southern cow counties would be taxed out of existence if the state government was controlled by the northern business interests.

Andres Pico introduced an 1859 joint resolution in the California State Assembly calling for the withdrawal of the counties of Los Angeles, San Diego, San Bernardino, Santa Barbara and San Luis Obispo from California, and the formation of the Territory of Colorado. Pico told the legislature that passage of the resolution was "the only salvation of our properties and happiness." The northern part of California had little or no interest in whether or not the southern cow counties left California. Both houses of the legislature readily approved Andres Pico's resolution, and the voters of the five counties concerned ratified it. However, with the onrushing events of the Civil War and the known sympathies of southern California being strongly pro-Confederacy, the bill establishing the new territory died in the Congress.

The urge for separation of the state readily survived the dislocations and readjustments of the Civil War. David Berry, the founder of Pasadena, was convinced in the seventies that California would shortly be divided and Los Angeles would be the new state's capital. The early 1880s showed the great ranchos of southern California in the main broken up and agriculture flourishing while mining in the northern part of the state was no longer of major importance. Still a strong tide for state division was running again below the Tehachapis because of the difference in climate, type of agricultural products and the substantial commercial and political domination of the state by San Francisco and its satellite areas. Meetings were held in 1881 urging state division. Again in 1888 the separation movement surfaced with a division bill receiving support in the legislature. The young Los Angeles Chamber of Commerce not only strongly advocated separation but proposed the purchase of Baja California, from Mexico for inclusion in the new state of Southern California.

The state division agitation died down with the collapse of the Boom, but there remained limited rapprochement between the north and south portions of California despite the sharp increase of population in the southern cow counties. Foreign immigrants, usually Catholic, settled in San Francisco during the 1890s while the region south of the Tehachapis tended to be populated by emigrants from the East, Midwest and South, primarily Protestant. Los Angeles became one of the prominent centers of the Temperance Movement, to the Bay City's initial amusement and then dismay. Again, San Francisco had developed a strong organized labor movement while Los Angeles remained violently open shop or, as the unions argued, anti-labor.

After the turn of the century it was becoming painfully evident to San Francisco and the North that a major shift southward of political and commercial power would occur in the years ahead. In 1900, the region below the Tehachapis had only about 350,000 residents, less than a third of the total of the north. Two decades later the southern region had three-quarters of the number living in the north, and Los Angeles had become California's largest city.

Population equilibrium between the two regions did not end the economic jousting nor serious proposals for state division. One would suspect that the North and South of California will persist in their marriage, but it is safe to predict that the uneasiness in the union will continue.

CHAPTER 6

"Intemperance and impurity are iniquity's Siamese twins"

The small town of Los Angeles had well over a hundred saloons after the Civil War and was a ripe if unwilling candidate for the massive ministrations of the national antiliquor societies. In two decades Los Angeles changed from a hell-roaring frontier town to a sober, God-fearing and rather dull little city with sixty churches. In the interim it had become a nationally recognized center of the aggressive antiliquor cause. The transition was a capsulized version of a country-wide morals reform movement spearheaded by women at the grass-roots level. Their initial target was alcohol.

A prebreakfast dram, toddy or shot glass of hard liquor, the first of a number throughout the day, was a common and well-recommended practice in the generations prior to the Civil War. Depending upon the section of the United States and the regional preferences the liquor might be applejack, peach and grape brandy, corn and rye whiskey or West Indian rum and a domestic version made of Caribbean molasses. Liquor consumption continued during the day with a periodic swig of rum considered appropriate for lightening the daily tasks. This tippling might be a rum break at 11:00 A.M. and 4:00 P.M. in a small urban factory or nipping on a jug strategically placed at a corner of a field being plowed. Even prisoners in the local jails usually received their daily gills of liquor. Los Angeles lawyers and courthouse politicians had Peach and Honey at John Schumacher's during the noon hour. Several of these potent peach-brandy concoctions were thought to provide a solid base from which to plead an afternoon case.

Only dangerous or outrageous intoxication carried stiff penalties. The routine drunken husband reeling out of a saloon after too many drinks, while leaving his day's wages behind him along with a wavery "X" on a tab evidencing additional debt, was of no interest to the general society of the times. Somebody, however, was concerned. This was a sternly moralistic and reform movement growing apace in the settled areas of the country. The tenets of the movement included the prohibition of all liquor along with a modest amount of women's rights and strictures involving tobacco, card playing and theatrical productions. Most of these doctrines were later reflected in the so-called Blue Laws, passed by most municipalities around the country.

The Quakers were probably the first group to form what came to be called the "Temperance Movement." The term was a misnomer because the Movement promoted the notion of total abstinence from alcohol or "Demon Rum" as it was increasingly being called in the liturgy of Temperance. And Demon Rum included by this definition beer and unfortified wines. Almost unwittingly Temperance scored its first success at the national level with the 1834 passage of a law forbidding sale of liquor to Indians under federal jurisdiction.

The evolving Temperance Movement could not accept the concept of moderate drinking. One Temperance leader expressed this view well: "I would that no person were able to drink intoxicating liquors without immediately becoming a drunkard. For who, then, would . . . drink the poison that always kills, or jumps in the fire that always burns?" Or as another said: "Men who drink now and then in a respectable manner without exposing themselves to reproach . . . are the recruiting officers in the devil's army."

The original premise of the Temperance advocates (also termed "the Drys") was that each person should convert himself and that liquor prohibition laws were neither desirable nor necessary. Gradually the Drys became convinced the coercion of the weak or thoughtless individual by law was required, the social-engineering concept of a century later. The "no-license" through "local option" device appeared to be the most ready vehicle to accomplish this. The individual states were urged to empower their townships to submit a no-liquor-license proposition to the township voters. With the adoption of local option, the legal sale of liquor in a saloon would be stopped eventually because the saloon's liquor license would not be renewed. The evident weakness of the Dry township plan by local option was that Demon Rum moved in from the surrounding Wet or legal liquor districts. The cure for this was alcohol prohibition at the state level and someday throughout the nation. One could even dream of an entire world wherein alcoholic beverages would be prohibited. The key to all of this splendid thinking was local option. After the Civil War, state after state in the East and the Midwest authorized township elections. Temperance was on the march.

When the rural and small-town districts, the bellwethers of the Movement, truly began to dry up, an interesting aspect of liquor prohibition appeared—a sharp increase in the use of patent medicines in these localities. Advertised to be highly desirable tonics and sold in good-sized bottles, the most widely used contained a substantial percentage of grain alcohol. Pe-Ru-Nu was one-third alcohol in a pint-and-a-half bottle and sold for $1.10. Another favorite was Lydia Pinkham's Vegetable Compound (more than one-fifth alcohol by government analyses in 1902) and was recommended by the manufacturer for a wide array of female complaints.

Whatever the patent medicine foibles of some of their sisters, the bulk of the women of the United States by the 1870s and 1880s had clearly decided that the consumption of alcohol in any form should be prohibited. Raised for a generation or more in the increasingly savage denunciation of Demon Rum and its running dogs of Sin, Pauperism, Romanism and Rebellion, the women supported the antisaloon demonstrators. Naturally, the followers of a Carry Nation would set the fashion of breaking into the saloons, smashing the barrels with axes and sweeping the liquor bottles off the shelves with pokers. The obedient menfolk in the background supported their ladies whether they were really Dry believers or not. By this time it was evident to even the dullest of the men that the ladies meant business.

When the *Crusade Temperance Almanac* of 1875 asked the rhetorical question: "Who is left to [suppress saloons] but God and Women?" there was little question that God had relinquished His task to a more powerful force, at least for a time. Francis E. Willard, the driving Temperance leader, told her flock what they wanted to hear when she dramatically warned "of the inflamed nature of men, let loose from the 250,000 saloons of the nation upon the weak and unarmed women, whose bewildering danger it is to have attracted [their] savage glances. . . . Intemperance and impurity are iniquity's Siamese twins [and] every house of ill-repute is a secret saloon and nearly every inmate an inebriate."

"Saloon" is still a loaded and carefully unused word in the liquor-dispensing fraternity nearly a half-century after the repeal of the national prohibition amendment in the early 1930s. There is good reason. Once a synonym for an impressive apartment or drawing room it had too often come to mean in nineteenth-century America a drinking den filled with the reek of stale beer, wine and adulterated liquor. Associated with this saloon definition could be bullyboys and knockout drops along with the drunks and noisy semidrunks leaning against the walls of the establishment and vomiting into the gutter. With proper coaching, a few of the drunks were more than willing to expose themselves and shock the women Dry agitators demonstrating across the street from the saloon. Within this kind of framework the Temperance tableaus pictured the harried and desperate wife who sent her oldest youngster into the saloon to haul on the husband's coat and call out in a childish treble: "Father, dear Father, come home with me now . . ."

There was another side to the saloon argument. Unquestionably it was the poor man's club in the cities and a meeting place removed from his women in the villages and towns. The cluster of quietly gossiping men with a nucleus of young veterans of the war, the low-stake card games, and the land boomer or traveling drummer talking with the small businessman while the two stood at the bar were typical scenes in the tens of thousands of drinking places throughout the country. In addition to providing the customers newspapers, magazines and very often billiards, the saloon was a reference point for messages, mail and listings of available jobs. It usually had one of the first telephones in the neighborhood and often the only washroom and bathing facility.

The "free lunch" at the end of the saloon's bar was controversial, and the food served was generally good. The buffet might include some or all of such standard bar items as cheese, baked beans, hard-boiled eggs, salt herring, ham, Welsh rarebit, corned beef, soup and beef stew. The Drys insisted that the free lunch was an evil device to increase the consumption of liquor by association; much like inexpensive Las Vegas entertainment of today is to encourage casino gambling. The astute moderate drinker strongly disagreed with the position of the Drys. To him this was an opportunity for a thrifty and good lunch or a supper break in the long workday of the period. Saloon competition was intense and the quality of the free lunch a substantial factor in a saloon's financial success in selling liquor and beer. Unintentionally, the saloons pioneered in the serving of good short-order food, a practice subsequently picked up by the automats and dairy lunches and then the coffee shops and franchised hamburger stands. But whatever the prosaloon arguments might be, nothing could stem the incoming tide of Temperance.

Some fifty towns in southern California by the end of the 1880s had become involved in one form or another with local control or prohibition of the sale of liquor. Ontario and Coronado even had deed restrictions covering saloons. Pasadena had gone Dry and Pomona's ordinances subjected the town's saloons to detailed and harassing supervision. The character of the hired bartender had to be approved by the Pomona town council, and each saloon was to consist of only one room. Half of the room's windows on the street side were to be of clear glass so that a full view of the bar and its occupants could be had from the sidewalk. Saloon fees were set at a prohibitive level—$5000 for a Pomona permit and $500 for a six-month license.

Shortly after Los Angeles severely limited the number of saloons in the city in the late 1890s, the county extended local liquor option down to the precinct level. This simply meant that a neighborhood could eliminate its corner saloon at will. After the Los Angeles County option action, the *Pacific Wine and Spirits Review* sadly and correctly warned the liquor trade that ". . . unless the saloon men have the forethought to organize and fight, then this condition of affairs will spread throughout the state."

Drugstores became liquor and beer sales points for a time when the saloons dried up. A Wet who wanted a beer in Riverside of the 1890s went down into the basement of any of the principal drugstores. If the beer was to be drunk off premises, the main floor clerk was asked for "one shoe or two shoes." The clerk disappeared for a moment and then returned with a shoebox containing one or two bottles of beer.

There was one sure indication of the towering strength of the Temperance Movement and the rigid moral posture in the principal rural areas and towns on the South Coast. This was when periodicals like the Covina *Argus* could afford to joke mildly about the Movement and its adherents:

"It is whispered that a number of Covina girls got together at the close of the meeting last Wednesday evening and adopted the following 'platform':

> *"The man who takes the red, red wine,*
> *Can never glue his lips to mine;*
> *The man who chews the navy plug,*
> *Will in our parlors get no hug;*
> *Who smokes or chews or cuts a deck,*
> *Shall never, never chew our neck . . .*
> *Drink nothing stronger than red pop,*
> *Or in your laps we'll never flop . . ."*

Hard drinkers found the momentum of the Temperance Movement equivalent to facing a tidal bore, equally dangerous to their career and social survival. For some the answer was to mask or preferably hide completely the liquor addiction. One of these was Griffith Jenkins Griffith who reputedly reached a peak consumption of two quarts of whiskey a day while protesting publicly he did not touch liquor. The predictable alcoholic crisis occurred at the Arcadia Hotel in Santa Monica when his accelerating persecution delusions resulted in an attempt to murder his wife.

A short man with a high laugh, brilliant with an abrasive personality, Griffith J. Griffith had arrived on the South Coast during its first boomlet in the seventies and successfully built a land and business fortune. As the decades passed, the millionaire seemed to become more vain, more noisy and more irritating, with some acquaintances characterizing him as a midget egomaniac. Griffith was easy to dislike. Even in 1898 when he made a magnificent 3000-acre gift of hills and some bottomlands from the old Rancho Los Feliz for a Los Angeles city park, many of his critics mocked the gift as a worthless rockpile. Horace Bell went further in a satirical piece based on a legend that the donated lands were haunted by the ghost of Antonio Feliz, owner of the original rancho grant:

" 'What, oh, what can I do with this terrible property?' groans the Baron [Griffith].

" 'You can't sell it,' mused [his business] secretary.

" 'No.'

" 'You won't live on it.'

" 'I wouldn't spend a night on it for a million.'

" 'You have to pay taxes on it right along.'

" 'Horrors, yes, taxes-taxes.'

" 'I'll tell you what I would do,' announces the secretary, coming to life. 'I'd give the bedeviled place away.'

" 'Who in hell would take it—a place that is all taxes, no income and stocked with demons?'

" 'Donate it to the City of Los Angeles!' cries the secretary, an inspired look in his eyes. 'Give it to the city as a park and the municipal council will rise up and call you blessed. . . .' "

There were violent emotional reactions against Griffith before and during his trial for the attempted murder and resultant facial disfigurement of his wife. The press pictured him as a monster. Yet the millionaire was fortunate he lived when he did. Forty years earlier in Los Angeles, he would have been lynched. Griffith's lawyer, Earl Rogers, who had reluctantly taken the case, made a surprising and effective defense of alcoholic insanity, perhaps the first of its kind in the United States. Because of this the defendant received only a two-year sentence with provision for psychiatric treatment.

Griffith J. Griffith was a different man when he came out of prison—quiet, sober, still with an offbeat personality but somehow calm. He had found his cause. Prison reform and job placement of convicts absorbed him to the end of his life. Almost incidentally Griffith gave $100,000 in 1912 for the construction of an observatory on Mount Hollywood in his beloved park, and his will provided for the establishment of the Greek Theater. Griffith's works outlived his critics.

CHAPTER 7

"Grand rain—3.57 inches"

The massive Pacific storms birthed in the empty ocean between Siberia and Alaska determine the major weather systems for western United States and Canada. These storms sweep routinely through Washington, Oregon and the extreme northern part of California; and many hundreds of miles away, southern California lies on the erratic fringe of their weather patterns. The backbone of a mountainous California is its Sierra Nevada which runs much of the length of the state and is the first to feel the major land effect of the heavy and rain-laden clouds of the advancing Pacific storms.

The Sierras are raw mountains, a great block of granite tilted sharply upward on its eastern side and rising in a few miles to a maximum height of over 14,000 feet at Mount Whitney. The water-laden air from the Pacific Ocean dumps huge quantities of snow during the winter storms, through rapid adiabatic cooling when the moist air hits the western flanks of the high new mountains. A record of seventy-three feet of snow has been recorded during a Sierra winter season—this at 8000 feet. Sixty-five feet of snow have been logged in at Donner Pass, the main railroad route from Reno to Sacramento, with a yearly average of thirty-one feet.

Because southern California is on the fringe of these extensive storm patterns, snow levels in its mountains and rain in its valleys are usually much less than further north and can vary tremendously from year to year during the six-month rainy period. Therefore the arrival of the first substantial rainstorm in the fall of the year was a major event in the cattle and then the agricultural economy of the South Coast. With little or no rain since the previous spring, the countryside was parched, brown and dusty with large aimless cracks in the adobe clay ground. In a matter of a few weeks after the first heavy rain in late October or early November the yearly miracle of change took place. The green hills and valleys stretched to the gaunt mountain with their ridges of snow. The clay cracks healed, and the streambeds filled with water.

A benign climate and normal rainfall made this a wonderful cattle and agricultural country. However southern California was always in a precarious climatic balance. On a chance basis there could be scant rainfall over the critical six-month period or much of the precious water could be wasted if the rains occurred in a short period of days or weeks. During the Civil War a drought which lasted well over two years ended the Californio ranchos and cattle economy of the South Coast. Yet in 1884 Los Angeles had twenty-six inches of rain in February and March while there was none in the same months of the next year. The weeks of concentrated rain meant flooding of a good part of Los Angeles when the nearby river broke through its levees and turned the lowlands into vast lakes, with dead animals, wreckage and debris drifting in the mindless currents of the flooded areas.

These violent oscillations of rainfall forced an intense pre-occupation with the weather in both rural and urban areas of the agricultural South Coast. Henry W. O'Melveny was typical of this absorption when he entered rainfall figures in his daily business journal much as if he was cheering on a home team, with comments like "Grand rain—3.57 inches." The moment a newcomer accepted rainfall statistics as legitimate front-page news and conversation rather than a monumental bore, he had become a Southern Californian.

When the flowing rivers of the South Coast became dis-couraging and desultory trickles well before the end of the dry season, even the most amateur settler knew that his year-round water supply must come from underground. Very shallow wells of ten to fifteen feet near streambeds were hand dug, and water was brought to the surface with a bucket or a small pitcher pump. For depths up to a hundred feet an auger turned by a horse was often used, the auger bit design being similar to many present-day posthole diggers. For the deeper wells without artesian flows, windmills pumped up the water into tanks above the farmhouses.

A standard alternative to the auger method was the cable-tool rig working from a tripod tower two dozen or so feet high. A heavy iron chisel bit was laboriously wound up to the top of the tripod and then dropped in vertical guides much like a guillotine, with the bit slamming into the rock at the bottom of the hole. Both the auger and cable-tool methods required a blacksmith and his forge for the repeated resharpening of the indifferent biting edges of the metal tools. If the cap rock was thick and hard, days and weeks could go by while the hole moved slowly and expensively downward.

The decision by the settler to sink a well for water at a particular point in most districts was nerve-racking at the best and bankruptcy at the worst. Outside experts were consulted, local gossip was weighed, and local "water witch" practitioners were used by a good many. Insisting on silence while going about his work, the water witch or douser utilized a wishbone-shaped twig which he held with both hands above his head. Selecting what to him seemed the most propitious location on his client's parcel of land, the douser usually moved backward and forward in an east-west direction followed closely by a silent but heavy-breathing audience. At the spot where he felt the strongest downward pull on his upright arms the water witch would lower the twig to the ground and then ceremoniously hammer in a stake. The same procedure was repeated on a north/south axis. Presumably water would be found in the middle region between the two stakes. While some scoffed, most settlers believed the douser's skill enhanced the possibilities of finding the precious water. They were undoubtedly right. The douser did have a favorable record of success due to his familiarity with conditions encountered in nearby wells supplemented by empirical geologic knowledge like a tipped rock stratum welling up water during heavy rains.

The most spectacular sources of underground water were artesian wells. San Pedro stagecoaches on their way to Los Angeles would detour to point out the novel sight in a semiarid country of a flowing well bubbling to the surface under its own pressure. The well had tapped a subterranean channel of water moving toward the sea. Such channels were filled from surface water seeping through intervening rock strata, and much of this seepage could be many miles away from a well bore. The gravity flow of the water moving down the subterranean channels provided the pressure to raise the water to the surface—in some instances strong enough to form a mushrooming kind of a fountain. With understanding of artesian possibilities, wells were bored to depths of 40 to 200 feet and eventually 1000 feet. The Gospel Swamp people around present-day Fountain Valley and Springdale in Orange County loved to boast, and with good reason, about their flowing, bubbling wells. They solemnly warned the new settler that he had to be careful with fence postholes, or he would have a string of unwanted artesian wells following him across his property.

Beyond the water wells of the individual settlers, however, southern California badly needed a broad scale yet integrated irrigation concept suitable for its particular requirements. This notion generated in an unlikely place—the Colorado Desert.

For those who had to cross it, the Colorado Desert was an abomination of desolation. Forming the far southeastern portion of California, its waterless burning stretches, shifting sand hills, alkali flats with their penetrating dust and the keening wind for days on end were notorious to Westerners, well used to all of those things. To propose seriously that such a region could support a prosperous agricultural economy was patently absurd even if, by some impossible chance, Colorado River water could be made available. Yet all of this was what Dr. Oliver M. Wozencraft foresaw even before the Civil War. His plans were dismissed with hard laughter, and he was considered simply a small fanatic who dealt in large fantasies.

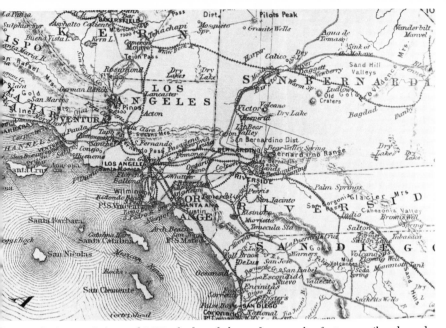

The South Coast of the mid-1890s had a skeleton framework of steam railroads and a dirt road system for teaming. From *California of the South* (1896).

The great railroad rate war of 1886-87 brought a national rush to the South Coast with the Southern Pacific depositing 120,000 people in Los Angeles during one year. *Courtesy of Title Insurance and Trust Company.*

The speculative froth of the land boom was most evident at parcel auctions like th Monrovia subdivision. *Courtesy of Title Insurance and Trust Company.*

Palm trees greeted Southern Pacific passengers coming out of the fine new Arcade Stati of the late 1880s in Los Angeles. *Courtesy of California State Library.*

Elias J. (Lucky) Baldwin. A well-deserved reputation as a rake and libertine overshadowed his legendary speculative and land ⟨ac⟩quisition capabilities. *Courtesy of* ⟨T⟩*itle Insurance and Trust Company.*

⟨At⟩ the start of the Boom of the eighties Los Angeles' population was about 12,000. This ⟨188⟩5 photograph shows Spring Street looking north from First. *Courtesy of Title Insurance* ⟨and⟩ *Trust Company.*

Manuel Dominguez. In contrast to most Californios, he and his heirs managed to keep the bulk of Rancho San Pedro land intact. *Courtesy of the Dominguez Estate.*

Isaias W. Hellman. The premier Western banker of his generation, Hellman's conservative practices carried southern Cailfornia through financial panics. *Courtesy of Security Pacific National Bank.*

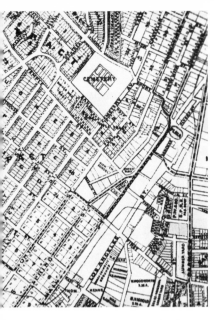

During the Boom of the eighties H. J. Stevenson's 1884 map of Los Angeles was a required reference. The central portion of the map is shown here. *Courtesy of Los Angeles Public Library.*

e Chinese were hated as a group in California but loved individually. *Courtesy of Se-ity Pacific National Bank.*

The California missions were wrecks after generations of neglect. Beginning in the 189
Charles F. Lummis headed an effective mission restoration group. *Courtesy of Title Ins
ance and Trust Company.*

Flowing artesian wells in a semiarid country like the South Coast impressed new settl
particularly in the Gospel Swamp area of the new Orange County. *Courtesy of T
Insurance and Trust Company.*

George Chaffey. Often-times ignoring sound business counsel, he brought large-scale irrigation to the United States and Australia. *Courtesy of Title Insurance and Trust Company.*

The relief map shows the Imperial Valley (Colorado Desert) just before a rampant Colorado River filled Salton Sink, minus 235 feet below sea level. *Courtesy of Title Insurance and Trust Company.*

Packing oranges had become a production procedure by the mid-1900s. Research was just showing the importance of careful fruit handling. *Courtesy of Los Angeles County Museum.*

The famed gravity railroad of Ontario utilized two mules to pull the car up a long grade; the photograph shows a return trip. *Courtesy of Title Insurance and Trust Company.*

A wondrous dragon, 200 feet long and carried on the heads of local Chinese, was a feat of the 1894 La Fiesta de Los Angeles. *Courtesy of Title Insurance and Trust Company.*

Trackwalkers lead a Southern Pacific passenger train in 1905 across Salton Sink. By mischance the Sink was rapidly filling with Colorado River water. *Courtesy of Southern Pacific Company.*

A sea wall 200 feet wide at the base and nearly two miles long, the San Pedro breakwater was built of rock hauled in by railroad. *Courtesy of Title Insurance and Trust Company.*

The first teaching hospital on the South Coast. California became a regional symbol of man's triumphs over disease. *Courtesy of Huntington Library.*

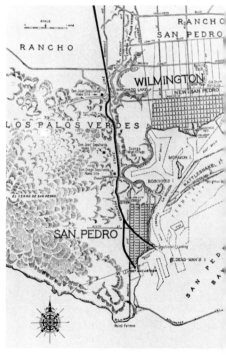

This 1925 map of San Pedro Harbor shows the location of Dead Man's Island, Wilmington Lagoon and Rattlesnake (Terminal) Island. *Courtesy of Title Insurance and Trust Company.*

ne ladies back their whaleboat down in San Diego Bay near a steam yacht and a fast, ff-rigged sloop. *Courtesy of Title Insurance and Trust Company of San Diego.*

Frank Wiggins. The powerful and effective Los Angeles Chamber of Commerce was due in substantial part to the organizing work of Wiggins and C. D. Willard. *Courtesy of Security Pacific National Bank.*

Henry E. Huntington. Eventually known as the Trolley Man, he built the famous interurban system of the South Coast with its "Big Red Cars." *Courtesy of Southern Pacific Company.*

Pick-and-shovel work built this double-tracked horsecar line on Los Angeles' Main Street. St. Vibiana Cathedral is in the background. *Courtesy of Security Pacific National Bank.*

The expensive Los Angeles cable car system, best symbolized by "the great San Fernando Street Viaduct" over the railroad yards, was bankrupt in 1893. *Courtesy of Security Pacific National Bank.*

Trolley line construction required tower rigs for the overhead network of wires. Obviously, OSHA and its safety regulations had not yet arrived on the South Coast. *Courtesy of Security Pacific National Bank.*

The elegant Victoria of the 1900s is in front of one of the bon ton stores on Broadway between Second and Third streets in Los Angeles. *Courtesy of Los Angeles County Museum.*

William Mulholland. This famed aqueduct and water engineer accumulated friends and enemies with equal vigor. *Courtesy of Los Angeles Department of Water and Power.*

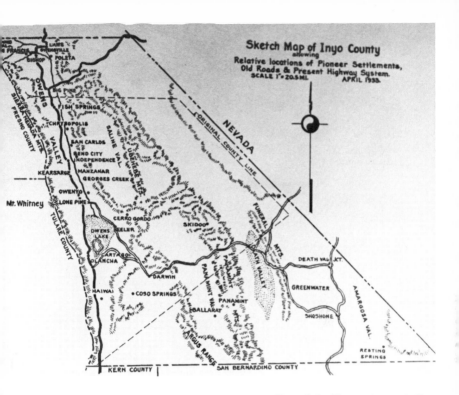

Sketch Map of Inyo County showing Relative locations of Pioneer Settlements, Old Roads & Present Highway System. SCALE 1" = 20.5 MI. APRIL 1933.

East of the Sierras, Owens Valley in Inyo County was the water collection point for the controversial Los Angeles Aqueduct, completed in 1913. From *The Story of Inyo* (1933).

The Owens Valley aqueduct to Los Angeles, 250 miles long and an engineering triumph, was built over and through most difficult topography. *Courtesy of Los Angeles Department of Water and Power.*

Ocean bathing was popular at Venice in the late 1900s. The people clustered at the water's edge are holding on to a surf rope attached to a buoy. *Courtesy of Los Angeles County Museum.*

Typical of beach tent cities of the 1900s was this one on the Silver Strand below the Ho Coronado and across San Diego Bay. *Courtesy of Title Insurance and Trust Company San Diego.*

Several years before his death the elderly visionary who was still dreaming his particular impossible dream talked at length with a young Canadian engineer. Wozencraft made a convert. He was able to convince the engineer, George Chaffey, of the long-term feasibility of irrigating the Colorado Desert. But of more immediate importance, the Wozencraft conversations reinforced Chaffey's convictions that the semiarid plains to the west of San Bernardino and Riverside could be systematically watered and the soil would be fertile.

Chance brought George Chaffey to southern California in 1880, and he had no background in the novel and challenging field of irrigation. Chaffey had worked on his father's freight boats in Canada and was a Great Lakes ship designer and builder until he visited his father who had just retired and moved to the small town of Riverside. After seeing the accomplishments of the Riverside Colony and its irrigation use of Santa Ana River water, the thirty-three-year-old engineer was excited about the vacant lands extending over the horizon to the west of the settlement. This was the rank amateur in water development who was destined to become the greatest irrigationist of his time. During the next quarter of a century he would remake the agricultural economy of a good part of southern California and Australia.

Probably the most important characteristic of George Chaffey was his vast reservoir of energy combined with a receptive and curious mind which welcomed and understood the explosion of man's knowledge in the nineteenth century. He needed all of this ability at times to counteract some of his astoundingly poor business decisions. In later years he was fortunate in having one of his sons who ably advised him on such matters. Unfortunately, Chaffey had a dismaying habit at times of ignoring the advice. Powerfully built and fairly tall, the irrigationist looked older than his years because of a heavy square beard turned prematurely grey and a thinning hairline. Chaffey had the reputation of a personable man who was also a born leader. Yet he was reticent to a fault in refusing to express himself to large groups or answering newspaper attacks. In a small meeting he listened attentively and talked brilliantly with his normally hooded blue eyes sparkling while he gestured home a point. But above all else to those who knew him well, Chaffey was a born risk taker.

Thanksgiving Day of 1881 was the date that George Chaffey with his younger brother, William, launched an irrigation career. They bought the Garcia ranch fourteen miles west of San Bernardino together with some adjoining acreage and called it the Etiwanda Colony. A year later they acquired 6700 acres of Rancho Cucamonga twenty miles west of San Bernardino along with the Kincaid water rights and one-half of the surface rights in the San Antonio Canyon below the 10,000 foot Mount Baldy. The Chaffeys paid about $60,000 for the land and rights, which they named the Ontario Colony.

The validity of the Etiwanda purchase was reasonably evident to outsiders, the Ontario decision definitely was not. Looking south from San Antonio Canyon and bounded by two boulder-strewn washes a mile to three miles apart was a narrow strip of land extending in a gradual downward slope for seven miles with the far reaches disappearing into a purple haze of heat devils and sagebrush. This was strictly coyote and jackrabbit country which might support a single head of cattle on ten to fifteen acres of land. The people of Pomona six miles away were convinced that George Chaffey was simply a younger and crazier Wozencraft when they heard how he proposed to provide water for his extensive Ontario project.

The irrigationist recruited men to dig a lateral tunnel of over a half-mile in length into the dry streambed of San Antonio Canyon along with another lateral tunnel to the west of the canyon. While the local gossips did not realize it, Chaffey had a sound geologic basis for his decision. He was convinced that a tunnel into the gravel and rock bed would tap a major and dependable pool of subterranean water percolating down through the rock structure and not lost through surface runoff from the canyon mouth below Mount Baldy. The water he anticipated was there, and the land was fertile.

George Chaffey had another important reason for his Ontario

site selection. The gentle but continuous slope to the south along the entire length of the tract made efficient gravity irrigation from the water source possible at minimum costs. Forty miles of concrete pipe (made on the site) distributed water to the highest point of each ten-acre parcel. The final major element in the Ontario plan was a simple yet ingenious scheme which insured irrigation use representation in water management of the colony. This was the establishment of a mutual water company owned and managed by the water users, wherein each parcel holder had voting shares of the company proportionate to the number of acres owned to the total colony acreage. The interlocking elements of the Ontario water plan became the model for all of the South Coast land developments on the alluvial fans below the mountain canyons.

The town of Ontario was a planned community. A 200-foot-wide Euclid Avenue was laid out so that its base was a fountain near the Southern Pacific tracks and its head at the mesa of the Sierra Madre foothills seven miles away. The center park strip of Euclid Avenue had a gravity railroad, both a practical transportation and promotional feature of the colony. Two mules hauled a rail car up the gradual grade to the mesa, and then solemnly rode back down on a tender attached to the coach.

Along with transportation George Chaffey was determined that his new town would have a college, a campus of the fledgling University of Southern California. He allocated one-half of the town lots to the college for endowment funds and twenty central acres for the campus. Neither Chaffey brother was a strong teetotaler but they correctly estimated the rising tide of Temperance. Each of the deeds of the Ontario tract provided for a reversionary clause if there was sale of alcoholic beverages on the parcel. The Ontario Colony had all of the ingredients for a solid promotional success including its famous fountain whose water volume was turned up prior to the arrival of a passenger train.

The Royal Australian Irrigation Commission arrived on one of those Southern Pacific trains in 1885 to inspect the Ontario Colony. The chairman, Alfred Deakin, later his nation's prime minister, had heard of the irrigation success of Ontario after the commission members had included southern California on its itinerary because of the climatic and soil resemblance to many parts of their own country. With the ubiquitous eucalyptus, first introduced on the South Coast from Australia around 1870 and widely planted, Deakin's group found the regional similarities were even more pronounced. The Chaffey brothers were much impressed with the Australian chairman who had early recognized that "a weakness of George Chaffey [was] to be always on the watch for some new wilderness to conquer." The upshot of the Deakin meeting and later communications was that the Chaffey brothers would go to that far land and introduce systematic irrigation into Australia.

The first Australian location selected by the American irrigationist was not prepossessing: "A Sahara of hissing hot winds and red driving sand, a howling carrion-polluted wilderness. The only thriving thing was the rabbit [the scourge of Australia] which increased miraculously, for there was no grass." But George and his brother, W. B. Chaffey, who joined him after selling their Ontario properties at the beginning of the Boom were convinced of the irrigation possibilities of the remote subcontinent. The Chaffey brothers' experience in Australia was a record of magnificent success and then, with the international business depression of the mid-1890s, a memorable failure.

A not-so-ebullient George Chaffey and his family returned to the South Coast in 1897. Soon the irrigationist and his son, Andrew, were involved in profitable land and water development matters in southern California. But again Chaffey reached for his particular star over the strenuous business objections of his son.

The irrigationist's experience in Australia with the deserts and hissing winds there had persuaded Chaffey that the concepts of Oliver M. Wozencraft of so long ago could now be implemented. He would bring water to the Colorado Desert. His vision saw an extraordinarily productive land with broad prosperous farms and supporting market towns.

The Colorado River of another geologic period headwatered in the Rocky Mountains and emptied into the Gulf of California at just about the point where Mexico, California and Arizona now meet. What subsequently became the Colorado Desert, and much of which is known as the Imperial Valley, then was an extensive indentation of the Gulf with the northern waters lapping at the base of the San Jacinto Mountains near today's Palm Springs and San Gorgonio Pass. The deepest part of the sprawling bay and, for that matter, a good part of the Gulf of California itself lay only fifty miles southeast of these mountains at the Salton Sink. During the passing ages the violent Colorado slashed its course through what came to be called the Grand Canyon. The debris of the river's tempestuous floods formed a mammoth delta which eventually cut off the northern bay from the Gulf. With an increasing aridity cycle in the region the inland sea gradually dried up and became a parched sandy desert underlaid with a deep rich silt deposit of the long-departed sea. George Chaffey proposed to move Colorado River water to these lands. Unfortunately his choice of a corporate vehicle to accomplish the task was a poor thing indeed as his son had been quick to point out.

The California Development Corporation in 1899 was not long for this economic world. Clearly, the company was going to collapse under its own ineffectiveness in the next few months. Seven years before John C. Beatty with his own brand of water promotional imagination commissioned C. R. Rockwood to make an engineering survey dealing with the irrigation potential of the Arizona side of the Colorado River. While Beatty's venture fizzled out, it did induce Rockwood to become an irrigation promoter himself and he was one of the organizers of the California Development Corporation in 1896. After a variety of futile paper transactions which resulted in the accumulation of little money and no irrigation work, the surviving principals—A. H. Heber, S. W. Fergusson and C. R. Rockwood—approached George Chaffey through his friend of two decades, L. M. Holt. After discussing the group's proposal with his son, Chaffey told Holt he would not become involved with the Rockwood venture.

A few months later, over the violent objection of Andrew, Chaffey completely reversed his position and impulsively ex-

ecuted a contract with the California Development Corporation
—a company destined in a few years to become a notorious name
throughout much of the United States. Shortly after signing the
contract, Chaffey discovered a number of representations or
warranties were inaccurate. To his dismay, among other things,
the irrigationist found that the company did not own either
the indispensable Mexican lands or the key acreage at Pilot
Knob where the main irrigation canal would tap the Colorado
River. He may have been dismayed but he stubbornly refused
to jettison the contract.

For a pittance George Chaffey had contracted to do a great
deal in a hostile desert environment. He was to provide the
money to construct a lengthy canal system from the Colorado
River which would deliver a minimum annual water total of
400,000 acre feet. In return, the irrigationist was to receive
twenty-five percent of the stock in a company which was mostly
on paper and, at a later date, $60,000 in cash or water rights.

Astride the direct route from the Colorado River to the
planned water distribution center was an impenetrable barrier
of sand dunes fifty miles long and twelve miles wide. Chaffey
decided to have the main canal detour to the south until it
reached the dry and ancient channel of the Alamo River in
Mexico. He thus was able to use forty miles of this riverbed
which ran westerly and then bent back to the United States
border and the Salton Sink, the lowest part of the old sea. Just
south of the border the new canal left the Alamo channel and
continued northward to the center of the first valley district
to receive Colorado River water. Chaffey accomplished all this
for about $100,000 while establishing two new townsites—Cal-
exico and Mexicali. Water was delivered to Calexico in May of
1901, only thirteen months after the irrigationist signed the
contract. In another year there were 400 miles of lateral canals
and irrigation ditches. The euphemism, Imperial Valley, was
selected by Chaffey to replace "Colorado Desert" with all of
its past sinister connotations.

Still the new associates of the canal builder were restless and
greedy. Once the water was turned into the lateral canals they

saw large and quick profits and had small interest in central channel improvement and maintenance, primary concerns of Chaffey. Finally, even the irrigationist could see that he was in a hopeless minority position regarding company priorities and distribution of funds. He sold out his position for about the same money he had invested, with no recompense for his time, accomplishment or risk. At least he received his capital back, more than could be said for the outcome of some of his Australian episodes. Equally important, he finally convinced himself that heed should be given to his son, Andrew, on financial and contractual matters.

For the Southwest it was a tragedy that George Chaffey left the Colorado Desert when he did. Incredible technical mistakes followed miscalculations there in the next few years. The wild Colorado, one of the great rivers of North America, was turned by man's doing into the Salton Sink instead of its natural home, the Gulf of California. H. T. Cory, the engineer who finally stopped the appalling flood, and only then because of maximum backing of the Southern Pacific and the Federal Government, wrote about Chaffey's conquest of the Colorado Desert:

"He acted with such decision and energy that he fixed and determined the lines of its development irrevocably; so wisely that its success has been phenomenal in spite of the mistakes made after he severed all connection with it, so many, so grave, and often so inexcusable, as to assure disaster to any ordinary enterprise."

The channel of the Main Canal to the Imperial Valley paralleled the natural levee of the Colorado River for several miles below the canal intake at Chaffey Gate. After the regular summer flood of 1904 the stretch of channel alongside the river was badly silted with the resultant reduction in water flow through the canal. Dredging machinery was inadequate, and neither capital moneys nor George Chaffey's sure technical touch was available. Irrigated land sales to new settlers in the Imperial

Valley were booming, and there would be heavy water demands in the next summer season, less than a year away. Thus the stage was set for a train of grave mistakes and miscalculations in estimating Colorado River flow.

C. R. Rockwood, chief engineer of the California Development Company, and his other managing associates had a neat solution to their silting problem. Rockwood proposed to make two small bypass cuts through the natural levee four miles south of Chaffey Gate and across the Mexican border. The silted canal section then could be cleared at leisure and, as a pleasant by-product, the Mexican intake could be used as a pawn in a running controversy with the fledgling Federal Reclamation Service. The fatal decision was made and Cut No. 2 and Cut No. 3 (the Rockwood Cut as it was known ever after) were opened into the Colorado River beginning in late September of 1904. Cut No. 2 was closed by Christmas, usually the annual low-water point of the Colorado River flow, before the days of upstream dams. The Rockwood Cut was left open, according to the chief engineer, because permission from the Mexican government could not be obtained for well over a year to install a control gate at the new intake point.

Whatever the flimsy rationale, C. R. Rockwood's failure to close the cut in one form or another was a deadly technical error. The Yellow Dragon, as some called the silt-laden Colorado, had five 1905 winter floods. The Rockwood intake cut was widened dramatically by clawing currents. The pushing waters down the Main Canal took out the lightweight dams all along the Alamo and then followed the ancient riverbed until the rivulets of Colorado River water entered the deep, dry Salton Sink, the first elements of a great flood. With almost a biblical feeling of fatalism, the Imperial Valley settlers watched helplessly while a major river of North America ran amok.

John Tangney, the maintenance superintendent for a stretch of Southern Pacific tracks between San Gorgonio Pass and Yuma, Arizona, was having a difficult time convincing his superiors in Los Angeles that he was not seeing a desert mirage. Tangney reported he was filling gunnysacks with sand to buttress his railroad track from rising waters, and that track was fifteen feet above the bottom of Salton Sink. Eventually, even the San Francisco headquarters reacted in July of 1905 after the *Golden State Limited* was just able to splash through at a crawl with a man walking ahead.

A hurried meeting was called by Julius Kruttschnitt, the senior Southern Pacific operating executive, and Edward H. Harriman was consulted. After the railroad's engineers reported that most of the waters of the mighty Colorado were being diverted into the Alamo and thence to the Salton Sink rather than the Gulf of California, the Southern Pacific decided to become involved. If the diversion continued, surely the Imperial Valley and its vast agricultural potential would disappear under water. A $200,000 loan was made to a dazed California Development Company for leveeing what sections of land it could against the enveloping waters while the railroad engineers laid out a plan of attack.

Forty-three miles of the main line of the Southern Pacific between Mecca and Old Beach were eventually involved in the rising waters. As the flood rose, the railroad kept moving its line higher on the shoulders of the Salton Sink, or the Salton Sea as it was now beginning to be called. Two years after the Colorado pushed through the Rockwood Cut, the surface of the Salton Sea was minus 146 feet below sea level at its lowest point which meant the maximum depth of water there was 89 feet. Parts of Superintendent Tangney's roadbed and sandbags were 74 feet below the whitecapped surface of an unlikely sea.

After a temporary dam from an island in the Colorado to the west bank of the river was taken out in 1905 by an unexpected November flood, the Southern Pacific finally recognized the strength of the adversary. Epes Randolph and his key engineer, H. T. Cory, building the railroad south of Guaymas in Mexico, were given the closure of Rockwood Cut as a responsibility. Their decision was to utilize a rock-dam type of construction, and Randolph told Cory to go ahead with the operation. The engineer laid a railroad line north to the Yuma/ Los Angeles tracks of the Southern Pacific and tie-in with rock quarries along the route. His first task was to raise the natural levee above and below the Rockwood Cut, now grown to an alarming half-mile width. Then Cory commenced the construction of two massive rock jetties, leaving a 600-foot gap through which the mainstream of the Colorado River rushed toward the Salton Sea rather than the Gulf of California.

Now the difficult task of sealing the gap was at hand. To connect the two jetties Cory first built a railroad trestle on piles driven down through the pulling current of the Colorado. While the trestle work was going on, a lace of wire cables intermeshed with heavy brush to form a foundation mattress was fabricated ashore. After the 600-foot mattress was sunk on the downstream side of the piles, the rock-fill operation commenced from railroad cars on the trestle. Finally a concrete head gate was mounted in the center of the dam, and H. T. Cory could report to Epes Randolph in September of 1906 that the Rockwood Cut had been sealed. He was wrong.

Less than a month later, the Yellow Dragon flicked its tail, and the Colorado floodwaters took out the new head gate and a section of the rock fill. Cory and his team went back to work. Rock was dumped into the gap with loaded cars rumbling in from as far away as Los Angeles. The break was sealed in a little more than three weeks and again the work crew scattered. And again, this time in early December, the Colorado broke the rock barrier.

By this time H. T. Cory's epic struggle with the Colorado was front-page news. President Theodore Roosevelt made a direct appeal to E. H. Harriman, the railroad magnate, to use every means at hand to repair the break. Harriman issued orders that Cory's requirements were to receive absolute priority throughout the Southern Pacific system. The engineer's requirements were harsh indeed. He demanded ten-ton or more chunks of granite to stand up to the restless, probing fingers of the

Colorado current, totaling up to more than a hundred thousand cubic yards of rock—and he wanted the material forthwith. A thousand or so men worked at the dam site and hundreds more were in support. Again a trestle was built out over the break and the rock was dumped in—80,000 cubic yards in one feverish fifteen-day period. Finally, on February 11, 1907, Cory and his exhausted crew had the breach sealed, and this time it held.

The Southern Pacific had forced the Yellow Dragon back into its natural channel, but more than a generation would pass before the Colorado's appalling floods could be controlled by upstream dams.

CHAPTER 8

"The reverberating cracks of bark splitting on mature orange trees in the deep still cold"

The second echelon of settlers moving into the sprawling and semiarid South Coast found the lands nearly as inhospitable as their predecessors had a score or so years earlier after the Civil War. Blustery, dry santana winds of the fall and winter months still piled bulky tumbleweeds roof high as they raked the plains and hills while "filling all the air with clouds of dust and seemingly concentrating all their power at the mesa's edge, thundering at our doors day and night as if in rage . . . and bent upon the destruction of ourselves and all our effects."

Along with the santanas the new settlers learned expensively that the region's rainfall was dangerously erratic, and much of it could be concentrated in a few heavy storms. After solid winter rains the wild mustard and other weeds grew astonishingly. Dinner-plate-sized sunflowers in places like the central San Gabriel Valley stared into the eyes of a man on horseback. The farmers had found the only effective way to strike down the saplinglike stalks supporting such huge blooms was to have several horses spread out fan-wise and drag a section of sharpened train rail through the sunflower forest.

Once the fields were cleared and crops planted, the settler discovered that the animal and insect life had voracious appetites. Hordes of jackrabbits and periodic plagues of locusts chewed on the crops and the kitchen vegetable plots. Coyotes rapidly developed a taste for the settlers' chickens, and gophers carefully pulled down young plantings into their tunnels. Near the game-bird flyways transient geese and ducks stuffed themselves with ripening grain. Mountain lions remained a threat to stock in the canyons, but the bears which the Californios detested had retreated to the mountains and few of them were left. However, there were plenty of three-foot-long bobcats in the hills who casually and painfully educated the household dogs, while eagles with a wingspan of six feet drifted overhead to carry off young lambs.

In addition to everything else, women in the remote farmhouses had a gnawing fear while the developing blight of the economic depression of the 1890s spread throughout the United States. Men were being laid off in the factories and shops of the Midwest and East by the scores of thousands. The nation was in economic turmoil, and poverty was on the march. Unemployed men by the hundreds were dropping off freight trains in southern California. Dirty, hungry and sometimes desperate, these bands of rootless men were certainly leavened with a share of child rapists, sadists and murderers. The specter of a rapacious tramp or hobo shambling into a farmhouse, with the children huddling in and clutching the farm wife's skirts while she stood at bay before the kitchen stove, was real enough to generate horror stories for a generation.

One thing was free and plentiful for the recent settler. That was advice on how to live and eat and given by experts, people who had spent at least a season on the South Coast. The outlander was advised to "sleep with the constellations as a canopy" even though the temperature ranges made such a procedure rigorous indeed a good share of the year. He was told that coughs and colds were scarce and that ". . . small wounds or scratches which would have proved troublesome elsewhere, healed up with marvelous speed." There were strong views on clothing: "The old-timers among the men found a blue woolen shirt, blue overalls, slouch hat and boots about all that was necessary any time of year; the women wore calico dresses, and perhaps other things; native children usually wore neatly fitting tan suits."

Robert Hornbeck dispensed some good advice on eating

habits during the hot months when he told the recent settlers that "the American usually insisted on beefsteak for breakfast and roast beef, boiled beef or corned beef and cabbage, coffee and pie for his dinner [at noon]. After his usual breakfast or dinner it was small wonder he felt the heat." On the other hand Hornbeck advocated a monumental assortment of food for breakfast during the cool months on the South Coast:

"Cantaloupes, oranges, grapefruit, coffee, toast, fresh ranch eggs—fried or poached, fried chicken, hot biscuits, fried mountain trout, liver and bacon, beefsteak Spanish style or with mushrooms, pork or mutton chops, corn fritters, sliced tomatoes and cucumbers, wheat cakes and maple syrup. Be sure and start the day right. If the stomach is O.K., the head and muscles are bound to be so."

A special kind of a miracle would have been required for the wife of a recent settler to provide the type of a breakfast Hornbeck recommended. The first crop of the farmer was usually barley and a scanty one at that. Generally dry-farmed, the settler had to be convinced that the soil was only to be plowed to a depth of three or four inches. This was to take maximum advantage of the light rains during the sprouting season after the fields were sown in the middle fall. Depending upon the erratic timing and amount of the winter rains, the height of the crop varied dramatically—in fine years high as the withers of a horse and in miserable seasons only six inches or so. A ton of barley hay an acre was considered a good average yield with a selling price of ten dollars a ton, and steam haying equipment routinely was being used in the 1890s.

A recurrent nightmare to the barley farmer during the dry months was the cascades of sparks from the steam agricultural units and locomotives. A grass fire could wipe out a year of work and the family's lives with only a few minutes of burning. Ten thousand acres of blackened fields and ruined hopes in one such fire near Puente, spread from the sparks of a locomotive, was evidence enough of that.

Most farmers set out fruit trees after their grain crops were established. Pears, plums, apples, peaches and cherries were all tried with varying degrees of success. The best cash crop of the deciduous fruits was dried apricots. The crop was picked in the summer, the fruit cut immediately in halves and then placed on redwood trays. The trays were loosely stacked over a pit containing burning sulphur and enclosed by cardboard. These "bleached" or "sulphured" apricots were then sun-dried for a week. The bright-colored and pliable dried fruit was ready for the market after a final ten days of bin storage, and traders paid from five to seven cents a pound for the fruit even during depressed farm prices of the 1890s.

Vegetable crops were planted between the young fruit trees and on land which was particularly suited for truck crops. Pumpkins, some of historic size, were raised for livestock food and cabbages, onions, table grapes and watermelons were profitable. One grower solemnly asserted that he lost nearly his whole crop of hillside melons to thirsty coyotes. The farmer claimed the coyotes nudged the melons until the gourds began rolling down the hill to be broken open when they struck the stones in the ravine below. There the coyotes presumably quenched their thirst from the succulent melon fragments. More prosaic crops were early potatoes followed by fall tomatoes. Picking of the tomatoes was underway by late summer and continued even into January. An Eastern market developed for this fall crop, with the tomatoes being shipped in the new Wells Fargo refrigerated cars.

Any orchardist understands the serious financial risk of guessing wrong on what trees to plant when the harvesting of the fruit or nuts is years away. A prime example of such a major miscalculation were the olive groves of California. The olive provided the world's principal cooking oil, and the South Coast variety of the 1890s was unquestionably equal in quality to the better grades of imported oil. An olive planting frenzy took place and within a few years there were 2,500,000 trees in California. But about the time the bulk of the groves were coming into production the California olive industry clearly could not compete on a cost basis with the just-introduced vegetable oils which satisfied most American tastes. Then the painful choice was to convert the groves to the relatively small pickled-olive market or rip out the trees for other plantings.

Bananas were grown as curiosities in the 1850s and sometime later an acre of the fruit was planted near Santa Barbara. As with mangos, the bananas were either of indifferent quality or matured in limited quantities. Pineapples showed equally poor results while papayas had more promise but the crop was still marginal. On the other hand the Japanese loquat flourished and was a popular fruit for a time during the 1900s. Tea, a close relative of the camellia, could grow in southern California but the quality was far inferior to its Asiatic competition. While the avocado was a native of Mexico and Guatemala, the fruit was not raised extensively if at all in the Alta California missions. There were a number of plantings in the 1870s on the South Coast, but the real awakening of the avocado industry was still several generations after that.

The English or soft-shelled walnut was another matter entirely. Next after citrus and sugar beets the crop became the symbol of the flourishing agriculture of southern California at the turn of the century. If walnuts with paper-thin shells could be grown in quality and quantity, there was an assured profitable market because of the few groves in the United States with most of the nuts being imported from Europe. The local walnut farmers found by cut-and-try experience what the bearing trees needed—cool and overcast weather while the groves were in bloom and moderately warm weather while the nuts were ripening. Too much fog was harmful, and the dry santana winds, fanning out from the desert passes, were worse. In favorable locations on the South Coast walnuts were replacing apricot and peach orchards and were considered a strong competitor to the best of citrus in profitability. Meanwhile, the expanding grape industry of only a few years earlier on the South Coast was in desperate difficulty.

The grape farmers around Anaheim were worried. The town was the center of the principal grape region of California with the associated manufacture of wines and brandies. In 1881 several alert growers had reported some shriveling of grape leaves on the vine. The next year showed much more of the blight with some of the oldest and strongest vines being affected. A Department of Agriculture expert was called in, but with no results. In succeeding years the blight spread inexorably throughout the grape acreage of southern California. The cause of the destruction was finally determined to be the leafhopper but a sure cure only became available in the late 1890s. By that time the vineyards and many of the owners were ruined, the land was converted to citrus, and the South Coast's long history of vineyards and wine was well on the way to being forgotten. That is, except for the furious energy of Secondo Guasti.

One of the earlier waves of Italian immigration deposited Guasti, a young man with the usual empty pockets, in Los Angeles where he first worked as a cook at the Hotel d'Italia on Second Street. Raised in the tradition of small vineyards of northern Italy, Secondo Guasti was involved in several tiny wineries around Los Angeles by the late 1890s, and he naturally followed with professional interest the identification and then the eradication of the Anaheim blight.

In the tradition of Wozencraft and Chaffey the Italian became obsessed with the idea that some of the desolate, dry and windswept regions of southern California could become prime agricultural land. Knowing that a grapevine sends its root system down to a depth of seven or eight feet, Guasti had convinced himself that thousands of barren acres with no prospects of surface irrigation lying between the Ontario Colony and San Bernardino could become fruitful vineyards. Hiring an assorted bag of laborers, the crazy Italian, as he was known in the district, dug an apparently aimless pattern of shallow holes on the idle plains, each time climbing down to feel the moistness of the earth as his father had done before him in Italy.

The prospecting digs confirmed Secondo Guasti's concepts. More to the point, in 1900 he convinced a group of his fellow Italian-Americans that they should invest $16,000 toward the establishment of the Italian Vineyard Company. Fifteen hundred acres of land were purchased and vines planted. The crazy Italian was right. The vines grew in the semidesert with no irrigation and the vineyard prospered. Eventually there were 5000 acres of vines stretching to the horizon, along with twenty-two miles of narrow-gauge railroad to transport the grapes to the winery on the property. Guasti could boast that his company had the world's largest vineyard and, very possibly, the noisiest and most interesting annual meeting of shareholders.

The vineyard company was closely held by intensely involved and hardworking Italian-Americans and their families. The annual meeting was unforgettable. The day was a combination of a secular feast, gathering of the clan, New England town meeting and fine safety valve for emotional people. In theory at least, the shareholders meeting was conducted in English. In fact the session shortly turned into machine-gun Italian, punctuated by staccato gestures, while the debaters preferably stood nose-to-nose and toe-to-toe. Violence if not mayhem appeared to be imminent. Presumably a corporate attorney was needed to answer officially annual meeting questions and ensure that some modicum of protocol was preserved in the general bedlam. William W. Clary often acted in this capacity:

"It was customary for the attorney to take the train to Guasti Station, where he would be met and conducted by carriage to a large hall. . . . The stockholders were Italian and they all attended. They were talkative and excitable. . . . Though sometimes it would appear to the attorney they were coming to blows, this never happened. . . . The entire day was set aside for the meeting and dinner, and no work was done at the winery. Dinner consisted of many courses, spaghetti and ravioli predominating. Comely Italian girls moved quietly up and down the room carrying large pitchers of red and white wine. No glass remained empty long. Toasts were drunk and those who had denounced each other in the morning were pledging each other's health in the afternoon. . . . Toward evening the party broke up. . . . The attorney was driven to the station, where he boarded the train and dozed happily back to Los Angeles."

Sugar was still for occasional use by a rich man only a hundred years or so before the Civil War. Cane sugar planting straggled into the West Indies after a leisurely and peripatetic trip to Europe from India. The tropical Americas shortly became the sugar-producing region of the world while the appetite for the sweet rapidly mounted and the cost went down.

Hawaii, a separate island kingdom, became a major sugarcane producer almost overnight in the early 1880s when cheap irrigation water was available. Encouraged by the successful artesian experience of southern California, wells were driven through the hard volcanic rock cap of the Islands. From depths of less than three hundred feet, ten- to fifteen-foot geysers of water pressed up through the well holes. The waters spewed over the arid acres on the parched leeward side of the Hawaiian mountains. These were the lands which formerly would only support a head of cattle for every twenty acres.

Claus Spreckels in the late 1880s was the principal contractor for the cane production of Hawaii while using San Francisco as his base in an attempt to form a sugar monopoly west of the Mississippi River. If he was to hold, let alone improve, his business position, Spreckels recognized he had to make a difficult decision. His cane sugar contracts with the Big Five families of Hawaii were due to expire in 1890, and he knew the Big Five were eager to refine and market their crops. The recently formed Sugar Trust was encroaching on his domains in the western half of the nation, none of whose regions could grow sugarcane. He had followed the technical progress in his native Germany with sugar beet production, and there was a strong probability that beet sugar could be produced economically in California. And finally, Claus Spreckels sensed that there was a good possibility of lobbying through tariff protection for U.S.-grown sugar. If this could be accomplished, both the Caribbean and Hawaiian suppliers would be placed at a disadvantage in the booming U.S. markets.

The Western sugar magnate made his decision because the neatness of the apparent solution appealed to him. Spreckels would control an extensive beet sugar industry in California which would form his farming and refining base while he lobbied for a protective sugar tariff in an increasingly favorable Washington climate. German beet seed for planting was imported and a prototype beet refinery facility was built in California at Watsonville. In only a few years this had become the biggest U.S. sugar factory.

Spreckels' spectacular operations in California and initial success in tariff lobbying brought competition from two shrewd operators, the Oxnard brothers. Robert Oxnard had been refining Hawaiian cane sugar in San Francisco while his brother, Henry, had a beet sugar plant in Nebraska. The brothers selected Chino in southern California to be the base of their beet operations because of the sandy loam soil. Sugar production by the mid-1890s reached 10,000 tons annually, from 7500 acres of beets.

Higher tariff protection for domestic sugar brought a new surge of beet planting and factory construction, even after Hawaii became a U.S. territory. The Oxnards built the model refining plant of its day in Ventura County on a hundred-acre parcel adjoining a townsite named after them. Thousands of acres of peat lands in and around Gospel Swamp, named for early evangelistic squatters and inland from Huntington Beach, originally had been rejected for the profitable beet plantings. The experts believed that the roots would be large and watery with little sugar content. However, an experimental crop proved very successful, and there was a rush in Orange County to plant sugar beets, a crop which ultimately supplied five nearby factories.

To its considerable surprise in the early 1900s, the South Coast found it was one of the principal sugar-producing regions of the United States.

Mrs. Eliza Tibbetts of Riverside was the rather unlikely reason that oranges became the largest fruit crop of southern California. Since her friend, Mrs. William O. Saunders, had gone to all the effort in 1873 to send her two small orange trees from Washington, D.C., Eliza planted them near her kitchen door. Not only was this to keep gophers and rabbits from them but also to pour her dishwater around the two young trees. Her "disputatious and eccentric" husband, Luther, had refused to buy Riverside irrigation water.

Prior to moving out west, the Tibbettses had lived in Washington, D.C. One of their neighbors was William O. Saunders who headed a division in the Department of Agriculture which had been allocated the obscure citrus-fruit specialty. About the time the Tibbettses left Washington, the United States Consular Office in Bahia, Brazil, sent several young trees to Saunders' division. Other trees were budded from them and a dozen or so good citrus were developed. Several of them were tried in Florida with unsatisfactory results. Then Mrs. Saunders suggested sending two of them to her friend somewhere near the village of San Bernardino in the wilds of southern California. The young citrus liked the Riverside climate and Eliza's treatment; the two trees bore a few oranges in the season of 1876. The fruit was outstanding and buds from the Tibbetts' citrus were successfully transferred to seedling orange trees by Josiah Cover and Samuel McCoy. The California citrus industry was born with the Washington Navel orange, which Eliza Tibbetts' progeny was finally called.

The young citrus industry received a major assist when J. R. Dobbins recognized that the seasonal maturation of the Valencia was substantially later than the Washington Navel. This meant southern California could have oranges in the prime Eastern market most of the year, presuming the growers could survive citrus tree diseases and freezes while solving their fruit-marketing difficulties. These survival "ifs" were hard and dangerous.

Raising citrus was easy, if one believed only a small part of what each wave of land boomers told the eager newcomers. The boomers could certainly demonstrate that young groves of the Mrs. Tibbetts' type of oranges had sold in the early 1880s at a thousand dollars an acre—a tremendous price. However, few mentioned the fact that the vast majority of settlers were neither able nor would remotely consider gambling such large sums of money on the planting or raising of the delicate citrus. Orange trees needed years to bring to fruition, and there were the continual worries of insect infestation and the loss of a year's crop in several nights of frosty weather. Harvested fruit showed a disastrous tendency, for unexplained reasons, to deteriorate rapidly while being shipped to market. Perhaps all of these hurdles could be surmounted, and then the grower would find a temporary market glut which meant ruinous selling prices.

The South Coast did not become one sprawling citrus area in a year or so. Instead a laborious parcel-by-parcel transition occurred while field crops, vineyards or orchards became unprofitable and risk money was slowly accumulated. The expensive conversion was usually made with a kind of grim fatalism, and the hope that the citrus type selected would be best suited for the district and the parcel's location in the district.

Limes were early recognized to be a poor cash crop, both because of frost sensitivity and indifferent fruit flavor. The Florida grapefruit (or pomelo as it was known earlier) was introduced in the 1880s and some of the fruit grew to the size of footballs. But even with improved strains, the local grapefruit crop had neither the succulence nor the sweetness of the Texas, Arizona or Florida competition.

Lemons were far more adaptable to the South Coast than the grapefruit. While considerably more sensitive to frost than oranges, the productive season was substantially longer, the fruit stored well, and lemons shipped better than oranges. When Thomas A. Garey successfully introduced the juicy and seedless Eureka variety with its smooth and thin skin, the South Coast had another fine citrus product. Perhaps the outstanding citrus grove of the 1890s was the 500-acre Leffingwell establishment east of Whittier. Initially with a hundred acres in lemons, C. W. Leffingwell ran a model citrus operation for the day incorporating technical advances which only came into general use years later. His lands were generally frost-free and watered by deep wells. Chemical fertilizers were extensively used, and the trees were systematically pruned and shaped for maximum fruit production and picking. A prime innovation was this grower's insistence that his fruit be picked, handled and shipped with maximum care. Not surprisingly, the Leffingwell fruit sold at premium prices.

Gophers liked the tree roots of the young citrus groves. Settlers were convinced that precocious rodent leaders directed their hordes to fresh groves by long underground treks. The farmers fought back—trapping and poisoning the little mammals. In one all-out effort in the 1890s, five hundred of the rodents were killed in a grove over a three-day period. Still the virus, molds and insect pests were a far greater worry to the orchardist. At the very time the Boom townsites of the eighties were being laid out along the rail lines of southern California, two of the region's prime agricultural crops were being destroyed by insect pests.

In black despair the growers watched helplessly while their hundreds of thousands of producing grapevines withered and died. Then the citrus growers saw the cottony-cushion scale and its scale bugs move remorselessly from one citrus grove to another. Spray and fumigation techniques accomplished nothing, and the groves died. More and more citrus growers were bankrupt, and the land with rows of dead trees lay fallow. Then word of a possible last-minute reprieve for the remaining groves rocketed through the countryside in 1889. The Australian "lady-bird" beetle could destroy the scale bug and most of the citrus was saved.

Fighting insects with insects dramatized the benefits of agricultural research, and the procedure became a standard defense against citrus infestation. Fumigation and spraying techniques improved. Tents were placed over the citrus trees and mixtures of sulphuric acid and cyanide were utilized as the killing agents. A combination of costly spraying and fumagiation appeared to be the only systematic answer to the insect pests. There were some dissidents because of the cost, one of whom utilized a spectacular, albeit unsuccessful, procedure:

"A gleaming white orchard in Charter Oak, covered from the base of the tree to the widest spread of branches with common whitewash, is attracting the attention of ranchers from all over the county. It is the ten acres of S. W. Funk . . . and is an experiment in killing all kinds of scale and vermin."

Citrus was a luxury; an orange in a Christmas stocking was a treat in most families. Certainly, luxuries were the first to go in the economic depression of the mid-1890s. Citrus prices declined precipitously in the Eastern markets and, even so, the individual grower found he was forced to ship his fruit on consignment. This meant that the grower underwrote all the fruit packing and substantial railway shipping charges with his oranges being sold at whatever might be the current price in a distant city's wholesale market. Many a grower found he would have been money ahead if he had let his oranges rot on the trees.

Some type of a cooperative or coordinated marketing system had to be devised, if citrus was to be sold on a broad-scale basis in markets thousands of miles away. Most growers were willing to try any arrangement, for "no plan can be worse than the want of one which now affects us." After establishment of a number of ineffective local associations, a central marketing agency under the leadership of T. H. B. Chamblin and then A. H. Naftzer was formed in 1895. This agency eventually evolved into the California Fruit Exchange, and it was surprising that the central marketing activity survived in any form during the early years. Plagued by hostile private shippers concerned with losing control of a rich crop, growers who were learning laboriously to hang together rather than hang separately, and association management distinguished for its inexperience, the central exchange wallowed in deep difficulties. Still, real progress was made in broadening the national consumption of oranges by reducing distribution expense. Total shipments in 1902 were triple the 7000-car figure of 1895. This was a fine record but now the continued loss of fruit in shipment became a major cost concern.

The central marketing agency was learning painfully after the turn of the century that there was an inflexible upper limit on the growth of the orange industry. This was the expensive loss of fruit by decay even when shipped in iced refrigeration cars. The transportation loss, always taken for granted, now demonstrably forced selling prices above the ability of a developing mass market to pay. By fortunate coincidence the solution came shortly after the economic problem came into full focus. G. Harold Powell and his associates in the U.S. Department of Agriculture were convinced after four years of work that most of the fruit decay was due to blue mold. This potent fungus was entering the fruit through punctures, abrasions and bruises of the skin accumulated from the time the orange was picked. With a demonstrated solution the results were dramatic. The valuable fruit was handled and washed most carefully, with prime citrus wrapped in tissue paper.

From a sales viewpoint the decision of the California Fruit Exchange to select a brand name and advertise the product was nearly as important to the South Coast citrus industry as Powell's successful investigations of fruit decay. The Exchange's board of directors in 1907 authorized a $10,000 advertising appropriation, with the understanding that the Southern Pacific would provide matching funds. The advertising campaign headlined by "Sunkist," the premium brand name, was concentrated in the Iowa market. The sales jump in the test region was three times that of the national increase during the same period. The fantastic citrus success story of southern California was underway, but the perils were still there—the prime one being weather.

The citrus districts always braced themselves for the long nights of December and January. These were the months when frost could ruin a crop and sometimes a grove. The only defense against the silent cold of a winter night was smudging from pots spaced among the trees. The growers had found that a layer of smoke over the citrus tended to hold the existing heat from the intruding cold, hopefully until the morning sun would raise the temperature. The choking pall of smudging also spread over and onto the nearby ranch and town buildings, leaving an oil film coating on the outside walls while the smudge's greasy tentacles snaked through door and window crevices.

Fueling and firing many scores if not hundreds of smudge pots in the dead of a cold night was a back-breaking, stumbling operation carried on amid the eddying oily smoke. Smarting eyes, heavy coughing, and miscellaneous burns were an accepted part of the smudging activities. Eventually oil-burning heaters, which actually raised the grove temperature, replaced the pots but only some of the labor and none of the discomforts. Unfortunately, heaters and certainly pots could only do so much under conditions of prolonged and severe cold. The fearsome "Great Freeze of 1913" amply demonstrated that.

The reverberating cracks of bark splitting on mature orange trees in the deep still cold of a massive freeze could sound the death knell of a citrus grove. The sap was freezing and its expansion was rending the trees apart. The noise brought many an exhausted and dazed grower to stupefied attention after hours of breasting the chilling northern gale and then fighting the still cold and the choking smoke through the previous night of smudging. He remembered now with a kind of sick nausea the old wives' tales of this kind of a catastrophe. The half-forgotten stories were true, and there was no reprieve. Many of the old trees were dying, the young trees were already dead, and the fruit had dropped off all of them. The cause was a northern santana which brought a devastating cold in its train.

The breeding grounds of the santana winds of southern California are in a high pressure area of northern Nevada, southern Idaho and occasionally a good deal further north. These dry winds rush first through the southern desert mountain passes and, if voracious enough, over the mountains into the South Coast plains and out to sea beyond Catalina Island. When a true northern santana can take off without interference from another clockwise high movement in Canada and head due south bringing very cold air in its skirts, God help southern California and its citrus if no local weather pattern intervenes. None did, beginning January 4, 1913.

The cat's-paws of the northern santana arrived quietly on the South Coast during Saturday forenoon. By early evening the lashing of the eucalyptus and the strumming of the electric power wires meant more than a fresh gale to a worried citrus grower. The weather was too cold. This was a "new sort of norther" and more than disquieting because of its low temperatures. The word soon passed that a few old settlers were remembering 1879 when the Riverside canal was frozen after a similar wind. Worse yet, some of the Florida emigrants were talking again about their own norther of 1895 whose following cold wiped out much of the Florida citrus groves.

The chill gale rushing over the mountains howled all Saturday night and all day Sunday, while a thin layer of ice formed in puddles. The wind precipitously dropped to nothing at dusk on Sunday and the quiet was far worse than the gale. Soon the dreaded cold came. Between 7 to 11:30 P.M., the temperature varied between fifteen and eighteen degrees at the Citrus Experiment Station in Riverside. A sustained temperature of twenty-seven degrees for a few hours will freeze oranges because the expanding juice breaks the membrane of the juice sacs.

The plight of the typical grower, with neither the best smudging or heating equipment nor the material and forces to man effectively what he had, was desperate if the cold should continue. The hated santana for a time seemed a blessing when the wind velocity in the predawn hours of Monday, January 6, picked up and the grove temperatures moved to the high twenties. But again the wind dropped about dusk on Monday and then the temperatures went to the same level or lower than the previous night. Those growers who had not given up were shambling wrecks of fatigue as they waited with a dull dread for the third and final night of the freeze. The answer was not long in coming. Redlands, San Bernardino and Pomona showed a low of eighteen degrees before dawn.

For many citrus localities the temperatures were below freezing for nearly sixty hours. So many of the groves looked "as though they had been swept by fire"; the young trees were killed, a large number of the old trees survived the badly split bark and limbs but lost all of their tip growth. The value of the undamaged portion of the orange crop from protected areas was ruined because frozen oranges dumped on the market made the entire South Coast harvest suspect. Bankruptcy was common and many families lost their land.

Still, citrus survived, and expanded, and then expanded again.

CHAPTER 9

"The people of your district are a set of idiots"

Later generations on the South Coast have found it difficult to believe that the empty waters off the mouth of Santa Monica Canyon comprised a bustling port in the mid-1890s. And if Collis P. Huntington had had his way—which he nearly did—the present-day San Pedro/Long Beach breakwater of nine miles would have stretched instead from above Topanga Canyon to Venice.

The Long Wharf of Huntington's Southern Pacific moved straight out to sea for most of its 4300-foot length, beyond the 33-foot depth at low tide. Completed in 1894, railroad tracks were laid out to the end of the wharf off Santa Monica Canyon. A mooring buoy system was installed so that ships laying alongside the pier were breasted off by lines to the buoys. The completed facility, called Port Los Angeles, was supposed to have cost a million dollars; two-thirds of this figure was probably more accurate. The Long Wharf was immediately utilized for unloading coal from Australia and lumber from the Northwest. A systematic sales campaign was launched for the new port supplemented by maximum economic pressure on the ocean shippers, which was considerable. For northern coastal traffic the saving of a half-day's time over San Pedro, the long-time harbor for Los Angeles, was emphasized. A free train for influential shippers was always available to the new Southern Pacific port with dinner and wine at the Hotel Arcadia on the Santa Monica Palisades.

Collis P. Huntington, a difficult man to please, was satisfied with the rapid progress of Port Los Angeles. His railroad controlled it absolutely; there would be no repetition of the San Pedro mistakes. Huntington was ready now to make his big push for Federal funds, to build a long breakwater at his Santa Monica location. This began with quiet, serious lobbying in both houses of the Congress during the mid-1890s.

The San Pedro advocates for a deep-water harbor had not been idle during the controversy's limbo period of the previous two years. A Free Harbor League had been formed headed by L. W. Blinn, Harrison G. Otis, W. D. Woolwine and John F. Francis. The League supplemented and extended the pro-San Pedro activities of the Los Angeles Chamber of Commerce and its general manager, Charles D. Willard. The Chamber's principal and most effective effort was a letter-writing program directed at each congressman and his immediate coterie of supporters. The program was carefully organized and letters written only on the basis of long and substantial friendships, all made before the South Coast migration. Since the bulk of the South Coast population was recently from somewhere else this was not difficult to arrange. A New York *World* editorial provided the theme of these letters: "Mr. Huntington's Santa Monica enterprise throughout its entire extent is as exclusive as though it were surrounded by a Chinese wall."

Huntington's power move for his harbor funds again surfaced unexpectedly in March of 1896. Earlier that winter agreement had been reached between the Cleveland Administration and congressional leaders on a reduced total for the Federal river and harbor budget for fiscal 1896-97. This was duly reported to the Free Harbor League and the Chamber of Commerce by the freshman senator from Los Angeles, Stephen M. White, and Representative James McLachlan whose district included the South Coast. Both recommended only making a $400,000 appropriation request for inner harbor improvements at San Pedro and postponing the deep-water harbor proposal. This was done and a four-man group headed by W. C. Patterson appeared before the House Committee on Rivers and Harbors. The South Coast delegation was pleased with the ready assurances of Binger Hermann and other key members that the

San Pedro appropriation would receive a "do pass" recommendation. In late March of 1896 W. C. Patterson, back in Los
Angeles, received a letter from Congressman Hermann which
stunned the San Pedro advocates. In it, Hermann blandly
dropped a bombshell:

"At this hour, I have succeeded in securing for San Pedro
. . . the entire $392,000. . . . This is a great victory. Santa
Monica secures the same advantage; the amount for completion
is much larger. . . . Of course some event may happen by
which we may suffer the loss of the items contained in the bill.
If one goes, the other must take the same course."

This was a superb one horse/one rabbit maneuver engineered by the wily Huntington—$3,000,000 for Santa Monica,
$392,000 for San Pedro with the threat of a double appropriation
or none at all. The San Pedro forces were nearly demoralized.
So was James McLachlan, House member from the South Coast,
after being read off by Binger Hermann when he objected to
the Santa Monica action of the House committee:

"Well, you are by all odds the damndest fool that the whole
God-damned State of California ever sent to Congress. . . . The
people of your district are a set of idiots that don't know when
they are well off, if they can't take a double appropriation and
two harbors. . . . If you won't take Santa Monica, you don't
get San Pedro."

Recognizing that Hermann was not bluffing, the Free Harbor
League and the Chamber of Commerce made a hard decision.
They would not support the double harbor appropriation. Binger
Hermann forthwith moved that both items be struck from the
house bill and this was done.

The time had now arrived for the junior senator from California to meet his own political destiny in the two-harbor war.
The principal battle was about to take place in the United States
Senate. Stephen M. White, then in his forties, had entered the
upper house in 1893. He already had encountered considerable
Los Angeles criticism for not taking a more active part in the
skirmishes and confrontations with the Santa Monica advocates
during the intervening period. Perhaps time was required for

White to recognize the quality of the opposition and his own opportunities in combating it.

After being admitted to the Bar in 1874, Stephen M. White had come from San Francisco to Los Angeles where he worked for and subsequently was a partner with John D. Bicknell, a well-known attorney. The young lawyer successfully handled the trial work for the firm while establishing a reputation for being an orator in the tradition of the day and a man who liked his whiskey. Bicknell & White grew into the largest law firm on the South Coast until the total involvement of the junior partner in politics resulted in the dissolution of the firm in 1888. After several tries White had been elected District Attorney and then went on to become a state senator and served as presiding officer of the Democratic National Convention. He came into the U.S. Senate on the coattails of Grover Cleveland, who was serving his second term in the White House. The freshman senator continued to maintain his Los Angeles law office in the old Temple Block over the Reception Saloon.

Stephen M. White was coldly infuriated with the handling of the South Coast harbor subject by Binger Hermann and the other congressional colleagues who had given him the appropriation misinformation. He now fully recognized that his real adversary, Collis P. Huntington, was "the shrewdest, most persistent and remarkable man" he had ever met. If anything could be salvaged for San Pedro, White decided that could only be with full Senate consideration and national newspaper coverage —unheard of for a river and harbor appropriation. Such relatively minor matters were always worked out in log-rolling sessions before and after committee meetings.

Equally clear to White was that this newspaper coverage could only be accomplished by projecting the individual, Huntington, as the antagonist against the people of the United States, with the anti-San Pedro senators cast as Huntington's pawns. If Senator William P. Frye of Maine, noted for his long-time opposition to the San Pedro harbor location, could be trapped into taking the Senate floor and defending Huntington, White felt sure this would precipitate a full-scale Senate debate.

In his committee discussions with Frye, White increasingly raised the name of the railroad president and referred to Huntington as "your principal," to the obvious and growing irritation of the Maine senator. The Californian knew he had his man when Frye announced on May 11, 1896, that he would reply on the following day to the remarks of Senator Berry of Arkansas who had given a closely coached speech against Huntington on the floor that day. When Frye was recognized by the chair, senators strolled in from cloak and committee rooms and the press gallery filled up in time to hear the Maine man say with strong emotion:

"Oh, it is too paltry to undertake to stop any legislation with that cheap demogogical cry that because Huntington has done it, no help can be given to Huntington. . . . Mr. Huntington is not bulling the stock markets, nor bearing them. He is not cornering wheat or flour. He is engaged in enormous enterprises, the results of which are building up the commerce of this republic . . ."

With Collis P. Huntington being spiritedly defended by a senior senator on a minor appropriation matter, the United States Senate woke up. Members of the upper house clamored to be heard on both sides. White was delighted. The major newspapers of the nation reported and editorialized on the Senate debate, and a mounting tide of telegrams and letters was received by the Congress from all over the country. The bulk of the Senate after five days of controversy was more than willing to accept what superficially appeared to be a compromise offered by Stephen M. White—establish a $3,090,000 appropriation for a South Coast deep-water harbor and let an independent technical board select the location.

To partisans on both sides, the California senator's proposal was no compromise but a likely victory for San Pedro because two other technical boards had selected that site. The House went along with the Senate's plan for the South Coast harbor over Binger Hermann's violent objections. Under the provisions of the congressional act a five-man harbor location board convened at Los Angeles in December of 1896 and organized under the chairmanship of Rear Admiral John G. Walker. Four months later the Walker Board submitted its report recommending San Pedro to Russell A. Alger, the Secretary of War in the recently elected McKinley Administration.

At the apex of his career Stephen M. White accepted the congratulations of the San Pedro partisans while announcing he would not run for a second term. Collis P. Huntington continued to be pleasant to White and noncommittal on San Pedro. The senator finally learned that the railroad president never gave up. Month succeeded month after the Walker Board's report and Secretary Alger still had not ordered bids for the harbor construction. This action was only taken after strong lobbying pressures developed in the Congress and on President McKinley himself. Two full years elapsed after the Walker Board's report before the first barge-load of rock was dumped for the San Pedro breakwater. A decade had gone by since Senator William P. Frye of Maine had wondered aloud whether the whole South Coast was worth the out-of-pocket cost of building a deep-water harbor.

Start of the breakwater construction certainly merited a major celebration, something which would hopefully rival one of the best South Coast parties ever, also held at San Pedro nearly a half-century earlier. In 1853 Phineas Banning along with David W. Alexander gave a Fourth of July celebration at the desolate little roadstead port, for two thousand of their Californio friends who came from Santa Barbara down to Sonora. That wonderful party had lasted for a solid two days of barbecues, drinking, betting and feats of horsemanship punctuated by appropriate oratory and miscellaneous brawling. The 1899 Harbor Jubilee Committee really had an impossible act to top, but it tried. Twenty thousand people came to San Pedro for suitable speeches, barbecued beef and beans along with five tons of clams baked in open pits. Stephen M. White was the principal speaker on that day, April 26, 1899, and all agreed his florid oratory was in excellent form. Most of the people who heard

White speak came to the San Pedro Jubilee near Point Fermin by way of the Terminal Railroad. The Southern Pacific, in a fit of pettishness, refused to provide additional train service from Los Angeles for the occasion.

The breakwater bids came in. The winner was Heldmaier and Neu of Chicago, who asked only $1,300,000 to build the 7,450-foot breakwater extending out to the 52-foot contour, and to be finished neatly from the low tide line with massive rectangular stone blocks. The breakwater was to begin 1800 feet from the Point Fermin bluffs with the water gap left to provide tidal scouring action. Rock was quarried by the Chicago contractor at Catalina and towed across the Channel on barges.

Because of failure to meet time dates during the first year of construction the War Department abruptly canceled the breakwater contract and rebid the project. This time the work was awarded to the California Construction Company of San Francisco who bid just under $2,400,000. The San Francisco company utilized a completely different approach in bringing in and laying down the quantities of rock required. The cost-time determination was made to move the rock by rail from San Bernardino County and the upper end of the San Fernando Valley. The flatcars were run out on a wooden trestle over the waters of the open bay, and railroad cranes dropped the rock from the flatcars into position. The ubiquitous Southern Pacific hauled the rock for a decade until the structure was completed in 1910.

An engineering determination was made to close the inshore 1800-foot gap giving a total breakwater length of 9250 feet ending with a 70-foot lighthouse called Angel's Gate. The local newspapers loved to recite this array of statistics and many more as well. All agreed the most impressive was the size of the rock wall approaching two miles in length. The sea wall was 200 feet wide at the base and had an average height of 64 feet. The end result was a fine job, but the inner harbor approaches would continue to be tumultuous during a major southeast storm until additional miles of breakwater extensions were added many years later.

Old friends were distressed with the rapid deterioration in health of Stephen M. White, still in his late forties. The sad note of Henry W. O'Melveny in his private journal of December 1, 1899, explained the concern:

"Worked this afternoon at White's office . . . White was there. His is one of the most lamentable cases in the world. . . . Having achieved his ambition early in life . . . he is now a physical and mental wreck. He is today suffering under delusions."

The young wolves were moving in on their professional kill when Stephen M. White was slowed down by his heavy drinking. Earl Rogers, a soon-to-be famous criminal lawyer and a tragic alcoholic in his own right, led the pack. According to Rogers' daughter, a local reporter told her of the time Rogers used White's drinking habits to outmaneuver the famous trial lawyer and politician. Dan Green of the Los Angeles *Examiner* described how the young attorney had unblinkingly watched White dawdle repeatedly over lunch even on trial days while he sipped his whiskey. This particular day was no exception and the famous ex-senator came into the courtroom late and found the key witness "had been on and off the stand. He swelled up and said to Rogers in a whisper like a calliope, 'That was a damn dirty trick, Earl,' but of course he couldn't say it into the record without admitting Rogers had made a fool of him."

Like swatting a kelp fly, Rogers' maneuver was nothing to reminisce about, even to himself.

Human ordeals fortunately have an end. In the instance of Stephen M. White, death finally came before dawn on February 20, 1901. Henry W. O'Melveny's simple entry in his journal summarized the feelings of many for the tortured man "Requiescat in pace." At his funeral, Harris Newmark turned to Harrison G. Otis and suggested a fund drive to raise a monument for White—an unheard-of thing for the South Coast. Otis was enthusiastic and $25,000 was shortly subscribed for a bronze statue representing White standing with one arm outstretched. It was placed in front of the ornate courthouse, the symbol of the South Coast, on Poundcake Hill and was moved subsequently to the present Civic Center of Los Angeles.

The big, bald old man watched his contemporaries die and men like Stephen M. White, half his age, fall apart. Approaching his eightieth birthday, Collis P. Huntington seemed endowed with eternal life and limitless energy. Moving into advanced age, the last survivor of the Big Four—Leland Stanford had died in 1894—was even more autocratic and blunt of speech, if that was possible.

As always, he was oblivious to any invective or vituperation of the newspaper editorial writers. Worse yet for the crusading newspapers he was a difficult man to cartoon. Collis P. Huntington showed none of the obvious personal foibles of the other robber barons of the period which a young editor like William Randolph Hearst could pick apart at his leisure. The railroad magnate had no political or social ambitions, and no desire to change anything unless it was of benefit in his own affairs. To him titles were meaningless and philanthropy was an incomprehensible aberration of his wealthy friends and associates. Remarks to the press such as "I will never be remembered for the money I gave away" and "you can't follow me through life by the quarters I dropped" was pure Collis P. Huntington.

During the mid-1890s the railroad magnate was Uncle Collis to the host of California people who feared him and his Southern Pacific. Uncle Collis was looked upon as a powerful Scrooge-like character who was a near and unwanted relative. And with good reason. Huntington could travel from Newport News to San Francisco via Los Angeles over his own rails. His control of shipyards, steamship lines and vast land and timber holdings plus the many thousands of miles of railroad gave him an immense fortune of over $75,000,000 (or nearly a billion in mid-1970s dollars) and equally immense power which he believed in using, preferably with the bludgeon approach.

When the news of Uncle Collis' sudden death in August of 1900 clicked off the telegraphs on the South Coast, the report almost seemed too incredible to be true. Collis P. Huntington and the rest of the Big Four had forged their California transportation monopoly before a good share of the population was born and before the majority of the remainder had ever thought of immigrating to California. And for many railroad shippers, the magnate's death was the best omen for a new century of freedom.

The Long Wharf at Santa Monica Canyon did not survive Huntington's death by too many years. This was indicated in a 1914 report: "Eaten by worms, battered by the waves, deserted except for Japanese fishermen, that wonder of marine architecture is rapidly falling into decay."

The great harbor war on the South Coast was over—but not really. During the years of breakwater construction passed, there were sober reappraisals of the San Pedro deep-water harbor project. Even Charles Willard reluctantly admitted that " . . . it is as though a community should construct an enormous bridge with its approaches so small as to make a great deal of the structure useless." Willard was correct. No provision had been made in the outer harbor for handling deep-draft vessels beyond the five-fathom line by means of long docks from shore. And the idea of building railroad tracks on the breakwater to inexpensive stub docks there was soon given up because of the demonstrable threat from southeast storms. Equally discouraging, there was no substantial inner harbor in back of the 400-foot-wide entrance between the two jettys at Dead Man's Island, and certainly no real money to finance one.

None of this surprised San Diego with its empty and beautiful natural harbor. The port developments in the open Bay of San Pedro only a hundred miles north had always seemed to be a bad and expensive joke compounded with idiocy. The San Diego *Union's* description of Phineas Banning's "goose pond" in the tidal lands of Wilmington Lagoon in the 1860s and 1870s was not that far off target. And the freshly cut white rocks of the magnificent breakwater glinting in the afternoon sun was simply a symbol of another fiasco and caused the San Diego newspaper to refer contemptuously to the new San Pedro seaport as a "harborette." Again the designation was apt. To cap it all the San Diego people took bittersweet enjoyment in pointing out that the major political victory spearheaded by Stephen M. White would be eventually meaningless because most of the potential inner harbor lands at San Pedro were controlled by the Southern Pacific and a good deal of the remainder was in the hands of the Phineas Banning heirs.

The furious disputes over San Francisco Bay's tidal and submerged lands had brought into focus by the turn of the century the overriding public interest in such properties. In conflict with this premise, the State of California had provided for private railroad rights-of-way and terminals to be granted in perpetuity on these lands. An alert Southern Pacific, whose legislative connections were impeccable, had utilized this state provision to gain effective control of all approaches to navigable waters on the San Pedro side of the inner harbor while its railroad right-of-way neatly split the mud flats of Wilmington Lagoon. Most of the remainder of the potential inner harbor belonged to the heirs of Phineas Banning; and their title to these tidal and submerged lands was valid because the lands were included in the basic U.S. patent of Rancho San Pedro.

Los Angeles clearly believed in its own manifest destiny. The city proposed to cure the embryonic deep-water harbor's legal and financial problems and at the same time become a major seaport. The latter was to be accomplished even though the city's southern boundaries were at Slauson Avenue, many miles away from the two little harbor towns, San Pedro and Wilmington. Los Angeles neatly solved this by annexing in 1906 a half-mile-wide and eighteen-mile-long corridor (or "Shoestring Strip" as it was popularly known) to the perimeter of the two harbor towns.

Though still landlocked, the next move of ambitious Los Angeles was to establish a harbor commission and immediately pressure the State of California to file suits against the Southern Pacific and the Banning Company for the purpose of invalidating a number of different tidal and submerged land claims. A pivotal case finally reached the U.S. Supreme Court. In a noted decision the Court held that these lands were subject to public use for purposes of commerce and navigation.

Concurrent with the litigation actions, Los Angeles pressed ahead toward its objective of becoming a major seaport. This first required the consolidation of San Pedro and Wilmington with Los Angeles. The enabling act, bitterly fought by the Southern Pacific, passed the state legislature, another sure sign of the coming end of nearly two score years of railroad domination of the state government.

The delicate municipal consolidation maneuver required a favorable vote in the city and each of the two harbor towns. There was strong special interest opposition, which played on a wariness felt by the small communities toward the motives of powerful Los Angeles. A masterful annexation steering job was done by A. P. Fleming and Thomas E. Gibbon with the use of consolidation committees in each of the municipalities. Men like Stoddard Jess, William D. Stephens, Joseph Scott, Maurice H. Newmark, John T. Gaffey, James H. Dodson and F. S. Carey hammered out an agreement which was approved by the voters of all three communities in 1909. Los Angeles finally had its seaport. But one other ingredient was required—money to develop the harbor. This the courageous city voters would have to provide.

Most everybody was a newcomer in the Los Angeles of the early 1900s though the city's population was at the 200,000 mark. There must have been something about the climate and the times which would make a transplanted and conservative Iowan or upstate New Yorker vote for huge municipal obligations and agree to build projects potentially of tremendous community value but of no proximate benefit, particularly when the continuing influx of population meant an immediate driving demand for more schools, streets and sewers in a city with a small manufacturing base and some debilitating labor unrest. These immediate requirements and restraints did not stop the long-range projects.

The people voted overwhelmingly in 1905 and 1907 for a total of $24,500,000 of bonds for an unbelievable 250-mile aqueduct to be constructed over some of the most difficult terrain in the world. In mid-1970 monetary terms the aqueduct cost would exceed a quarter of a billion dollar commitment or about

$1300 for every man, woman and child in Los Angeles at that time. Not content with this, the growing city in 1910 approved a $10,000,000 harbor contractual commitment while voting an immediate $3,000,000 in bonds. These moneys were spent in the next few years within the framework of a master plan, the essential elements of which were followed for the next half-century.

The initial outer harbor improvement was to reclaim the submerged lands running from Timm's Point (near present-day Signal and Miner streets) out to sea toward Dead Man's Island. These dredge-filled lands where Municipal Pier No. 1 was constructed formed a rough triangle abutting the curving bluffs and were reached by steep and unpaved San Pedro (Viaduct) Street, then by a wooden trestle, and later by a concrete viaduct.

Much of Wilmington was a mass of reeking tidal mud. This was the primary area selected for inner harbor development, and the first phase was a unique street improvement project undertaken by Homer Hamlin, the City Engineer of Los Angeles. Hamlin proposed to raise the tidal morass from the waterfront back eight blocks to the business district. To provide a natural grade above high tide, this required as much as eight feet of material to be dredged from the proposed inner harbor sector extending from Wilmington to the Turning Basin in San Pedro.

The dredged material was deposited in the Wilmington streets and "naturally, the mud and silt overflowed on the adjoining lots, and thus the property owners got their lots filled and raised along with the streets. If any property owner refused to sign the petition, his lot was surrounded by a dike and left at its original elevation." Uniform concurrence of all the lot owners was not long in coming. Mud oozing through the crevices of the enveloping dikes and the ponding of gummy water on a confined parcel with the resultant remarkable stench would soon persuade any obdurate property owner to sign up for Engineer Hamlin's project.

From a duck pond to a harborette to one of the major deep-water ports of the world in a generation or so seemed such a short step to the people involved. For them perhaps it was.

CHAPTER 10

"Here's abundant prosperity to the Pacific Cable Company"

A modest network of local steam lines plus the two major railroads served the South Coast during the Boom of the eighties. Los Angeles considered itself sort of a minor league metropolis with standard and narrow-gauge roads coming in from most directions. And in the central district, horsecars on railroad tracks were determining the direction and growth of the small city.

The horsecar was no anachronism in the expansive age of steam and mechanical technology. Los Angeles had had its first single-track line in the early 1870s, not far behind the establishment of similar systems elsewhere. The horsecar made sound economic sense, and there were a hundred thousand horses (and mules) in the transportation networks of several hundred U.S. cities and towns in the eighties. The small cars pulled by one or two horses had developed into a sensible and economic rig, well accepted by the public. Some of the horsecars had plush seats, overhead straps for the standees, stoves, oil lamps and advertisements mounted on the wall at standee eye level. There was straw or sawdust on the floor to warm the feet and absorb dollops of tobacco juice; smoking was not allowed in the car itself. Chewing tobacco had an unusual but useful function for the crew: "Out on the back platform the conductor also had his cud, traditionally used as a weapon-within-the-law with which to dislodge impudent lads caught stealing rides by clinging to the rear of the dash."

Because Robert M. Widney built a residence out in the country on Hill Street between Fourth and Fifth, Los Angeles and the South Coast had its first urban transportation in 1874. Widney's real estate office was near the Plaza and reachable in the winter months only by horseback over and through the muddy morass of the streets of the town. He found a number of other people along the prospective route who would contribute, and the result was a horsecar line, on which unfortunately the cars routinely went off the tracks at several of the curves. Widney, never noted overmuch for his sense of humor and definitely not appreciating the salty comments of the town, redesigned the curves himself and shortly thereafter sold the line to John F. Hollenbeck and Stephen C. Hubbell.

From this beginning the horsecar lines spread out to all quadrants of Los Angeles. Traffic increased to the extent that there were "early bird" cars prior to 6:00 A.M. and "owl" cars operating after 10:00 P.M., considered locally to be a high level of urban accommodation. Each horsecar in service required about ten trained animals. An experienced horse (and an occasional mule) was a valuable commodity distinguished by long tenure and certainly not mistreated nor casually put aside. One legendary horse in Chicago logged over 103,000 miles through the winter ice and snow and the oppressive summer heat over a period of twenty-two years. While track and equipment costs for a horsecar line were relatively low, operating costs definitely were not. This forced serious consideration of alternative forms of public urban transportation, initially steam-propelled vehicles and then cable cars.

The environmentalists of the day formed vociferous and broad-scale opposition to the clanking, smelly and puffing steam vehicles on the city streets. Horses ran away, property owners complained of the noise and stack smoke, and passengers warily sat in the attached cars having heard about boiler explosions. The steam "dummy" was sort of an answer to some of the objections. This was a tiny boxlike locomotive with a vertical boiler and exhaust steam mufflers along with aprons hung over the connecting rods. These devices were intended hopefully to quiet the suspicions of nearby horses tensing themselves to rear in their carriage shafts. Many of the dummy steam lines prospered, primarly in the suburbs. However, another modern development of the day, the cable car, appeared to provide the best competitive answer to the horsecar in the urban areas.

The cable car was a melding of the age of steam and the basic inventions of John A. Roebling who pioneered in wire rope and cable design shortly before the Civil War. Andrew Hallidie first integrated these concepts in aerial tramways for California mines utilizing an endless moving wire cable. Hallidie then became absorbed in a revolutionary urban transportation idea—why not lay an endless cable in a tunnel immediately under the car track and utilize a powerful central steam engine to move the cable on its sheaves and blocks? The system would require some device which the car could use to grip and then release as required the constantly moving cable in the tunnel. The hills of San Francisco provided a rigorous test in 1873 for Hallidie's transportation system. The grip man started the car moving up the steepest grade at a uniform speed by simply clamping the cable with an ingenious mechanical grip. He stopped the car by releasing the clamp and setting the car's own brakes.

The cable cars were immediately popular in communities with all types of terrain. The cars were quiet, fast for the day and there was no dummy locomotive smoke. If managed and maintained properly, cable lines were much less expensive to operate than horsecars. But financing a cable system was something else again; the initial construction cost was very high. James F. Crank and Isaias W. Hellman, the local horsecar financiers, soon found this out when construction commenced in 1888 on the lines of their Los Angeles Cable Railway Company. They lost no time in soliciting outside capital and brought in a Chicago traction group which folded the Crank/Hellman transportation interests into the Pacific Railway Company. It cost the Chicago syndicate a hundred thousand dollars a mile to build a double-track line in Los Angeles. The investment for ten miles of cable lines of both single and double track, three steam powerhouses and miscellaneous land and equipment totaled nearly $2,000,000. These were private funds being spent in a small city of 50,000 people. In mid-1970 dollars, the per mile cost of the double-track cable line system would be roughly equivalent to building a mile of freeway in a suburban district.

The principal elements of the expensive cable network were completed in the fall of 1889 and the Los Angeles *Times* could report in an excess of hand-rubbing, civic satisfaction that "the system of the Pacific Railway Company of Los Angeles, taken as a whole, is probably the largest and most complete in the world. Besides the cable roads, having a total length of 21 miles, there are 24 miles of horsecar lines. The great San Fernando Street Viaduct, where two tracks are carried upon single pillars over the Southern Pacific Railway Yards, stands alone as a feat of engineering skill. . . . Let there be nothing but good feeling. . . . Here's abundant prosperity to the Pacific Cable Company and a long life and excellent health to Colonel J. C. Robinson."

Toasts to the cable company and the superintendent, James C. Robinson, were premature. A few weeks later the spanking new cable railway system was damaged seriously by what appeared to be a casual and irresponsible decision by Robinson:

"Heavy rains on the night of December 24, 1889, flooded all three powerhouses [with the water pouring in through the cable tunnels]. The Christmas dawn showed not a cloud in the sky, but not a cable car was running anywhere in the city. Robinson was on the job, dashing here and there, pushing the work of his track gangs in removing sand and silt from the cable machinery. When a business acquaintance joshed him about the lack of cable car transportation, Robinson bet him a cigar the cars would be running by one o'clock. At one o'clock, although hours of work were still necessary to put the cable system back into condition for safe operation, Robinson ordered the engines to be started. The abrasive sand and dirt was ground deeply into the cable and sheaves and the exemplary equipment of Los Angeles' 'ideal' cable railway was badly damaged; however, Robinson won his cigar."

Quantities of money were required to repair the cable railway which the financially stretched Pacific Railway could ill afford. But there was a far stronger force already at work which would shortly obsolete most cable systems for mass transportation. This was the genius of a young American engineer by the name of Sprague.

The U.S. Naval Academy faculty and the graduating class of 1878 knew that Frank J. Sprague was a brilliant fellow. But nobody envisaged that this tall, skinny ensign would revolutionize a good part of the world's mechanical propulsion and transportation only a decade later. Sprague was a legitimate scientific genius nourished in a sound mathematics and engineering discipline at the Naval Academy. And this training and his basic capability could be used to a maximum because of the repeated scientific breakthroughs of that part of Sprague's century. Those were heady times indeed for technically oriented people coming out of the schools and colleges.

The young ensign had become completely absorbed in the equally young art of electricity. His total dedication and his ability to wangle assignments to appropriate technical conferences and meet their leaders was a source of wonder, some amusement, and outright irritation to many of his shipmates. Added to this was his involvement in experiments and calculations leading to a volume of correspondence around the world and the filing of a number of patent applications dealing with electricity. Not too surprisingly, the Navy and Sprague in a few years reached a parting of the ways.

Thomas A. Edison, the electrical inventor, offered the precocious junior naval officer a job at his Menlo Park, New Jersey, operation and Frank Sprague joined the famous laboratory in 1883. The extent of technical rapprochement between the new employee and the Edison team was fair at the best. Hopefully each learned something from the other. The Menlo Park operation had blown a thousand or so different shapes of glass bulbs for its continuing experiments on incandescent lamps. When Sprague, the young theoretician, was casually asked to compute the volume of one of these bulbs, the former naval officer gave a correct answer after some prolonged calculations. The Edison group leader chuckled and quietly suggested to Sprague that an infinitely easier and faster approach would be simply to fill the experimental bulb with water and decant off the contents into a measured flask.

Sprague laughed at himself and never forgot the empirical lesson. A bit longer time was required for his employers to appreciate his theory and systems approach to the infant field of detailed wiring calculations. The established Edison procedure was to construct a precise model map of the proposed area installation down to an individual peg for each house with turns around a peg to show the number of electric lights ordered for the house. To Sprague this was absurd. He knew the use of mathematical formulas incorporating wire sizes could eliminate much of this work. The Edison people eventually bought this idea, but in less than a year Frank Spargue went his separate professional way to the mutual relief of both parties.

The fresh generation of the Spragues in physical science could only have survived and blossomed because of a corps of empiricists headed by men like Edison and Alexander Graham Bell. Only a Sprague in turn could provide the needed research link to another type of person dealing with conceptual mathematics, epitomized by the young physicist, Albert Einstein, who published his quantum and relativity theories in 1905.

Frank Sprague became the nemesis of the cable car lines of the world just as the owners of the systems were commencing to receive adequate returns on their heavy investments. This unlikely unholy angel was in his late twenties when he invented a heavy-duty electric motor and then demonstrated the ability to control a number of these components in unison. Sprague next solved the problem of integrating his spring-mounted trolley motor with a reliable gear-meshing procedure. Learning from his Edison experience, he put together a team, nearly as young as himself, to prove that he had an electrical streetcar or trolley system which worked. By the end of 1888 Frank Sprague had laid the groundwork for a whole array of industries.

Some of the people involved in the elaborate cable car system of the Pacific Railway Company of Los Angeles may have been following Sprague's work. Certainly most had not. Electrical streetcars had been resounding failures. Leo Daft's trolley system, built during the Boom out to Pico Heights and Berendo Avenue, was a fiasco. The investors still winced when the subject was brought up. They remembered only too well that the electric dummy (locomotive) hauling a tiny passenger car crawled to Pico and Alvarado streets and then refused to climb a very modest grade. A cable line system even on flat or moderately rolling land such as Los Angeles should surely be the nucleus of any urban transportation system.

Yet in an incredibly short time there was available to eager Los Angeles entrepreneurs a rugged and fast street railway system featuring reliable electric motors, an alternating current distribution network, motor speed controllers and air brakes. The trolley system was as cheap to operate reliably as the cable lines and far less costly to construct. The districts surrounding Los Angeles could be serviced inexpensively at relatively high speeds and paid for by land development along the car lines. This meant that local capital would be readily available because of the evident appreciation and growth opportunities.

The one missing ingredient in such a pleasant scenario was abundant amounts of reliable electric power over and above the rising electric lighting requirements. This was forthcoming.

There were loud arguments in Los Angeles saloons over an unusual company proposal which the Common Council had on its 1882 agenda. In a town of flickering gas light, coal oil lamps and tallow candles, the proposal was nothing less than the installation of seven electric arc lights scattered about the community of 11,000 population. Each light was to be mounted on a 150-foot-high mast in order to illuminate as much area as possible. There was a hornet's nest of opposition to the arc light plan. The list of objections was extensive—chickens would molt, cows would dry up because they would be kept awake, and the light could cause color blindness and be the ruination of ladies' complexions.

A beleaguered Common Council recognized the lighting installation could end up as a costly failure and possibly do some of the things which were feared. However, overriding these considerations was the underlying feeling that the town must somehow shake off the deadening aftereffects of the depression of the late seventies. The lighting project's boosters felt that it would be the "best advertisement that Los Angeles could have."

Arc illumination was still a rarity in the United States even though it had been used on a few Paris boulevards fifteen years earlier. The Brush Electric Company proposed the Los Angeles installation of seven arc lights (subsequently raised to ten) along with a program for forty or so arc lights in commercial firms. All of this would justify a small powerhouse to be located in an old vineyard at Alameda and Banning streets. The sense of the town was to go ahead and the Common Council approved the arc lighting proposal. Two 50-horsepower steam engines provided the power for two Brush machines—one of which generated 3000 candlepower for town lighting and the other 2000 candlepower for commercial service. The power lines were installed, the high masts erected, the carbon points of the arc light were tenderly adjusted and the system was ready.

The word went out to the South Coast. On New Year's Eve of 1882, the arc lights were to explode into an unknown kind of brilliance. Farmers and ranchers bundled flocks of sleepy children in their wagons and drove to the tops of a hundred hills for the never-to-be-forgotten view of an island of manufactured light emerging from the grip of a land of darkness.

The tiny electric company was a success even though the carbon points of the arc lights required changing daily. Expensive coal was the fuel source and would remain so for some time until satisfactory fuel oil burners could be devised. At the turn of the century the electric company had its poles covering most of the city, was putting the wires underground in the central district, and was maintaining a thousand street lights. The generating equipment had changed in the new plant at Alameda and Palmetto streets—still Brush for arc lighting but Westinghouse alternating current for the Edison-type of incandescent lighting and 500-volt direct current for commercial power service. The seemingly insatiable power demands for the Sprague-type trolley systems brought in competition to the established operation from what had evolved into the Edison Electric Company. But the longer-term solution to expanding trolley requirements was an alternative approach to steam power—use of the energy of the brawling mountain streams of southern California.

Hydroelectric power on a major scale came to the South Coast because Metcalf Dodsworth built an ice plant in 1890. He first thought of locating the plant, which would use electrically powered machinery, in Ventura County until he discussed the subject of freight rates with his good friend, J. C. Stubbs, the general freight agent for the Southern Pacific, notorious for its arbitrary freight rate rulings. While Dodsworth should not have been surprised because of the long-standing policy of the railroad to charge what the traffic would bear, he could scarcely believe the number when Stubbs set a freight rate at just about the difference between the cost of producing the ice and the selling price. Fortunately, Dodsworth had an alternative. The Santa Fe had recently completed its own line from San Bernardino to Los Angeles, and the railroad not only quoted him reasonable freight rates but offered to buy his surplus ice from the proposed factory site near the mouth of the San Gabriel River Canyon at Azusa.

Utilizing an existing irrigation ditch and a flume with a drop of sixty feet, Dodsworth had ample river flow to turn the water wheels of his electrical generator. One of Dodsworth's partners, William G. Kerckhoff, who was making his own fortune in the lumber business, became intrigued by this novel idea of using flowing water to generate electricity. Kerckhoff was determined to supply electricity to Los Angeles and its trolley lines nearly twenty-five miles away. His San Gabriel Electric Company, with the technical input of Allan C. Balch, collected the river water far up the canyon with a nine-mile conduit to the spinning wheels of a powerhouse near the mouth of the canyon. Hydroelectric power officially arrived on the South Coast in June of 1898 when needles on the dials at the Third

Street Receiving Station in Los Angeles moved to positions showing 16,000 volts were being delivered over the miles of transmission lines.

More power was on the way. After Edison Electric consolidated several hydroelectric installations around the Santa Ana River headwaters, construction of an eighty-three mile transmission line to Los Angeles was begun. Technically speculative, as it was the longest transmission line to be undertaken for its day, the Santa Ana River delivered 33,000 volts to the receiving station on East Fourth Street below Main in January of 1899.

Los Angeles for a time had ample electrical power—enough for all of its needs, including the Big Red Cars and a developing interurban network which would be unequaled in the world.

CHAPTER 11

"This was scarcely odd,
because they'd eaten every one"

However tenuous the excuse for most of them, extravagant military titles proliferated on the Western frontier. In California Phineas Banning and David D. Colton acquired the designation of "General" from a Civil War militia which was ill-defined and mostly on paper. Moses H. Sherman had to reach even further for his military title. He had himself appointed Adjutant-General of the empty Arizona Territory in 1883 and ever afterward insisted on being referred to as General Sherman.

There did seem to be a strong positive correlation between the ability to accumulate power and money and the personal liking for a prestigious designation. In M. H. Sherman's case when he was age thirty-seven he was one of the very well-to-do men in his territory and was still looking for a fresh business opportunity. During a long-time association with his brother-in-law, Eli P. Clark, Sherman found his destiny in trolley railway lines on the South Coast.

At first glance the possibility of successfully establishing a trolley system in Los Angeles appeared to be minimal. The small city only had a population of 50,000 in 1890 and yet its streets carried expensive cable railway lines, recently built by Pacific Railway. The Los Angeles *Times* summed up the general feeling that the cable system had to do no more "than relax and watch the money roll in from a populace which enthusiastically applauded its service and well-located lines."

The *Times* was wrong. Less than four years later the cable company was in financial receivership and shortly thereafter fell into the waiting arms of Moses H. Sherman. The Arizona general was not standing ready at the appropriate time and place by unlikely chance. Those intervening years had been a record of misfeasance, mistakes and miscalculations by Pacific Railway, complemented by an onrushing trolley technology and exploited by Sherman, a shrewd tactician and an excellent salesman.

The Sherman group tacked together several rickety trolley lines in the city and folded them into an 1890 Arizona corporation called Los Angeles Consolidated Electric Railway Company, immediately abbreviated to LACE. With optimistic forethought typical of Sherman, he standardized his trolley tracks on a narrow gauge of three feet, six inches—the same as the cable lines. While foolishness and greed continued to gnaw at its vitality, the cable system was also struck a competitive frontal blow.

Under a clever populist guise of monopoly control, the so-called "five-block law" was passed by the state legislature. This was due in good part to the efforts of William E. Dunn, Sherman's representative, who lobbyed through the legislation. Dunn, later counsel and confidant of Henry E. Huntington, coolly and successfully advocated the notion that a local rail line could utilize the track of another system for five city blocks and repeat the procedure elsewhere along the competing line. Now Sherman's trolleys in the prime business and commercial districts were able to use the cable line tracks at will in preferred locations. The advantages to the trolley entrepreneur were evident; to the cable system shareholders the law was a prelude to disaster.

Sherman's LACE selectively utilized the cable system's tracks at four prime locations for a nominal and court-assessed cost of $15,000. Last ditch attempts of Pacific Railway to raise money for electrifying its cable lines failed, aided in part by an effective Sherman campaign of fact and rumor dealing with the weaknesses of Pacific management and the basic financial structure of the company. Pacific Railway was sold in receivership to the highest (and only) bidder, LACE, in mid-1893. By this time, LACE itself was mortgaged to the hilt, but Sherman then nor later was ever held back by such financial facts. He acquired local lines in Pasadena and commenced construction on a trolley line from Los Angeles to Pasadena—the South Coast's first interurban which opened for service in 1895. Meanwhile, however, Sherman and his partner, Eli P. Clark, were encountering some real Los Angeles trolley competition.

The displaced Pacific Railway investors had a silver lining to their black cloud, albeit a very small one. The Sherman/Dunn five-block maneuver had not gone unnoticed. Another shrewd and capable outlander with money to support his ambitions was determined to establish a local trolley position. The shining green trolleys of William S. Hook must have given a seriously overextended Sherman a bilious feeling as they ran down key sections of the LACE under the five-block law, while Hook's people assiduously circulated facts and rumors dealing with the Sherman lines' insolvency. The result was that the bondholders of LACE threw out the Sherman management and renamed the system the Los Angeles Railway Company.

Other men might have been depressed and certainly intimidated by the bondholders' takeover of their holdings. But not so with Moses H. Sherman. He and his brother-in-law somehow extricated the Pasadena interurban from LACE before the bondholder takeover and proceeded to double track the popular interurban route, calling the interurban the Los Angeles and Pacific Railway. Sherman then scrounged money to fashion together four embryonic lines which became the basis of an interurban road from Los Angeles to Santa Monica.

Sherman's route, to the bay town, was viable even a half-century later. The track went south on Hill Street from the central district to Sixteenth Street (Venice Boulevard) and out past Arlington Heights to Vineland (Venice Boulevard and Vineyard), thence diagonally across to a desolate stop in the wheat fields and wild mustard, originally called Morocco and shortly thereafter Beverly, where the track turned toward Santa Monica. The cars stopped at Sawtelle, a village which had grown up just south of the Old Soldiers' Home, already housing nearly 2000 veterans in its new, white wooden buildings. With flags flying and a band playing, the first trolley on April 1, 1896, arrived in Santa Monica at the terminal atop the bluffs on

Ocean Avenue. Some of Sherman's critics believed he had energetically mortgaged himself to build an interurban through a vacuum to nowhere.

A solid case could be made that M. H. Sherman's optimism had leapfrogged his judgment. Beyond Arlington Heights the ranch country flowed to the ocean. Santa Monica, the highly promoted Zenith City on the Sunset Sea a generation earlier, was a dozing, tourist-oriented community which had reacted only lethargically to the strenuous Port Los Angeles efforts of the Southern Pacific. Still Sherman was sure there was a major potential in the line because he was convinced Los Angeles would move west. When his second set of creditors closed in on his trolley enterprises, it found the Santa Monica interurban had been carefully extricated from the creditors' grasp and remained with the promoter. At this point many of General Moses H. Sherman's contemporaries were convinced he utilized mirrors in his financial magic and juggling acts.

Sherman's magic mirrors in fact were his consummate salesmanship combined with a type of brassy nerve which somehow kept his shaky trolley enterprises afloat for a time. A minor regional capitalist like Sherman who operated with no monopoly or government subsidy had somehow to obtain what borrowable funds were available in an area where there was a strong demand for capital. I. W. Hellman and other San Francisco money interests felt "he could talk money out of the birds in the trees," and they went to some lengths to avoid meeting with the trolley promoter for that reason.

At the same time Sherman's ability to stretch his credit with his suppliers was almost legendary. A story was told of one irate and hard-bitten vendor of railroad ties who was determined to collect personally $30,000 of long-overdue invoices. On leaving the trolley promoter's office, wrapped in a self-satisfied smile, he was asked by another creditor in the anteroom whether he had been successful in collecting his money from Sherman: "Oh, better than that," he happily replied, "I sold him $30,000 more ties."

A compulsive worker over a long lifetime, M. H. Sherman

would readily admit to an impressive list of illnesses, both past, present and unquestionably in the future. Either consumption (tuberculosis) or a kind of galloping asthma brought him to Arizona Territory when a young man, and circulatory ailments among a host of other diseases (according to Sherman) plagued him constantly until he died at nearly eighty years of age. Certainly the Arizona general was always conspicuous because of his constant complaint of being cold. Most of the year Sherman "wore an enormous, below-knee-length overcoat. . . . He was on at least one occasion mistaken in his coat for a theatrical character and his autograph solicited." One could be sure that the trolley promoter did not molt one feather at such a request.

Sherman was not as popular with his subordinates as with his peers. An operating detail man when he had the time and inclination, his loud and carrying voice was only matched by his brusqueness in overwhelming an unwary or errant employee. Still General Sherman with his weaknesses and strengths was the embodiment of a thousand regional risk-taking promoters. Always cash-poor, they were the men who dominated their regions for a time and then yielded to still stronger forces.

A powerful triumvirate quietly entered the South Coast and bought up the previous Sherman holdings—the local trolley system in Los Angeles and the Pasadena interurban. Two of the principals of the purchasing group were names to conjure with in California, Collis P. Huntington and Isaias W. Hellman. The other principal was known then chiefly because he was the favorite nephew of the aging railroad magnate. But by himself, Henry E. Huntington would shortly stand front stage center on the South Coast.

"No better boy than Ed ever lived." To receive such an accolade from Collis P. Huntington verged on the edge of the improbable. Also anybody who knew Uncle Collis well understood such praise of his nephew was not generated because of Henry E. Huntington's penchant for helping elderly widows across muddy streets. Young Ed or "H. E.," as he was generally known to his close business associates, had demonstrated the single-minded aggrandizement of power and money which appeared to characterize the Huntington clan. When Collis died in 1900, his loyal nephew was managing the Southern Pacific's trolley system in San Francisco and was fifty years of age. H. E. Huntington discovered he was an immensely wealthy man a few days later. His uncle's will provided that the principal elements of the estate would be divided equally between the fifty-year-old widow, Arabella, and the beloved Ed.

Old Collis P. Huntington had managed to hold the reins of railroad power in his gnarled but still powerful hands. His death automatically meant a major struggle over the Southern Pacific. After a few months of jockeying it was clear that Edward H. Harriman, chairman of the Union Pacific executive committee, would take over control. H. E. Huntington and Arabella sold their railroad holdings to the Harriman group. Each received about $40,000,000, roughly a half-billion dollars in mid-1970 buying power. Years later H. E. and Arabella would marry, and she would eventually be able to involve him in a single-minded pursuit of book and art collecting.

However, to expect the key representative of the Huntington clan in the prime of his life to retire forthwith and enjoy his enormous fortune was patently absurd. If H. E. Huntington could not run the Southern Pacific, he had a plan for building a barony of his own. He intended to buy strategic lands in southern California and exploit these properties with a network of interurban trolleys. Huntington believed his trolleys would provide a much more frequent service and greater short-haul efficiency than the steam lines in a region destined for major population growth.

The land could be bought and Huntington had the capital resources and solid railroad training to bring an extensive interurban system into being during an age of no automobiles, trucks or paved highways. He assembled a potent group of West Coast financial and technical people to organize and implement a corporation called "Pacific Electric." Isaias W. Hellman, Christian De Guigne and Antoine Borel had worked closely with

Huntington on the San Francisco trolley system. Jonathan S. Slauson was a South Coast landholder and promoter, John D. Bicknell served as legal counsel, Epes Randolph was one of the senior railroad engineers in the nation, and George S. Patton (his son was the World War II general) was a vociferous Democrat known for his anti-Southern Pacific position. And in the tradition of his uncle, H. E. Huntington believed firmly in utilizing debt leverage to accomplish his objective. Later, when bearded by Hellman on this, Huntington's blunt reply was simply: " . . . I wanted you [Hellman, De Guigne and Borel] as a partner because you were capable of raising money." And raise money the trio did—$10,000,000 in 1902 alone.

H. E. Huntington then was ready to make his move in southern California. His choice of Long Beach as a first terminal from Los Angeles appeared unlikely. The 1900 census of the beach town showed a population of 2000, monstrously inflated according to some. On a bid basis he acquired a trolley franchise in the town for $9,600, a rich price, and only because he was bidding against the William S. Hook interests. Long Beach was delighted, the competition was a major windfall for the municipal budget.

The Long Beach interurban was not to be a one-shot promotional trolley if Epes Randolph had anything to do with it. Randolph, the general manager, established the engineering specifications of standard-gauge, heavy-duty rails with matching ties, roadbed and bridge structures for a balanced railroad system of the day. This was no flimsy line so typical of the early South Coast trolley systems. Smaller editions of the Big Red Cars, as the Pacific Electric was popularly known a few years later, arrived at the Long Beach terminal in 1902, less than nine months after receipt of the franchise. Most of the route from East Ninth Street in Los Angeles was on private right-of-way including the center of American Avenue (Long Beach Boulevard).

Long Beach merchants, so often denied what they considered to be their just due, could not believe their fortune while they watched the just-opened interurban system deposit a load of passengers every fifteen minutes at the terminal on Ocean Boulevard during the morning of the Fourth of July. In a state of bliss the local newspaper estimated there were 30,000 visitors in the little town and on its magnificent beach, the bulk of which came by trolley. Whatever the number, Long Beach loved it and Henry E. Huntington, with his spreading interurban network, became a conjurer of good fortune for all the striving small communities and surrounding farm lands of the South Coast.

In contrast to his Uncle Collis, who deliberately gave the impression at times of a shaggy gray bear who walked and talked like a man, H. E. Huntington always presented the appearance of an urbane, kindly gentleman. Tall, broad shouldered with a clipped mustache and the beginnings of a substantial paunch, the interurban magnate radiated quiet confidence and command. He was a familiar and prepossessing figure in his gray suit, immaculate linen, spats, and wide-brimmed hat when he traveled leisurely in a carriage about the South Coast examining prospective land purchases. Touted and courted as the lodestone of property appreciation in southern California he discovered that much of what he did was newsworthy. Actually, a rather shy man, Huntington had a deserved reputation for detesting reporters. Yet he gave Harry Carr of the Los Angeles *Times* a major news story because the cub reporter was frightened enough and likable enough that Huntington took pity on him:

"I waylaid Mr. Huntington as he was going through the Southern Pacific Depot on his way to his private car with a bevy of gentlemen who looked like money. It was impossible for anyone to have looked as scared as I felt . . . [when] he sent his party ahead and we sat down on a bench.

" 'What is it you want?' he said gently.

" 'I—I don't know, sir. The City editor sent me to get a story.'

" 'Well, now, let's see . . .'

"Whereupon he handed me some information that stood the

town on its head. . . . Mr. Huntington was about to start the great system of interurban railroads that now spreads like a network all over Southern California . . ."

The trolley system envisaged by Huntington required quantities of reliable electric power which he was convinced must be under his control. The hydroelectric utilities of William G. Kerckhoff and his associates developed over the previous decade seemed to offer the best potential. The merger vehicle was the Pacific Light and Power Company, incorporated in 1902, with Huntington holding a majority of the stock. Other than himself the board of directors consisted of Hellman, De Guigne, Borel, Kerckhoff, Kaspare Cohn and Henry W. O'Melveny (shortly replaced by Allan C. Balch, an early electrical engineer). The board forthwith voted a $10,000,000 bond issue for expansion, the size of which demonstrated the influence of Huntington.

With an effective troika of adequate electric power, local trolley systems and an interurban network, the regional transportation and associated land empire of Huntington mushroomed. His Pacific Electric bought land near Alhambra and even 2000 acres deep in Orange County east of La Habra. Acquiring local trolley lines in Riverside and San Bernardino was an evident beachhead for an interurban line paralleling the Southern Pacific and the Santa Fe. Pacific Electric track crews moved toward San Pedro and the harbor from Dominguez Junction even as the Southern Pacific lethargically talked about seeking an injunction to prohibit the trolley magnate's crew from crossing the steam road's tracks. During a spring night in 1903 a crossing frog was installed on the Southern Pacific tracks and the trolley railhead shortly thereafter reached the harbor.

E. H. Harriman, who controlled the Southern Pacific and was the most powerful railroad man of the 1900s, was originally amused, then irritated and finally angry with Huntington. He made the decision to put the Southern Pacific into the interurban business on the South Coast. Shortly after buying up

Hook's narrow-gauge trolley from Los Angeles to San Pedro, Harriman with a good deal of relish was able to suggest to Huntington that they meet in San Francisco at Huntington's convenience.

The trolley magnate's convenience turned out to be practically forthwith when he learned I. W. Hellman and Hellman's two associates, De Guigne and Borel, had unilaterally and secretly sold all of their interests in Huntington's ventures to his arch rival, E. H. Harriman. Hellman had placed forty-five percent of Huntington's transportation ventures in the enemy's hands without obtaining a final refusal offer from his principal. Jackson A. Graves was an invited witness by Hellman to an unusual conversation between the banker and Huntington shortly after the sale:

Hellman: "When we went into this deal, did not you fix the amount that it would cost us?"

Huntington: "Yes."

Hellman: "When we had spent that much money, did not I then sell ten million dollars' worth of Pacific Electric Railway bonds for the use of the project?"

Huntington: "Yes, that is correct."

Hellman: "When that money was gone, did not you begin to call on us individually, you putting up your share and calling on us for additional money?"

Huntington: "Yes. I could not build railroads without money. And if I had told you what it was going to cost, when we began the work, you never would have joined me."

Hellman: "Did not I come to Los Angeles and remonstrate with you, telling you that I was not going to break myself on this project, that De Guigne and Borel had borrowed all the money they could, and were worrying over the matter considerably?"

Huntington: "Yes, you made that complaint to me."

Hellman: "And did I not beg you to buy our stock, and you laughed at me?"

Huntington: "Yes, I thought you were worrying without reason."

Hellman: "You refused to buy our stock. Then, did I not tell you that I was going to get out, and if you did not buy it I was going to sell it?"

Huntington: "Yes, and I told you to go ahead and sell it. I had no idea that you could find anyone on earth who would step into your shoes."

Hellman: "Then you acknowledge here, before Mr. Graves, that I gave you every opportunity to buy it?"

Huntington: "That is correct. But I wanted you as a partner because you were capable of raising money."

After a little more conversation Mr. Huntington rose to go, and Hellman, still seated, said:

"Now, what are we to be, friends or enemies?"

Mr. Huntington extended his hand, saying, "Friends."

The definition of "friends" in Graves' report of the foregoing dialogue was open to interpretation. Huntington and Hellman did not have a great deal to do with each other after the episode.

Initially it appeared that E. H. Harriman had seriously misjudged his man. H. E. Huntington was constitutionally unable to have an outside ownership of forty-five percent critically looking over his business shoulder. Harriman knew this and expected the trolley magnate to sell out. Huntington did not. Instead, he immediately organized the Los Angeles Inter-Urban Railway. In several years the young company had more track mileage than the Pacific Electric, partially due to the fact that Huntington had a number of routes still in his own name when the Southern Pacific made its surprise purchase from the Hellman group.

When the railhead of an interurban trolley reached a village or development, property values shot upward. Typical was the deserted stretch of beach and marsh land between Santa Monica/ Ocean Park and Ballona Creek. Abbot Kinney, a multifaceted personality and a conservationist of a sort, determined to build a Venice of America featuring handsome residences on canals with arched bridges and even including some imported gondoliers with their Venetian boats. Kinney's project opened with a flourish on the Fourth of July, 1905, when the just-completed Los Angeles and Pacific extension from Santa Monica brought 40,000 people to his Venice.

Three days after the Venice opening, Henry E. Huntington let it be known that he was buying large amounts of land in the Redondo Beach district and was considering building additional wharves for deep-water vessels. Shortly thereafter, his company announced the purchase of the Los Angeles and Redondo Railway Company. Immediately, Redondo found itself in an unbelievable land frenzy. The real estate offices were surrounded by yelling people just off the trolley, pushing and shoving for a place in line to purchase anything. "They bought heaps of sand and holes in the ground; they bought in one breath and sold in the next; they bought blindly and sold blindly." Then sanity finally returned, as suddenly as it had left.

The Moses H. Sherman group sold its Los Angeles and Pacific to the Southern Pacific in 1906, despite repeated assurances to Huntington that the company intended to remain independent. This sales news was received with nearly the same amount of bitterness by Huntington's associates as the surprise Hellman sale to the Southern Pacific three years earlier. The trolley magnate (or Trolley Man as the newspapers were beginning to call him) continued his interurban expansion, but the careful Southern Pacific moves had accomplished their purpose. H. E. Huntington had developed other interests, and two years after the death of Edward H. Harriman, he sold his interurban system to the Southern Pacific and its Pacific Electric. In return he gained full personal control of the local Los Angeles Railway and Pacific Light and Power.

The Pacific Electric with its Big Red Cars became a magnificent regional railway system with the Huntington acquisition in 1911, the equal of any in the world. It had 600 miles of line and a daily schedule of 1400 trains, and for years afterward the network would continue to expand. Running times of the Red Cars during their heyday from central Los Angeles to suburban depots was impressive by optimum freeway standards of a later day.

Los Angeles To	Miles Distance	Minutes Running Time	No. Round Trips Daily	Schedule Year
Long Beach	20.4	48	54	1913
Pasadena	11.2	39	70	1911
San Bernardino	57.4	125	7	1916
Santa Monica	17.1	52	38	1911
Venice	14.8	38	53	1911

With the Pacific Electric's extensive rights-of-way strategically located throughout much of the South Coast, the persistent question raised a half-century or more later was *why and how did this fine mass-transit system disappear?*

The answer lay simply in the continued erosion of the interurban trolley's ability to make high speeds on its own rights-of-way. There was an exploding public demand for automobile roads. And to stretch the highway dollar/mileage to the maximum, the new roads simply cut across the interurban tracks rather than building expensive viaducts over them. Then principal streets were widened by the easy expedient of eliminating trolley rights-of-way and paving around the rails.

Year after year the trolleys were forced to reduce speeds, yet still the interurban/automobile accident rate skyrocketed with the Big Red Cars the prime object of public and newspaper abuse. When running times continued to mount and fares increased because of drop-offs in patronage, commuters left the Pacific Electric in droves, changing to automobile transportation. So the vicious circle tightened on the interurban system until a day came in April of 1961 when there were no more Red Cars. For the public and its elected representatives, like the Walrus and the Carpenter, " . . . this was scarcely odd, because they'd eaten every one."

Most Los Angeles people in the 1900s were less than fifteen minutes away by local trolley from the just constructed Huntington Building (later known as the Pacific Electric Building) and its interurban center. The largest structure in the city by far, and costing $1,700,000 in 1905, the nine-story building was located by H. E. Huntington at Sixth and Main streets, on the outskirts of the central business area. A tourist attraction in its own right, the interurban center was the departure point for transportation to the well-publicized Catalina Island.

Every newcomer to the South Coast had heard of the benign climate and wonders of the Island and its town of Avalon, twenty-seven miles from San Pedro dock across the open sea and forty-nine miles from Los Angeles. Yet a tourist could have a leisurely breakfast in his city hotel or boardinghouse and be in Catalina for lunch. The total time from the Huntington Building to Avalon pier was three hours. This was a marked improvement over the first yachting party to Catalina, given by Phineas Banning in 1859. His Los Angeles guests left the town at dawn by stagecoach for the twenty-one mile run to Wilmington, jouncing over the rutted track and inhaling the clouds of irritating adobe dust. After breakfast, Banning then took his guests by steam tug down the narrow winding channel of the muddy San Pedro estuary, across the bar with its cresting waves near Dead Man's Island and out to the *Active*, a U.S. Coast Survey ship, rolling in the roadstead anchorage near the present lighthouse. The *Active* arrived off Catalina after a two-hour passage.

By the time of the interurban trolley, Santa Catalina Island waters according to Charles F. Holder had become world renowned for their "extraordinary sea-angling with rod and reel, the region being, apparently, the meeting ground of many great game fishes caught nowhere else. . . . Here is the leaping tuna, the long-finned tuna, the yellow-fin, the white sea bass, the leaping swordfish that jumps and outfights the tarpon, the yellowtail and many more, any one of which would make any place famous, and to catch some of which, scores of anglers cross the Atlantic and continent yearly."

Holder, a noted naturalist, sports fisherman and professor at the Throop Institute, went on to write that Catalina had "the climatic charm of the Riviera without its summer heat and the delights of its winters without the cold winds which sweep down from the Maritime Alps." Professor Holder's books were widely read and preserved. The writer's copy of the naturalist's classic *Channel Islands of California* was published in England in 1910, and an Indian friend found it, carefully rebound, in a New Delhi book stall in the 1970s.

Catalina Island in the 1900s was a sheep ranch and a wild goat range on the flanks of precipitous mountains which rise abruptly from the sea. Twenty-two miles long and containing 45,000 acres, the Island has a substantial lee side protected from the long Pacific swells. There was and is one town, Avalon, located in a bight on the quiet side near the Island's east end.

In the late 1900s Avalon had a summer population of seven to nine thousand, probably more than the town had sixty or so years later. The community then was well served by three steamers, the largest of which carried 800 passengers. The town climbed the hills and canyons with the Metropole and the other principal hotels situated on the waterfront along with the Tuna Club and the Pavilion, the latter used for dancing and concerts. The golf links (whose hardpan fairways were becoming legendary) and the tennis club courts were back up the main canyon several blocks beyond the acres of a summer tent city shaded by eucalyptus trees just entering their early prime.

The fresh water supply of the town was expensive, possibly erratic, and a man who had a cistern for water storage was the envy of his neighbors. These same cisterns, now crumbling and most long forgotten, are a source of dismay in some new house construction as the Avalon neighbors of the writer discovered in the mid-1970s. Avalon's water was pumped from a limited number of wells and brought from the mainland by steamer and barges after the turn of the century. Seawater was used in toilets, hydrants, and the sprinkling carts which kept the street dust down. Fire in the wooden town was a substantial worry for the Banning brothers who owned the Island and a good part of Avalon itself.

In the tradition of his father, Phineas, and the opinion of

many in the 1900s, William Banning was the finest amateur six-in-hand coach driver in the West. Unquestionably, his rugged island's terrain and the coach road spiraling down from the summit to Avalon was the place to demonstrate his skill. Banning and his brothers, Joseph and Hancock, bought Santa Catalina Island (other than Avalon village) in 1892 from the James Lick estate after George R. Shatto and an English mining syndicate were unable to meet their mortgage payments. While Shatto had control, a townsite was laid out at Timm's Cove (he renamed it Avalon) during the Boom and a typical substantial wooden hotel, the Metropole, was completed there in 1888. Sheep ranching, sports fishing and tourism expanded under the Banning ownership; and the coach road into the Island's interior was extended from Avalon all the way to Howland's Landing toward the west end of the Island beyond the Isthmus.

The section of coach road which ran from Avalon to the 1500-foot summit towering above the town on the northwest was the most famous or notorious, depending upon one's point of view on mountain coaching. A six-horse team required an hour and a half to reach the summit from Avalon. William Banning could make the coaching run down the steep switchbacks of the fifteen-foot wide rock/dirt road in eighteen minutes, about the same time which would normally be made by an automobile on a far better roadbed in the 1970s. The Banning brothers gave the Catalina coaching concession to George Greeley. A ride "down the hill" with this famous professional driver could be made in Banning's time if, as Charles F. Holder put it, you particularly *desired* speed (Holder's italicization):

"With foot on the heavy brake, lines well in hand, Greeley starts his team, the horses gaining speed until all six are seemingly on the dead run down the incline. The party have left their nerves on the summit, so there is nothing to mar the complete enjoyment of the rush. Now the horses make a sharp turn, the leaders entirely disappearing around the bend; but so deftly is the brake used that the coach turns safely. . . . Now they turn at the head of the canyon, rising on the incline, and dash out on the loop, the leaders seemingly in air, turning so quickly that they are going one way and the coach almost another. . . . There is a roar of wheels grinding over a hard road, a musical clanking of buckles and trappings, the snap of a long whip. . . . All six horses are running loosely in the harness. The horses dash out seemingly in space, then wheel around and start down the lower train, sending clouds of dust over the edge of the precipice and [the coach] rolls into Avalon amid the cheers of the people who have been watching the descent."

The steam whistle alerting the volunteer fire department of Avalon echoed off the mountains around the town even as an enveloping blaze jumped from one wooden structure to another. In the early morning hours of November 29, 1915, the flames spread with frightening rapidity; every firefighting facility was inadequate, and there was no help to be had. The people scattered—up the mountain flanks and out along the narrow oceanfront toward Descanso Bay and Pebbly Beach. That smoke-filled dawn found the bulk of the town destroyed, including the Metropole.

The rebuilding was longer and more expensive than anticipated. World War I would shortly engulf the country with its deadening impact on a tourist locale like Catalina. The Banning brothers put their beloved island up for sale, and William Wrigley, Jr., the chewing-gum entrepreneur, took over their interests on a two-step basis in 1919.

Wrigley's purchase became the symbol of another beginning on the South Coast, much as was the establishment in the same year of H. E. Huntington's library and art gallery in San Marino.

Standing on a spur track inside the Huntington estate, the private railroad cars, San Marino No. 1 and San Marino No. 2, were being readied for a transcontinental trip in the spring of 1927. Henry E. Huntington, a widower for three years, was traveling to Philadelphia for relatively minor surgery. One of the private cars would provide his living accommodations, the other had space for servants and kitchen facilities. Huntington made the trip and died shortly after the surgical operation. He was seventy-seven years old but had been doing many things since he earned his South Coast reputation as the Trolley Man.

The sale of his interurban holdings in 1911 had given H. E. Huntington full control of the Pacific Light and Power Company at the time the utility was considering a difficult hydroelectric development. The Big Creek region northeast of Fresno, situated in a Sierra mountain wilderness of deep canyons and a maze of high peaks, had the required dam and power sites, although the location was fifty miles from the nearest railroad and 240 miles from Los Angeles. Wagon-freighting thousands of tons of materials, machinery and supplies through the rugged terrain would cost up to twenty dollars a ton. Huntington had been raised with the Southern Pacific which had had the men to match any Sierra mountains. He told his people to build a standard-gauge railroad to the Big Creek from the San Joaquin Valley. The S. J. & E. Railroad (referred to as the "Slow, Jerky & Expensive" or more formally the "San Joaquin & Eastern") was completed with an assortment of 100 curves, some of them hair-raising, to the site of the first powerhouse in the summer of 1912.

Only 157 days were spent in construction which meant bolting trestles to sheer rock walls in some of the gorges. The upper grades required Shay and Climax gear-type locomotives which clattered and clanked at five miles an hour. For exercise, at the beginning of one of the innumerable tight curves, the passengers would leisurely step out of their coach, hike up the embankment and wait for their car to arrive as the train labored up the switchback. Tickets included lunches, and the "up" and "down" trains met at Stevenson's Creek where there were beer bottles filled with warmish coffee, thick meat sandwiches, fresh pie and fruit. Big Creek power came fully on line in January of 1914, its transmission towers carrying an unbelievable power load for the day of 150,000 volts.

The very success of the Big Creek project brought H. E. Huntington up to a basic dilemma—should he expand his position in the power distribution field, which could only mean more time away from his recent and absorbing vocation of being both a bibliophile and an art collector? Huntington loved the library room of his San Marino home and "this tall, erect, portly master of the house, with his bald dome and fastidiously trimmed mustache, spent every afternoon working on his books. He clambered up and down the ladder in search of a volume he wanted, and he strenuously objected to being disturbed while he was reading . . ." There was a sensible and profitable merger match of Huntington's electrical power holdings with the Southern California Edison Company, and he decided to sell.

The Huntington Library and Art Gallery was established in 1919, and the Trolley Man became the Founder, a sort of an odd bibliophilic fly in amber for much of subsequent literary posterity.

CHAPTER 12

"What a great blessing this conquest has been for mankind"

For those in mid passage during the years of immense medical progress to have watched their children die horribly of diphtheria and then some years later to see a final solution to the dread disease could only awake aching memories of what might have been. Diphtheria killed three of Harris Newmark's children (all sons and aged nine, five and three) in less than two months. The torture of the Los Angeles merchant and his wife, Sarah, in 1879 while futilely watching the writhings of a desperately ill child can be understood from a description of the course of the disease when there was no diphtheria antitoxin available:

"The condition begins with a sore throat and with repeated attempts to expel, by spitting, the membrane that forms in the throat. If the disease continues, severe paralysis prevents swallowing and injures the heart. . . . The physician would frequently be called in the middle of the night to the bedside of the gasping child. Then he would suck the membrane from the throat by mouth-to-mouth contact or through a tube, if one was available. In severe cases he sometimes opens the windpipe with a knife to permit the child to breathe through the throat beneath the membrane. . . . There comes a period when breathing becomes impossible, and finally death."

An effective diphtheria antitoxin was announced by Emil von Behring in 1891, eight years after the germ or bacillus had been isolated by Edwin Klebs and Freidrich Loffler. The doctors who saw diphtheria before and after the advent of antitoxin strongly shared Morris Fishbein's feeling: "No one . . . who has actually seen a child with this condition, and who has then seen the marvelous effects of a suitable dose of antitoxin given early in the disease, can fail to appreciate what a great blessing this conquest has been for mankind."

The proposition that germs actually cause disease was successfully demonstrated in 1880. The work of Robert Koch and Louis Pasteur isolated the typhoid microorganism with a resultant cascade of medical knowledge. An array of diseases was traced to the invasion of the human body by germs. But diffusion of radical technical knowledge has always required time, far too much if the recipients were poorly trained and thoroughly conditioned in old habit patterns. Typical of this resistance to change was the medical profession and then its patients. Even a half-century after the typhoid breakthrough, a popular medical handbook for laymen found it necessary to emphasize that "anyone with a reasoning mind should be willing to grant that the germ actually causes the disease."

Well before the work of Koch and Pasteur led to the isolation of the typhoid microorganism, Joseph Lister in 1868 conceived the first procedures to counteract the development of pus in the human body. His antiseptic concepts revolutionized surgery. But again, comprehension and acceptance in the medical profession moved slowly. On the South Coast as in other remote regions, the 1890s had arrived before Lister's major scientific discovery was thoroughly understood and widely practiced. Before Lister's teachings, major operations were seldom attempted other than amputations and occasionally "cutting for kidney stone" and even so, death followed the incomprehensible infections in perhaps 50% of all surgical cases.

Primarily concerned about shock to his patient, a doctor in the pre-Lister era prided himself on his surgical speed. When tying blood vessels, he might hold the scalpel between his teeth. The lapel of the ordinary frock coat which he wore while operating was a convenient place to keep his needles in an orderly sequence for sewing up the wound quickly. Hospitals had a well-deserved reputation for being places in which to die. The admittance of a patient for surgery made everyone (including the patient) feel that condolences to the family should be readied.

Resembling in some ways the Keystone Kops in the movies of the next generation, many doctors reacted on a delayed timing basis to the continuing influx of knowledge from the medical research and teaching centers. Perhaps this was best typified by nineteenth-century man's dedication, like his ancestors before him, to curative hot springs and their baths. By drinking from the springs, inhaling their fumes, and soaking in the waters at various degrees of temperature, he was convinced these procedures separately or in combination cured many of the diseases afflicting mankind. The South Coast had more than its share of hot springs and reputable doctors who solemnly reported on the springs' alleged therapeutic value.

Pulmonary tuberculosis or consumption as it was generally called (and phthisis among doctors) supposedly responded to the waters at San Fernando because of the carbonic-acid gas and sulphur. Syphilis and rheumatism were noted for being cured at San Juan. And diabetes, dyspepsia and scrofula (tubercular lymph glands of the neck) were reported benefited at Santa Fe. Many cases of lung trouble such as pleurisy and bronchitis supposedly at once improved at Temecula while asthmatics also received "perfect relief" there. Under the sponsorship of reputable physicians these kinds of major curative claims continued to be made into the 1900s.

There was no shortage of recognized doctors on the South Coast after the Boom of the eighties, nor was there any scarcity of naturopaths, Chinese herb doctors, faith healers and an array of outright charlatans. Most of the doctors were able and devoted men; some were neither. They had come to southern California for the climate, their health or because of pasts they wanted to forget. Their out-of-town practice was handled with light spring wagons or buggies; doctors were among the earliest to experiment with horseless carriages. The state of the medical art (and dentistry, for that matter) in Los Angeles was probably no better or worse than any other remote urban area of the United States at the time.

Many of the more prosperous doctors and dentists of Los Angeles had their offices in the handsome Bradbury Block or on the first floor of Walter Lindley's building near Sixth and Hill streets. The third floor consisted of a six-bed hospital operated by Lindley. The "Buzzards' Roost" occupied the second floor and this was where young doctors and dentists were located. They handled overflow referrals from the established tenants in the prime office space below as part of the continued effort to develop their slim practices, and occupied their leisure time in the time-honored pursuits of young men, not least of which was having a satisfactory appreciation of the excellent Los Angeles beer.

A young dentist, William F. Kennedy, was representative of the type of men-about-town who inhabited the Buzzards' Roost. For an undisclosed reason, possibly unrequited love, on a hot Fourth of July Kennedy was desultorily but persistently bowling and drinking beer at Tony Zorb's place near First and Main streets. Likely stimulated by the noise of a marching band and certainly by a number of schooners of cold beer, Dr. Kennedy felt he should have his very own and large fireworks display. Action immediately followed this decision, a key but sometimes costly characteristic of a struggling young professional man:

"He hired a hack and drove to a fireworks stand. He threw back the top of his hack and had the vehicle filled with sky-rockets, Roman candles and firecrackers of all sorts and varieties . . .

"In front of the Grand Opera House some heartless wag threw a lighted match right into the midst of his newly acquired possessions. Things happened thick and fast. But Kennedy met the emergency. With the tails of his Prince Albert on fire, he jumped from the hack, threw off his coat, rescued the driver, unhitched the horse, and watched a fireworks display that included the unprogrammed distruction of the hack. It was an expensive Fourth of July for the young dentist."

Commencing with John S. Griffin, a principal characteristic of being a successful doctor in southern California after the Civil War appeared to be involvement in a great many things in addition to the practice of medicine. Joseph P. Widney was one of the chief proponents for breaking California into two states and was a co-author of a book extolling the South Coast's advantages. M. Dorothea Lummis (who later married the educator, Ernest Carroll Moore), a doctor who made her night sick calls in a buggy accompanied only by a police dog, was the driving force behind a variety of social service works including the Society for the Prevention of Cruelty to Animals. During the same period, John R. Haynes and his wife were nurturing the first elements of political reform in California.

But more energetic than most in fields removed from his immediate medical practice was Walter Lindley. He philosophized on the most humane way to execute a man (he favored hanging); co-authored the widely quoted book *California of the South* (it extolled the South Coast ad nauseam); and organized the California Hospital in the late 1890s. Lindley believed that the region needed and would support a teaching hospital for the South Coast's only medical school, which had been kept alive by the doctor instructors while the parent University of Southern California struggled for its own survival. Other than private nursing homes of a half-dozen or so beds, Los Angeles' hospital needs had been met with a facility operated by the Sisters of Charity, the French Hospital and a small county institution.

Establishing a major hospital along the lines proposed by Walter Lindley was a substantial undertaking for a city at the time with less than a hundred thousand population. An equally important consideration among Lindley's colleagues was the recognition that a group of doctors could seldom agree on anything. However, when Lindley indicated his willingness to manage the enterprise, a score of doctors swung over to his view and agreed to support and finance the proposed hospital. The California Hospital of a hundred rooms opened on June 1,

1898, with a staff of forty nurses. The venture was a success, drawing patients from the entire South Coast. Within three years California had 150 rooms, 75 nurses and 5 operating rooms, along " . . . with all the necessary attributes of a hospital with the comforts of a first-class modern hotel." Lighted by electricity and gas, centrally heated by steam and serving "the most nourishing, palatable and healthful food" California was most certainly "An Elegant Hotel for the Sick" by any previous standards.

For the California Hospital to boast of five operating rooms at the turn of the century was a sure indication that a brave new world of surgery had arrived. Now it was necessary to dissipate the public's ugly and desperate fears of all hospitals. Typical of the continuing campaign was the 1913 series of articles in the Los Angeles *Times* written by Jackson A. Graves who had entered California for major surgery. The high confidence level of Graves and his surgeon was such that Graves could report currently on his hospital sojourn for amputation of his leg far up the thigh:

"When I got to the hospital, the nurse wanted to shave my hip and thigh well into the groin. I took my own razor, sat up in bed, and shaved it myself. When I finished, she gave me a hypodermic and, I think with more frankness than discretion, said: 'I guess Dr. Bryant knows what he is doing, but that hypodermic is strong enough to kill a horse.'

"I told her I was a mule, and it would not kill me.

"Toward 11 o'clock they put me on a litter on wheels, and started me for the operating room. When we got to the door, Dr. Bullard, who was to administer the anaesthetic, said: 'Do you want to take the anaesthetic here or inside?'

"I answered: 'Oh, take me in and put me on the table . . .'"

As thorough understanding of antisepsis grew in the nursing centers, women who could afford the expense began to have their children delivered in hospitals, and the specter of the deadly childbed or puerperal fever moved far into the background. Typical of the radical change in attitude toward hospital childbirth was the writer's own family. One of three children, he was born in a hospital in 1915; his two older brothers had been born at home.

The cascade of medical knowledge and progress was nearly overwhelming to the early twentieth-century man. Life expectancy in the United States increased from 47.3 years in 1900 to 72.4 years in 1975 with the great progress occurring in the first two decades. No longer were the cemetery ceremonies dominated by the pathetic small caskets of children, or watched by shocked husbands whose young wives were suddenly dead from puerperal fever. That was a time for living, not dying.

CHAPTER 13

"Keep your coats buttoned, stars pinned on left breast on outside of coat"

The new Los Angeles stank a good bit less and its swarms of biting fleas had decreased markedly. This was real civic progress. In past years the town's smells and fleas were only exceeded by its homicide and violence in the attainment of a well-deserved notoriety.

Cesspools, a long-used system of human waste disposal, have always been a subject of absolute minimum interest to everybody except the persons who have to smell the effluvia when they overflow and worry about contaminated groundwater filtering into adjacent wells. For people in Los Angeles who were interested in cesspools (which included most of those who lived and worked in the town's central district), the triumphant hotel announcement of the Pico House in 1874 could be thoroughly appreciated: "The unpleasant odor of gas has entirely disappeared since the building of the new sewer." The town had just completed its first municipal underground drain built of brick and wood. Despite this propitious beginning sewer construction and waste disposal facilities did not keep up with the population growth of the 1880s. The odors from overflowing cesspools in the central district and decaying garbage of the meat markets and restaurants could combine into a remarkable stench, particularly on a hot summer day. The sewer and sanitation systems including a $400,000 sewage outfall to the ocean finally caught up with the municipality's requirements in the late 1890s. Garbage collection and disposal on a city-wide basis was underway several years later, and streets were cleared nightly of manure and debris by pull brooms drawn by mules.

Not only was Los Angeles gradually becoming sweet-smelling, a massive attack was being launched on its adobe clay streets with their clouds of biting fleas during the dry months. The adobe set into a cast-iron hardness during the summer season, but it still managed to throw off an irritating dust, yet if straw was laid on the streets, fleas were bred in astronomical quantities. In the rainy months the fleas were gone but the adobe clay was churned hub-deep by plunging wagon wheels into a black ooze with the consistency of oatmeal. After the end of a season of heavy winter rains in 1887, a vigorous crusade for paved streets and sidewalks was organized. One device for publicizing the issue was the erection in the downtown dirt streets of miniature mounds resembling graves with legend-bearing signs like:

BEWARE OF QUICKSAND!

FARE FOR FERRYING ACROSS, 25 CENTS

NO DUCK-HUNTING ALLOWED IN THIS POND!

BOATS LEAVING THIS LANDING EVERY HALF-HOUR

REQUIESCAT IN PACE!

The campaign was successful. Main was the first street laid with cobblestones and bricks followed by Fort (Broadway) and Spring. By the mid-1890s the city had twelve miles of paved streets with a good part of the paving asphalt, and 120 miles of graded graveled roads and cement sidewalks. These statistics were a source of immense gratification to a community who understood all too well what they meant in terms of comfort and convenience.

With its own unique flavor, Los Angeles drinking water came from zanjas (open ditches) until underground mains were laid beginning in the late 1860s. Wishful town ordinances such as "No filth shall be thrown into the zanjas carrying water for

common use . . ." were ignored by the little community's inhabitants, and the ditches were used to wash dirty clothes and
dispose of miscellaneous debris. The water in the zanjas came
from a flume behind a makeshift dam in the Los Angeles River.
A water wheel filled the madre (main) zanja from the flume,
and a gravity flow moved the water through the subsidiary
ditches.

With a large dose of enlightened self-interest, three of the
town's eager young men during Los Angeles' first boomlet in
the late 1860s were determined to provide a long-term and
systematic water supply for the municipality. Amid loud charges
of influence peddling, Prudent Beaudry, John S. Griffin and
Solomon Lazard received a thirty-year franchise from the Common Council to own and operate the Los Angeles City Water
Company. Municipal affairs of the day being what they were,
the influence allegations were undoubtedly true; but despite the
franchise furor, the private company successfully met the sharply
rising water requirements. At the turn of the century when the
franchise had expired, the city was in an aggressive municipal
utility mood and proceeded to buy the private water company
in 1902. The purchased water system included nearly 700 fire
hydrants with adequate and reliable water pressure, a contrast
to the futile bucket brigades from the zanjas of a generation or
so earlier.

As usual, San Diego felt it had to do more than Los
Angeles for its expanded municipal water supply. The smaller
city built a thirty-five-mile flume from Lake Cuyamaca to El
Cajon, a superior engineering effort for the late 1880s. Flume
design provided for gravity water flow in a six-foot-wide and
four-foot-deep wooden aqueduct across 315 trestles bridging the
canyons and gullys. The aqueduct-opening celebration in 1889
brought Governor Robert W. Waterman along with other influential people and their wives from around the state. The ladies,
suitably corseted and dressed for the outdoor speech making,
carried parasols for protection from the sun.

Someone had the fine publicity idea of having San Diego's
honored guests float leisurely down the flume with the gentle

current for a mile or so in shallow, flat-bottom boats to the point where the aqueduct dedication ceremonies would occur. Eight of the VIPs were carefully placed aboard each punt, installed on seats built nearly flush with the gunwales. One by one the boats were pushed off, initially drifting in a leisurely procession as planned. Then, almost imperceptibly, the top-heavy punts picked up speed in the flowing water and began mildly ricocheting off the sides of the curving flume. The passengers clutched each other, their hats and the seats while dodging the menacing points of the erratically moving parasols. The more the passengers shifted their weight, the more the boats rocked. This meant water occasionally slopped over the topsides. None of the punts quite swamped, but there was a bevy of damp dignitaries and damp, infuriated ladies helped ashore near the speakers' platform.

Providing water, streets, sewers and the other necessary municipal services required strong local government. Prior to 1887 all California cities and towns functioned under general state laws and were ineffective and usually corrupt creatures of the distant state legislature. In a precedent-setting move for local political autonomy, the home rule provisions of the state's general law were greatly strengthened, and California cities of more than 50,000 population were given the authority to have a city charter, subject only to the provisions of the state constitution. Los Angeles, swollen by the Boom influx from a little town of 11,000 only a short time before, was quick to utilize the charter mechanism. William H. Workman, a forceful man and the current mayor, chaired the Board of Freeholders. The board's proposed charter established a systematic administrative and financing municipal framework along with nine wards or districts, each of which elected a councilman. It was approved by the voters in 1889 and was the city's basic law until the present charter was adopted in 1925.

One agency which benefited from the strengthened city government was the public library although a good part of its reputation (or dubious public image on occasion) continued to come from some of the head librarians through the 1900s.

The first head, John C. Littlefield, was one of them. His asthmatic condition willing, Littlefield worked at his primary job which was to collect subscription fees for his tiny library, even though some public funds did become available in 1874. To alleviate his asthma, Littlefield smoked the dried leaves of the thorn apple. The nauseating odor of the smoke which trailed him wherever he went may have speeded the collection of delinquent accounts. Some subscribers would have done practically anything to be rid of him.

Young Mary E. Foy, with her mother less than a step in the background, was the first of a number of women who headed the Los Angeles library. Tessa Kelso was one of the best and a dedicated women's rights supporter to boot. Not only was she a systematic and energetic manager, she had an evident talent for offending the stiffening moralities of the former frontier town. In one instance Ms. Kelso filed a malicious slander suit against a local clergyman. The minister and his congregation had been loudly and repeatedly praying for her soul because she strolled through the streets puffing cigarettes and acquired French novels for the public library. To the surprise of many, she managed to retain the City Librarian position from 1889 to 1895 and supervised the facility's move to much larger quarters in the splendid new city hall on Broadway. However, Ms. Kelso's flair for personal publicity was handily topped by a master of such matters. This was Charles F. Lummis, the self-appointed arbiter and promoter of all things cultural on the South Coast. Lummis served as City Librarian for a few years in the 1900s on sort of a sabbatical leave basis from his other activities including civic reform.

Municipal elections, and all elections in Los Angeles for that matter, had always been casual and often fraudulent. There was no voter registration. Even in a close election a candidate who would pay over two dollars for a vote was considered a spendthrift, and the price dropped markedly for warm bodies which could be kept sober long enough to stagger into a voting booth. With the reform movement of the late 1880s in Los Angeles, the recently established office of the City Clerk, provided in the new charter, was given the responsibility for handling municipal elections. Probably the first honest election in the city's history was that of 1890, but civil service as a replacement of the spoils system was still in the distant future.

When John Bryam was elected to complete a term as Los Angeles mayor in the late eighties, ". . . he delivered himself into the hands of his enemies by appointing all six of his sons to the police force." Even the strong stomach of the small city rejected this amount of raw nepotism in an eighty-man police force already stretched to the limit of its capabilities, and Bryam was defeated for reelection.

The Common Council of the toughest little town of the American West had belatedly established a paid police department in 1869 which consisted of a city marshal, William C. Warren, and seven deputies. Not surprisingly in a town used to arguments followed by pistol shots, Warren managed to get himself killed in a gun battle with one of his deputies soon after his appointment. In the late 1870s a Los Angeles policeman was finally wearing a standard uniform—slouch felt hat, a hip-length coat of blue serge and an eight-pointed silver star badge. Shortly before the Boom and about the time the police department was authorized to install a single telephone, the total departmental inventory of equipment consisted of:

> Six dark lanterns, one horse and saddle, thirteen police stars, twenty rogue pictures, seven sets of nippers (handcuffs), and miscellaneous belts and clubs.

Law enforcement in Los Angeles near the turn of the century was infinitely easier than years earlier. It had become a quiet city which its hundred-man force, including a residential Bicycle Squad, could handle readily. The police uniform was up-to-date —a London-bobby type of helmet and a thigh-length coat with a high-button collar. A proud chief of police warned his force to "Keep your coats buttoned, stars pinned over left breast on outside of coat, and hold your clubs firmly." There was no question that local crime in Los Angeles was now considerably more under control than in Santa Barbara where a harassed mayor of the town wrote a fervid 1893 memorandum to his city marshal:

Sir: You will use every effort and means in your power and at your command, to keep out of Santa Barbara all confidence operators, thieves, thugs, house-breakers, sneaks, pickpockets, moll-buzzers, burglars, gopher-blowers, tramps, and their ilk.

The only reason that Los Angeles had not burned to the ground any number of times, as San Francisco had during the same period, was that its buildings were made of adobe bricks. In theory, the town had had a volunteer fire department since the 1850s, but in reality it was a disorganized bucket brigade. With the number of wooden structures built during the first boomlet after the Civil War and the storage of hay in many of these buildings, it was obvious that provision should be made for some kind of organized volunteer protection. A four-wheel, man-powered fire engine was purchased in 1871, primarily through donations of Calle de Los Negros gamblers, saloon keepers and whorehouse madams along with silver miners who used their facilities. The nucleus of a paid fire department was organized in the late seventies with the several volunteer companies placed under the command of an elected chief engineer. About the same time, horses, instead of men, were used to haul the apparatus.

The internal combustion engine had a difficult time replacing the Los Angeles fire horse. While the department first purchased automotive vehicles in 1907, the horse population finally peaked out at 163 animals shortly before World War I. The last piece of horse-drawn apparatus was not retired until the early twenties, and then not only with much sentimentality but with full recognition that fire-horse performance would not easily be surpassed.

A Los Angeles firehouse at the turn of the century was a proven and sensible entity of two stories with the apparatus manned by professionals and hauled by immaculately trained horses. The ground floor of the structure had a twenty-foot ceiling pierced by a circular hole with a highly polished slide pole. The heavy apparatus, either a hook-and-ladder rig or a steamer pumper with its vertical boiler mounted over a fire basket containing a smoldering bed of coke, was hauled by three horses and was positioned on a turntable. Ahead of the principal apparatus facing the street door was a quick-release rack suspended on overhead ropes. The rack held three sets of harnesses positioned above the points where the horses on signal moved from their duty stalls into place. The on-duty horses stood in shallow pens immediately in back of the apparatus and munched their hay from iron baskets filled from second-floor chutes. The floors of these stalls could be hosed down as they sloped backward to a narrow cross channel which led to a central floor drain.

The second floor of the firehouse consisted principally of a dormitory and poker area for the crew. Coal was used for cooking and heat while a parallel gas and electricity system provided lighting, along with kerosene lamps and lanterns for emergency use. A new firehouse had a toilet and even a separate office/bedroom for the company captain. But the principal fixture on the second floor was the gleaming six-foot top of the apparatus room slide pole protruding from its round hole in the floor. The proper sequential clanging of the big wall bell of the electrical fire alarm system brought the dormant firehouse into frenzied activity with the crew flinging on their clothes and sliding down the pole to the floor below.

The Gamewell patented alarm system appeared to be the epitome of progress for an electrical fire warning network in the small city where telephones were still a rarity. Wires from the firehouses fanned out on the utility poles to sixty-five station boxes, unlocked with a common key. The boxes were placed in strategic locations and adjacent to establishments open a good deal of the time, preferably with people living on the premises. Whether a good portion of newly respectable and Temperance-oriented Los Angeles knew it or not, the fire boxes were usually located near saloons, whorehouses, drugstores selling liquor in their basements and houses of well-known insomniacs with busy-body tendencies. To report a fire, the operator opened the box with his common key and pulled down a lever. This triggered the clanging bell in a sequential pattern at each of the stations, while a paper tape was simultaneously punched with this pattern showing the fire box location.

The firehouse responding to the alarm was expected to have the horses standing motionless, in their correct position below the rack of harnesses, within a minute of the company's alarm, ready for the dropping of the rack and the quick connect of buckles and chains. Whatever the interval, it was extraordinary how little time elapsed between the alarm, the clangor of the bell of the heavy apparatus, and the door flying up or open with the three-horse team exploding from the entrance. An unwary or deaf pedestrian literally scrambled for his life. Any small boy, and most of his elders, ached to be on the seat handling the three-horse steamer as, picking up speed and trailing black smoke, the brilliantly polished apparatus swayed and spun down the cobbled streets while the rig's steel rims and the horseshoes on flying hooves cast off most satisfactory showers of sparks. It was an exciting everyday spectacle. More important, the crews and the apparatus were efficient and effective in the protection of what was evolving into an attractive small city surrounded by a blooming countryside.

The principal low hills of Los Angeles had been finally scaled by the five-cent cable cars of the 1890s. Years earlier the town had casually bent to the northeast following along the base of the rising land to the west. The hills above the Plaza were considered worthless other than for a badly neglected Protestant cemetery and a not-so-occasional lynching. Gradually the town moved up the sloping arroyo called Temple Street where the high school and a much-admired brick courthouse had just been constructed. Large houses and mansions were also built on Olive Heights (or Bunker Hill as it was later called) which for a short time was the prime residential area of the town. The Crocker, Bradbury, R. M. Widney and Larronde residences were some of the homes built on the low hill. The turreted Crocker mansion, later the Elks' Lodge, was at the head of the tiny Angels Flight cable railway completed in 1901.

Beginning with the cattle prosperity of the 1850s, repeated forecasts had been made that the commercial center of Los Angeles would move southward from the Plaza district. The forecasts had always been wrong, and the construction of the Pico House and then the ornate Baker Block appeared to ensure the Plaza being the center of town for many years to come. Yet a decade later the movement south of the prime commercial district was well underway with the success of the Nadeau Hotel. Fort Street (renamed Broadway) was widened and the long-time center of the expanding city became forgotten and neglected.

A very old section of Los Angeles followed the base of the hills several blocks northwestward of the Plaza. It contained some of the town houses of the Californios but was principally settled in the early years by a number of emigrants from Sonora, the Mexican state. Sonoratown was always a community within a community having its own dialect and customs. The colony expanded substantially in the early 1850s with an influx of Mexicans who had come north to try their luck as miners in the goldfields and then drifted southward to Los Angeles. A half-century later the characteristic adobe rowhouses of Sonoratown still housed the Mexican colony along with a fair number of Italians and Slavs, although brick warehouses and blacksmith shops were taking over this old section of the city.

The "shameless bawds" from Bath Street by 1900 had moved their activities a few blocks south from their traditional locale adjacent to Sonoratown around Alameda and Bath (part of North Main) streets. There were 300 to 500 prostitutes concentrated in a half-mile stretch below the Plaza. This was the center of the Tenderloin district, with its assortment of saloons, blind pigs and gambling holes. Most of the tiny one-room cribs of the whores were near the Plaza on both sides of Alameda where the Southern Pacific passenger trains lumbered slowly down the center of the street toward the Arcade Station. Much to the embarrassment of the city's ministerial forces and Frank Wiggins, the active new secretary of the local chamber of commerce, the train passengers oftentimes received their introduction to Los Angeles via the whores' vigorous and ribald greetings.

The prostitute population tended to reflect the current ethnic mix of the city's single men, many of them European emigrants; most of the whores were Caucasian with reportedly "a brisk traffic in young French girls." There were a few black but an increasing number of Oriental prostitutes—the full row of Japanese cribs on the southern fringe of Chinatown were well patronized.

The crumbling adobe warrens immediately surrounding the Plaza had become a solidified Chinese ghetto even before the infamous Calle de Los Negros was made an extension of North Los Angeles Street in 1877. To titillate turn-of-the-century tourists, detailed maps of Chinatown often carried parcel legends such as "opium joint" and "gambling" which purportedly pinpointed such dens of iniquity. The guidebooks, after noting the strangeness of the sights of Chinatown and the strength of the unusual smells, became much more relaxed when they could describe other sections of Los Angeles.

Workmen lived near their work. The principal manufacturing district, such as it was, extended east of Main Street to the levees of the Los Angeles River, and many of the married employees had small cottages nearby, the first of them built there in the Boom of the eighties. Most of the single men, and there were many because of the influx of European emigration, lived in clapboard rooming houses and cheap hotels around the industrial and retail districts. They ate in boardinghouses or sat on hard counter stools in the "Best 10-cent Meal House in the City." There were many such restaurants, often operated by Japanese or blacks. Typical was the Mikado which featured every Sunday a "Turkey or Chicken Dinner with Wine and Ice Cream . . . or Pie." A competitor, the Sunrise Restaurant, offered twenty-one full meal tickets for two dollars. A laboring man needed meals of this price, when he was earning a dollar to two dollars a day in the 1900s.

The retail stores along East First and Second streets serving the workmen were operated by the typical ethnic groupings of Western America—the saloons and rooming houses by the Germans and Irish, the secondhand stores and pawnshops were Jewish, the barbershops were run by blacks, and the Chinese had the laundries. The Japanese were settling in this working-man's district which would shortly be known as Little Tokyo, and the Jews would go on to establish their base in Boyle Heights.

While Los Angeles' population tripled between 1900 and 1910, the foreign-born ethnic groups increased proportionately much more, led by the Japanese. Interestingly enough, the 1910 census showed that Russian and Mexican immigrants each constituted about two percent of the expanding city's population. However census figures in the United States for recently arrived immigrants have always been suspect because of major understatement. The foreigners were usually deeply suspicious of government as represented by the census takers. If they were seasonal farm workers such as the Japanese, they were not easily counted nor did they make any effort to be included in the census. The local Japanese association which kept track of its people estimated there were 10,000 Japanese in and around Los Angeles in 1907 after the San Francisco earthquake and fire brought many of them to the South Coast. Undoubtedly a good many Japanese returned to the northern city as rebuilding proceeded. But the official Los Angeles census figure of 4200 Japanese three years later was far off target.

The Los Angeles black community of the 1900s knew its glass of life was half-full and far indeed from being half-empty. The rising tide of their race from slavery a short two generations earlier continued to carry them forward. And those who lived on the expanding South Coast could see and feel the evident economic and educational opportunities of the region. Constituting only some two per cent of the population, the blacks lived in scattered clusters about the city, including a well-to-do district a few blocks west of Grand Avenue near Tenth Street, part of Highland Park, around Western and Santa Monica (Exposition Boulevard) Avenues, and the San Pedro Street/ Central Avenue area near Eighth Street. Many lived in single-family dwellings, and there was limited de facto segregation in perhaps the best developing system of public schools in the United States. Racial prejudice toward blacks, while always there, was at a minimum for a long time. The dislike, if not hate energies, of the dominant white population was directed against the Yellow Peril and the Oriental Menace—the Chinese and Japanese in California. In contrast, the blacks seemed like familiar acquaintances.

Black family bonds were strong, few of their race appeared in the police courts and the mothers could boast of a scattering of sons with advanced college degrees. A number of the doctors like George D. Taylor had graduated from Howard, J. Alexander Somerville had a degree in dentistry from Southern California in 1906 and J. W. Thomas in veterinary medicine from Pennsylvania the following year. Earning a living for a black was hard but not that much harder than the rest of the laboring force who had yet to see an eight-hour day. Many of the men worked as blacksmiths, barbers, cooks, handymen, teamsters and Pullman porters; the women might be domestic servants or practical nurses.

The black professional and business classes were expanding with the growth of Los Angeles and their own community; the Los Angeles Van and Storage Company, owned by R. H. Dunston, now employed thirty people. A sure sign of economic stability were the substantial churches—the Methodist Episcopal at San Julian and Eighth streets was built of brownstone and its members bragged that the building cost $40,000. There was a small cadre of rich people headed by Robert C. Owens who had built on the real estate fortunes of two of his grandparents, Robert Owens and Mrs. Biddy Mason. The younger Owens' paneled billiard room with its Navajo rugs was a source of considerable satisfaction to his people as they thought of the progress they had made and their conviction of greater opportunities through education which lay over the immediate horizon.

Viewed through the eyes of sodden discouragement with the

problems of many black young people a half-century later, the hopes of the black community of Los Angeles in the 1900s appeared to be the height of wishful thinking.

The city continued to leapfrog to the south and southwest with Grand Avenue (still called Charity by a few old-timers) having the "bon ton houses" on small parcels which caused one critic to comment acidly that "there was little excuse for putting a fifty-thousand-dollar house on a fifty-foot lot." The young West Adams subdivisions met this critic's criteria. With land parcels of an acre or more and with the snob appeal of street names like St. James Place, a variety of sprawling homes were built. T. D. Stimson erected a massive stone castle and the oil-rich Doheny family dwelt in something their expensive architect called a Renaissance mansion. Carl Leonardt was proud of his California copy of a half-timbered English country home and Artemisia Vermillion lived in an early example of the stucco Mission Revival period. All had grounds which typified the Easterner's concept of semitropical California—date and fan palms, magnolias, citrus as well as jasmine, rose and heliotrope, hedges of white calla lilies, red cannas and geraniums, and what came to be the symbol of winter on the South Coast, the brilliant red poinsettia. This was the flor de noche buena (flower of Christmas Eve) from southwestern Mexico and Guatemala.

Los Angeles could use an expanse of private lawns and grounds. It had few parks and Elysian was the only one of any size until Griffith J. Griffith made his 3000-acre gift in 1898. Park improvements were perennially in a state of suspended animation because of lack of funds. San Diego, with a shorter purse than most of its sister communities, came up in the nineties with an unusual approach for landscaping the naked City (Balboa) Park. The city leased thirty acres to Kate O. Sessions, a devoted gardener and civic supporter, for a nursery. For annual rent she was to plant at least 100 trees and give the city an additional 300 trees each year. As time passed, the park's woodlands demonstrated the success of the plan.

The southern boundary of the original pueblo of Los Angeles was Santa Monica Avenue (Exposition) which paralleled the railroad from the beach town. Long before, the Californios had had a casual but well-used racetrack and cock-fighting grounds just outside the pueblo lands near a trail leading to Grasshopper (Figueroa) Street. These grounds became Agricultural (Exposition) Park, and the present-day Coliseum was constructed in the 1920s on the site of the old racetrack.

A horsecar line from the Plaza went all the way out Main Street to Agricultural Park, but attempts at subdivision were unsuccessful during Los Angeles' first boomlet after the Civil War. Then three local entrepreneurs revived the idea of establishing a university in the district to promote subdivision land sales, first proposed by Robert M. Widney a few years before. The triumvirate—Ozro W. Childs, John G. Downey and Isaias Hellman—offered 308 lots for sale, with all of the proceeds to go to the Methodist Episcopal Church for the establishment of the University of Southern California. Another 300 lots of the subdivision were turned over to the church as an endowment for the fledgling college.

The University of Southern California opened for classes on October 6, 1880, in a spanking white, two-story building "standing in the midst of a vast stretch of unoccupied, uncultivated plain covered with a rank growth of wild mustard . . ." The writer remembers well the high-ceilinged rooms and particularly the squeaky wood floors of the structure when he taught an engineering course in the building nearly seventy years later. The young university appeared to have been organized at a fortuitous time, readily acquiring satellite campuses formed in real estate promotions. There was the Chaffey agricultural college in Ontario, a San Fernando site for a Maclay theology college and two seminaries in Escondido and Tulare. By this time the Boom was in full flower, and the remaining endowment lots of the original land promotion were readily selling at $1500 a parcel—more than five times the price of several years before. In rapid succession the university acquired a fine arts college in San Diego, a women's seminary in Monrovia and even some funds (and commitments) to build an observatory on Mount Wilson.

With the end of the frenzied land speculation a special kind of a Methodist miracle was required to keep the parent university afloat, even in a waterlogged condition. The fine dreams of satellite campuses turned out to be legal nightmares of liquidation.

The promoters and concessionaires at Agricultural (Exposition) Park across from the struggling university had snickered at the hardening moral tone of the adjacent residential district. The fulminations of preachers in the nearby churches against gambling, saloons, greyhound racing and asserted brothel solicitation were obviously futile because Agricultural Park was in county territory, just outside straitlaced Los Angeles. The situation changed almost overnight in the late 1890s. The University district and the churches found a leader in William M. Bowen, a youngish lawyer and Sunday school teacher. With twenty/twenty hindsight the concessionaires should have early recognized from a check of his background and a look at Bowen's tight-lipped, humorless mouth set in a square face that they had met a dangerous adversary. Yet racing at the Park still had substantial support in the metropolitan area. Boyle Workman and his father, the respected former mayor of Los Angeles, were Park supporters; and the younger Workman was impressed with the length of the bar at the track:

"Every year there were horse races at the park. John W. Griffin, who later married the daughter of Dr. David Burbank, ran a hotel there, and many track devotees remained at the hotel for the season. Under the grandstand was the longest bar I have ever seen. Nothing but beer was served. When a man stepped up to the bar, the bartender merely filled a schooner and sent it sliding down the bar's polished surface, with unerring accuracy, to the waiting customer."

Living in a strong Temperance community William M. Bowen and his adherents were less than impressed with full schooners of beer. Much more important, youngsters missed Sunday school to sneak into the Park. This was particularly offensive to Bowen, a dedicated lay teacher, who abhorred the ". . . crude pavillions bedecked with tawdry bunting, bawling concession-aires and . . . the cruel, debasing sport of 'coursing,' in which captive jackrabbits from the nearby open country were hunted down by hounds." The Sunday school teacher was an effective activist of his day. Bowen took the greyhound promoter into court and formed a Good-Government Alliance to promote the annexation of the University district, including Agricultural Park, into Los Angeles, noted for its strict moral ordinances. With the approach of election day rumors were rife that the Park concessionaires were hiring extra crews and registering them as voters to ballot against annexation. The lawyer-reformer was ready to challenge such illegal registrants and:

". . . with the dawn, Bowen and his sleepless band entered the polling place. . . . The day wore on at a desperate tension. Firearms bulged under coats; whiskey was dispensed with unstinted generosity within the Park, but not one of the illegal registrants, so eagerly awaited by the Good Government committee, attempted to vote. . . . The fight for annexation was won—by twenty-three votes."

With the forces of evil routed and his leadership assured in Agricultural Park matters, William M. Bowen was determined that his park would be beautiful and improved. Representing a substantial pork-barrel achievement, he was able to obtain city, county and state funds to finance his extensive development plans. The cornerstones of the art gallery-museum and state exposition buildings were laid in 1910 and the name changed to Exposition Park.

Reformer-cum-civic leader Bowen cast a long shadow. Not only did he create the first major cultural center on the South Coast, but three-quarters of a century would elapse before beer again was sold in the Park.

CHAPTER 14

"Vigorous and exquisite, strong and fine"

While the Temperance ladies were first sopping and then drying up the United States and the early forces of suffragettes were organizing for the right of women to vote, another element of the female power structure was conducting business effectively at the usual stand.

An anonymous and nubile daughter of a wealthy family was thinking seriously of marriage. In an 1890 letter to a friend from the Raymond Hotel she tells of her confidence in shortly becoming engaged:

"Mr. . . . has been quite as attentive as I care to have him unless I see fit to have him orate his little chestnut speech. If he does I shall pronounce his death sentence, i.e., so far as his bachelorhood is concerned. I really don't love him, but he would improve greatly I am sure under my gentle discipline. A man never amounts to anything anyhow until he does marry, and it is the wife after all who gives him his true worth. So I have decided upon one thing—he shall come to the point, that too very speedily. I will show you my ring when I see you—it won't be a cluster ring as you might suggest, for I alone shall be represented in that ring—a solitaire."

Marriage in her socially approved circle was the young spinster's only vocation. For this she had been trained in manners and remained a virgin. Love for or understanding of the young man she had selected was desirable but scarcely necessary. The bridegroom-to-be or the young lady herself hopefully adjusted to and improved each other with their individual disciplines.

The social structures underlying marriage around 1900 were

188

little different from that of many other periods except for one phenomenon. There was a pronounced stratum of emotional romanticism which stressed an idealized womanhood, far bigger than life. This roseate sentimentalism was brought into focus by the illustrations of Charles Dana Gibson and supplemented by the heroines depicted by contemporary novelists. Edith Wharton's sketch of Lily in the *House of Mirth* was typical: ". . . her long light step, the modelling of her little ear, the crisp upward wave of her hair . . . how evenly the black lashes were set in her smooth white lids and how the purplish shade beneath them melted into the pure pallor of the cheek . . . [and a] hand, polished as a bit of old ivory with its slender pink nails." This ideal woman was supposed to be "vigorous and exquisite, strong and fine" with the ability to blush beautifully at the appropriate time. Clearly, such a wondrous creature should be revered and protected by social conventions and mores which could very well be as stifling as cotton batting for some of those receiving the adulations. Los Angeles society, steeped in its own morality, was well equipped to conform to the contemporary social attitudes.

In stark contrast to an opulent Pasadena of winter visitors, Los Angeles society of the early 1890s was a small provincial thing. For its cotillions there was only the Kramer Dancing School or the Turnverein Gymnasium—so many cuts below the elaborate hotel ballrooms of a Raymond or a Green in Pasadena. The consoling grace was that any licentious excesses practiced by transplanted Eastern wealthy certainly did not exist in Los Angeles.

The bachelor attending a cotillion was expected to go to the party in the girl's family coach along with a chaperone. Being a principal center of the onrushing Temperance Movement "a man who appeared at such a party under the influence of liquor would have been ostracized. To have offered a girl a drink would have been an insult." The waltzing and two step of the cotillion went on into the early morning hours with a midnight supper usually catered by Al Levy's Cafe. There were no stag lines. Each girl had her own dance program with a pencil attached on a fancy string, and her level of popularity and party enjoyment revolved around the little program. This was measured by the rapidity with which her dance card filled, early in the cotillion, with the names of those she considered to be attractive or appropriate young men. Memorable dance programs were preserved as carefully as the faded bicycle racing ribbons of her escorts. These were relics of success and conquest.

The best-planned parties did have a few problems, humanity still being what it was. Boyle Workman described one such unexpected turn:

"Billy Garland and I invited two of the [Childs] girls to one of the cotillions. We invested in brand new tailor-made overcoats for this auspicious occasion. They were long coats of rough blue material, with black velvet collars. We were proud of our new attire. When we arrived at Kramer's Ballroom, the [Childs'] coachman was ordered to return at a certain hour. I suppose the time was long and the coachman needed amusement. When the cotillion was over, carriage and coachman were missing. Leaving the girls at Kramer's with their companions, we began a search. We finally located both, but the coachman was a sodden heap of humanity. Garland and I were for leaving him, but the girls would not have him deserted, insisting he must be taken home. So we heaved the coachman into the seat; Billy took the reins, and we started home. Alas, the motion of the coach did not harmonize with the coachman's copious draughts of comfort, and relief for the coachman spelled disaster to Garland's new coat."

Fortunately, men's abiding interest in the female figure was not dampened by the enveloping morality, the concepts of idealized womanhood and the heavy assortment of clothes a woman wore—vests and drawers for underwear, side-steel corsets and bustles, corset covers and dress protectors, chemises and ruffled, crackling underskirts, lisle and mercerized cotton stockings (silk stockings were two to three dollars a pair), waists and skirts,

ike many other cities, Los Angeles put its police in "London bobby" uniforms in the 890s. Here a residential bicycle squad pedals down Broadway. *Courtesy of Title Insurance nd Trust Company.*

Santa Fe passenger train of the late 1890s is about to leave its Los Angeles station. *ourtesy of Los Angeles County Museum.*

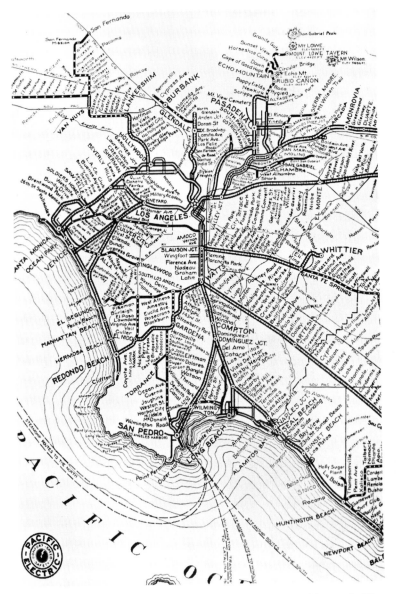

The Pacific Electric was a superb railway complex by World War I. The map shows a major portion of that interurban trolley system. *Courtesy of Southern Pacific Company.*

ken on the same day, these two delightful group photographs of the same Japanese-
merican women in their traditional and then 1907 Western dress was surely a sign of
ospering Oriental immigrants on the South Coast. *Courtesy of Los Angeles County*
useum.

Santa Monica Bay nearly had a great harbor. The beginning was to be Port Los Angeles, the 1894 Long Wharf off Santa Monica Canyon. *Courtesy of Security Pacific National Bank.*

The decline in th purchasing power of th dollar over the decades ca be seen in the graph whic contains key elements o U.S. industrial constructio costs indexed to a 1913 bas *Courtesy of America Appraisal Company, In*

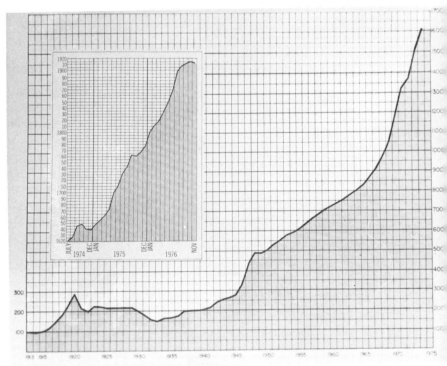

Collis P. Huntington. A titan and a tyrant, he left a heavy imprint on the South Coast. *Courtesy of Title Insurance and Trust Company.*

Stephen M. White. His Senate maneuvers helped defeat the Southern Pacific plans for a deep-water harbor at Santa Monica. *Courtesy of Security Pacific National Bank.*

Let's drill an oil well! Everybody wanted to in the 1890s and many did in the shallow, short-lived fields in central Los Angeles. *Courtesy of Title Insurance and Trust Company.*

Harrison G. Otis. To his enemies he was a bear who walked like a man; his friends felt Otis built the Los Angeles of his generation. *Courtesy of Los Angeles* Times.

Stub wharves for loading oil off the new San Pedro breakwater were tried for a time, but southeast storms made them impractical. *Courtesy of Title Insurance and Trust Company.*

n impossible picture
flying machines,
dirigible and a
alloon, it was made
ring the famous
)10 South Coast
ir Meet. *Courtesy
Los Angeles
ounty Museum.*

Charles D. Willard. Serving as a rallying point against the panzer tactics of Collis P. Huntington, Willard became a leader in the "Free Harbor Fight." From *Out West*, April 1909.

Tomas L. Duque. A successful banker and rancher, his numerous sons carried on the family name in an expanding South Coast. From *Out West*, April 1909.

f a treacherous coast and without radar, the express liners, *Harvard* and *Yale*, made the
n Francisco/San Pedro run in eighteen hours beginning in 1910. *Courtesy of Title In-*
ance and Trust Company.

e crowd in the foreground somberly watches the wrecked building of the Los Angeles
nes, bombed in the early morning hours of October 1, 1910. *Courtesy of Title Insurance*
l Trust Company.

J. A. GRAVES

H. W. O'MELVENY

J. H. SHANKLAND

This triumvirate of lawyers was deeply involved for many years in South Coast affairs—Jackson A. Graves, Henry W. O'Melveny and James H. Shankland. *Courtesy of O'Melveny and Meyers.*

The original San Pedro breakwater was faced rock above low tide; later breakwater additions were not. Alert small boat skippers caught in a fog near there remember this fact. *Courtesy of Title Insurance and Trust Company.*

An undulating plank road in the 1900s crossed the sand dunes of the Colorado Desert east of the Imperial Valley. Note the new road under construction. *Courtesy of Title Insurance and Trust Company.*

Longshoremen push an immaculate Detroit electric into the cargo deck of the *Yale* for a San Pedro/San Francisco passage prior to World War I. *Courtesy of Title Insurance and Trust Company.*

The wrecking crew pulls down the tower of the 1887 Santa Fe station in front of th
new San Diego railroad depot of the mid-1910s. *Courtesy of Title Insurance and Tru
Company of San Diego.*

By 1911 nickelodeons had opened in small towns like Covina and were running spec
features. From *Covina* (1964).

First called Morocco and then Beverly Hills, this was the interurban junction of the Santa Monica line as it looked in the early 1910s. *Courtesy of Security Pacific National Bank.*

Four of the great names of the early movies formed their own studio—Douglas Fairbanks, Mary Pickford, Charles Chaplin and D. W. Griffith. *Courtesy of Los Angeles County Museum.*

The Great White Fleet visited the South Coast in 1908. The 16,000-ton, coal-burning *Illinois* in the foreground was a typical Fleet battleship. *Courtesy of Title Insurance and Trust Company of San Diego.*

Henry W. O'Melveny. A respected lawyer and dedicated trout fisherman, O'Melveny liked to play cribbage with his mountain cabin caretaker. *Courtesy of O'Melveny and Meyers.*

Spanish-American War volunteers from the South Coast pause en route to the Presidio in San Francisco. *Courtesy of Los Angeles* Times.

With conspicuous secret service protection, President Woodrow Wilson is driven through central Los Angeles in the World War I period. *Courtesy of Los Angeles County Museum.*

By World War I the ubiquitous automobile was far along in replacing the horse as be seen in this photograph of Los Angeles' Broadway. *Courtesy of Title Insurance Trust Company.*

heavy hair switches and neck boas, high shoes (oxfords and slippers were still uncommon), cloth capes and the long coats called "automobiles." Indubitably, this was a female generation which did not admit to sweating and perspired only moderately. The men officially supported the notion that their women, and all women for that matter, should be fully clothed in public and the requirement also applied to actresses in the theater. The Riverside *Daily Press* expressed this authoritative view in 1891: "Ladies in tights are objectionable! We think the exhibition of women in tights on stage can serve no good purpose and tends to the demoralization of young men and boys."

Though women in tights were officially not acceptable, the Los Angeles *Times* enjoyed providing statistics on the perfect figure "for a young lady age 20: Height 5 feet 4 inches to 5 feet 4½, weight 118 to 122 pounds, bust 32½ to 33 inches, waist 21 to 22½ inches, bust over biceps 41 to 42 inches, ankle 6¾ inches; shoe size 3½." Later generations of women would find the shoe size of 3½ far harder to believe than the 21-inch waist.

Few respectable women or girls wore makeup and face powder, or used perfume. The pink fingernails of the idealized woman came from meticulous care and repeated buffing. She also bathed daily, used talcum powder and wore clean clothes. Cigarette smoking, even among Eastern society's avant-garde, was confined to the boudoir and was still mostly talk there. Yet it was not too many years before a cigarette company would have a daring advertisement featuring an attractive young woman telling a cigarette-smoking male to "blow some my way."

Divorce was possible and the rate was increasing during the 1890s. Yet the practice was considered discreditable even with strong justification. Reputable attorneys handled divorce proceedings reluctantly because of the time, emotion and community prejudice involved. Earl Rogers, the famed South Coast criminal lawyer, put the general professional feeling succinctly when he said that divorce cases were more trouble than they were worth. Henry W. O'Melveny went even farther after wrestling with the mother of a client whom he called "Mrs. X" in his journal:

"4/6 Mrs. X consulted with Shankland and myself. We told her there were no grounds for divorce on charges of cruelty. She directed me to employ detectives to have X watched. I engaged Insley with instructions to be on watch Saturday P.M. and Sunday . . .

"4/16 We called on Dr. Lasker. He says if examination were made proof would not be conclusive. The disease might have been in one case out of a hundred innocently acquired . . .

"5/14 We called [Mrs. X's mother] I desired to asure her that we could guarantee with no absolute certainty as to a decree but considered the chances more than even . . .

"6/25 [Mrs. X's mother] She talked around the bush awhile and then came to the point that she wanted us to reduce our fee. I refused to do so. . . . I did not like the criticisms and I told [her] so. A man who has a woman for a client is a damned fool."

There was not the slightest question in most men's minds that there were only two categories of women—the "good" as represented by their wives, daughters, sisters and women they conceivably might marry, and the "bad" which included the whores, hookers and harlots and anybody alse who crossed the demarcation line from virtuous to fallen. Because of this, the professional prostitute had limited amateur competition in contrast to the situation several generations later. It was a well-understood fact that "if a lady got involved in scandal . . . or was caught sleeping around . . . she moved or was moved over to the other side. A lady who could maintain her amateur standing while playing about had to be very clever."

While the good women stayed home for a while, the prostitutes had followed the men to California during the Gold Rush as commemorated in the satirical couplet:

The pioneers came in '49, the whores in '51
Between the two they then begat the Native Son.

The good women when they did come west found that their fallen sisters in the brothel and the crib were part of the customs of the expanding frontier. The Tenderloin district around Alameda Street south of the Plaza was the principal red-light section of Los Angeles and had a few hundreds of prostitutes in the early 1900s. San Diego was eagerly emulating its larger sister city in most things including vice, gambling and knockout drops for unwary seamen in its Stingaree area centered around Third and "I" streets. With some justification local Temperance leaders were emphasizing that San Diego was well on its way to surpassing Los Angeles during that city's dissolute heyday of a generation earlier. The Stingaree had seventy or so saloons and gambling dives with a hundred brothels and one-room cribs. A good share of the crib girls seated in the doors of their tiny barren shanties supported a lover who also served as her pimp or panderer. The prostitutes, recruited through poverty, aptitude or chance were often young when they went into the cribs, fourteen years of age in the case of Gabrielle D'Arley. Six years later she shot her pimp dead at a jewelry store as he was buying a wedding ring for his marriage to another woman.

Most good women on the South Coast might reluctantly accept the disorderly cribs and common brothels along with the vulgar "gents room" stories because they agreed with Blanche Lott when she sniffed: "Men. All of them have a gutter streak." However, the ego threat to this same phalanx of good women by a top turn-of-the-century fancy house was another matter entirely. Attractive house girls were conspicuous in expensive dresses and egret-decorated hats, promenading in carriages during the daytime and, equally annoying, sending engraved invitations to selected lists of gentlemen at their clubs.

Pearl Morton ran such a first-class sporting house in Los Angeles. Some of her girls were expected to play musical instruments well and all were trained to listen to and sympathize with their male customers, attentions often lacking in the men's homes. Divided by a broad entry hall with a wide staircase leading to the second floor of the sporting house was a huge front room covered with deep pile, red carpets and lighted by cut glass and gold chandeliers. A very young Adela Rogers, while tracking down her father, was impressed with the room's lush furnishings:

"The French windows were draped in red plush and there were big overstuffed chairs such as I have never seen before, and what seemed to be hundreds of little tables with gilt legs and glass or marble tops. There were two concert grand Steinway pianos, and full-length mirrors in magnificent carved gilt frames. . . . On the walls were huge paintings of rather fat ladies, some with a great many clothes on and some without any, all done in oils."

While most Los Angeles men may have had no difficulty in separating the "good" women from the "bad" women, there were strongly divergent views on the extent and depth of virtue and righteousness in the city. A prominent clergyman could proclaim with broad-scale support that the community was made up of "the highest moral and ethical citizenship" while another contemporary caustically commented that "Los Angeles was overrun with militant moralists, connoisseurs of sin and experts on biological purity." Doubtless, some of the old-timers had a sneaking nostalgia for the more relaxed days before the Boom of the eighties.

CHAPTER 15

"I'll have the damned thing taken out"

Fugitives from the frigid climates of the Midwest and East by 1900 somehow had convinced themselves that very little house heat was required to be comfortable during the reputedly benign South Coast winters. Their guests' forthright or diplomatic comments concerning the enveloping and devastating morning chill of a mid-December day in the barnlike houses were ignored.

Homes had no weather stripping or storm windows, and the wooden orange-crate construction worked with the expansion and contraction of the underlying adobe clay soil. Cold whistled in or oozed through the cracks and crevices depending on the wind or lack of it. Other than the coal or wood kitchen stove, heating in the typical house of the new Californian consisted of a small fireplace, in front of which "one could choose the climate he wanted from the torrid zone near the grate to the arctic in the bay window . . ." Portable and unvented gas heaters replaced the fireplaces in later years but these were turned off at night for safety. Under appropriate circumstances, the result could be walls dripping frigid moisture from condensation because of the cooling rooms. In the chilly bathroom, stoicism was required by any guest even though a tiny electric heater in a corner might give some slight moral solace to the shivering outlander. The late 1940s would pass before the average middle-class home on the South Coast was properly and safely heated.

Being both strange and foreign the sensible design of the Californio town houses and their thick adobe walls was ignored.

Instead the newcomers usually built two- and three-story houses of wood brought to the South Coast by steam schooner from the Pacific Northwest. There were two popular floor plans—a square consisting of four rooms with a central hall or a large oblong containing a six-room layout. The residences by standards of later generations were commodious, if for no other reason because of their twelve- to fifteen-foot ceilings. The first floor of the house was generally raised a few feet above ground level with a porch extending across the front. The windows facing on the porch were usually covered with heavy lace curtains or inside wooden blinds varnished yellow. The prevailing mode was to have small front and rear parlors separated by sliding doors supplemented by portieres of chenille ropes or strings of beads, shells or eucalyptus acorns. The front parlor, seldom used and infrequently aired, smelled of furniture polish and horsehair upholstery. Here was where formal calls were received and, after a death in the family, this was the lying-in room for the body.

While many homes were gas-illuminated in the 1890s a good percentage used coal oil (kerosene) lamps, and candles in the bedrooms. New houses often had dual chandeliers so that gas could be turned on if the erratic electric power failed. The kitchen, the nerve center of the home, was still dominated by a bulky cast-iron kitchen stove and an attached boiler, even though gas range sales were beginning to accelerate. Utilizing a coil pipe arrangement tied in with the coal or wood fire box of the big stove, water was heated in this boiler. The best method for bringing a cold stove up to standard heat in a reasonably short time was a matter of lively debate. Experts found undefined quantities of coal oil, rectified turpentine oil or sugar alone and in combinations to be effective. An amateur soon found that nonjudicious use of these additives in the confined fire box could send stove lids bouncing off the walls while the cook dodged out of their soot-laden trajectory.

A sure sign of being reasonably well-to-do was to own an imposing array of black walnut furniture upholstered in horsehair fabric; Mission Revival oak was only just becoming popular.

Dearly loved were the intricately designed Brussels carpets supplemented by ornate wall and ceiling papers. Equally admired was a plethora of shiny mahogany and yellow wood finishes on paneling and blinds. The best indication of some affluence was a small bathroom replacing the privy, chamber pot and commode. Many of the residences were converting tiny bedrooms or large closets for this purpose. The most appropriate finishing details of these expensive bathrooms were well-fitted wood paneling, preferably of somber mahogany color, a marble washstand with six-inch-tall faucets, a high claw-footed bathtub and a water closet. This last was the comfort symbol of the new age (the 1920s first began calling it a toilet), and the unit was majestically mounted on sort of a pedestal. The water closet's wood-faced water tank was hung just below the ceiling in the room's upper reaches above the flickering gas light. The reverberating roar of water dropping ten feet or so from the tank was itself almost a status index for a time.

Telephones had some commonality with bathrooms—both were initially installed in an out-of-the-way place and often on the second floor of the house. The preemptory ringing of this strange electrical instrument seemed always to come at the wrong time even though it might ring only once or twice a week. A housewife consoled the cantankerous, unfamiliar thing by calling to the contrivance in a loud voice, "I'm coming, I'm coming," while she labored up the stairs and ran to pick up the receiver. The idea that this obstreperous wall telephone could let somebody at will intrude into your house was shocking to many. Added to this annoyance was the capricious balkiness of the instrument itself. The frustration a full-bodied American head of household felt on becoming involved with a telephone containing a tinny voice which undulated and faded completely, only manically to revive for a moment, was enough to make him bellow to anybody within earshot: "I'll have the damned thing taken out!"

The cause of all the furor was the invention of Alexander Graham Bell who exhibited his telephone at the 1876 Centennial Exposition in Philadelphia. Five years later the Los Angeles

Telephone Company was organized with the office and exchange in the Baker Block near the Plaza and wires running to the establishments of ninety-one subscribers. A number of the business houses installed the new contrivance in a back room because "the customary noises around the store might interfere with the hearing, and so render the curious instrument useless." Many business and professional men refused to use the telephone; in their judgment business should be conducted face-to-face or by letter. Nevertheless the potentialities of Dr. Bell's invention yearly became more evident, and any number of entrepreneurs were counting down the first series of seventeen-year patents.

A Home Telephone Company was formed in Los Angeles to go into competition with what had become the Sunset Company and the new utility won a city franchise in 1898. There was no call interchange between the competitors' systems. The result, not by any means unique to Los Angeles, was that most users were forced to install a telephone from each of the competing utilities in order to utilize both networks of subscribers. This expensive and unsatisfactory condition ended in 1916 when the two Los Angeles utilities were merged into a predecssor company of Pacfic Telephone and Telegraph.

All-expense tours to California first became popular in the early eighties. Most prestigious were those conducted by Raymond and Whitcomb of Boston whose junkets cost up to $550. Rather than continuing to use the Del Monte Hotel on the Monterey Peninsula, the firm decided to build its own hostelry in present-day South Pasadena on a knoll just east of Columbia Street and Fair Oaks Avenue. The Raymond, completed at the peak of the Boom of the eighties, was for a short time the largest and most imposing hotel in southern California with 201 rooms and, unprecedented for its day, forty bathrooms. Open only during the winter season, most of the hotel's staff was brought out from Boston, considered the epicenter of the nation's civilized society. Much like the jet set of another age the Raymond's wealthy clientele was happily resort-hopping in the provinces because of the newfound freedom provided by the young national railroad network.

Like most of the large wooden hotels, the Raymond's life span was short. The building burned to its foundation on Easter afternoon in 1895 with the flames roaring several hundred feet from the ground and visible for miles. The just-designed electric fire-alarm bells alerted guests and employees and there were no lives lost. Fire hoses kept in the hallways, another advanced and publicized fire prevention feature, were unrolled and used, but inadequate water pressure and the stunning spread of the flames up the open stairwells made the fire-fighting efforts useless. In less than two hours the walls and roof of the Raymond had collapsed.

Most people thought it was Boom-talk froth when Elisha S. Babcock and H. L. Story announced their intent to build "the largest hotel in the world" on San Diego Bay, a structure which would be "too gorgeous to be true." The proposed location of the hotel and its surrounding subdivision was both absurd and appalling to anybody except a wild-eyed land boomer —a naked and desolate sandspit of a barrier beach noteworthy only for its innumerable jackrabbits and being across the bay from San Diego. And even in the heady euphoria of 1887, San Diego's optimists would have had difficulty in scrounging 25,000 inhabitants including every stray tourist who stepped down from the Santa Fe cars on census day. But the sensible people were wrong. Babcock and Story knew what they were doing, and a million dollars' worth of lots were quickly sold in what was called Coronado. Ferryboat service to San Diego was soon underway, and the promoters supplemented this with the Coronado Belt Line which circled the lower part of the bay into the small city.

Opening in early 1888, the gorgeous wooden Hotel Coronado, interior-balconied around a rectangular garden court, could justify any of the splendiferous adjectives describing it in an age which appreciated adjectives. The hotel's main dining room, designed with no pillars, was (and still is today) a most impressive public room. Seating a thousand comfortably, the dining hall was more than half a football field in length, nearly a quarter that wide and spanned by a thirty-three-foot ceiling. The great room was finished in sugar pine paneling, highly decorative and skillfully carved by craftsmen imported on the Santa Fe.

For its 399 rooms the Coronado had seventy-three bathrooms, an early indication of the Americans' eventual absorption in quantities of plumbing for all of their hotels. Typical of the deluxe resort hotel of the period, daily room rates were an expensive three to six dollars with suites considerably higher. Dual gas and electric fixtures were installed in 1894 making the Coronado at the time the largest structure in the world outside of New York to be so extensively lighted by electricity. So vulnerable to a racing fire, this huge wooden structure with its broad open stairwells has survived over the intervening years because of the installation in the nineties of a sprawling automatic sprinkler water system, a just-proven invention then and destined to be a prime life and property saver in succeeding generations.

Father Throop, the founder of the coeducational Throop College of Technology, was a Pasadena enthusiast. He had strong community backing and support. This was not surprising because the college head continued to say how fortunate he was to be living among such intelligent people, while seldom asking the citizens of the town for educational contributions. Amos G. Throop at eighty years of age had established a small liberal arts college (earlier called Polytechnic Institute) offering many trade type of courses—a young lady could even learn how to bone a basque in a dressmaking class. Not too many years later boning a basque would have been unusual material because Father Troop's school had become the California Institute of Technology.

In contrast to Father Throop, Professor Thaddeus S. C. Lowe knew he was an important man. Perhaps he was, but his 3,000,000 candlepower searchlight, the talk of the 1893 Columbian Exposition in Chicago certainly did not endear him to Pasadena. This blinding electrical light stabbed at will into the gas-lit streets from a 5,000-foot elevation above the city.

Being the most shot-at man in the Civil War was one of T. S. C. Lowe's claims to fame. As the head balloonist of the Union Army he had made more than 3000 ascents close to the front lines to observe enemy troop movements and direct cannon fire. Sometimes his balloon was in distant range of the rifled gun barrels of the Confederate infantry. After the Civil War the professor developed a widely used patented process for gas and ice manufacture which he utilized for several ventures on the South Coast. But the aging balloonist/inventor still had another driving ambition—to build a scenic railroad and hotel system on the side of a peak above Pasadena. Construction work was underway during the summer of 1892 on the flanks of Echo Mountain. A year later two cable cars, one ascending while the other descended, had made a successful run on the precipitous 3000-foot track.

Delighted with the public reaction to this scenic venture, Professor Lowe borrowed money to construct an electric trolley from his inclined railway to the 5000-foot level where his Alpine Tavern and Echo Mountain House were built and the controversial searchlight was mounted. The trolley offered spectacular views while winding up the flanks of the mountain and around horseshoe bends on trestles; there were moments when the tilted car seemed suspended in air. The professor had himself a major tourist attraction. Unhappily he also had high built-in operating and debt-repayment costs. These finally resulted in his losing control of the scenic railway enterprises and much of his personal fortune as well.

Pasadena had become absorbed in matters other than Lowe's searchlight and his financial problems. To its infinite delight the community found the town was becoming a center for winter visitors of considerable to great wealth who brought with them "an aristocratic and ultra-exclusive social life founded on Eastern models . . ." according to one writer. More accurately, the dynamic industrial expansion of the United States had grown continually larger crops of raw new millionaires, particularly on the Eastern seaboard. Their wives were eager and determined to emulate practically any version of an aristocratic and ultra-exclusive social life.

Whatever the reason, Eastern visitors to Pasadena appeared to be wealthier each year. Private railway cars such as Chauncey Depew's on the sidings excited little interest although the six-car private train of Cornelius Vanderbilt was an attraction. Balls, receptions and formal gatherings of all kinds followed each other in endless succession during the season. The outlanders also established a hunt club which brought some tongue-in-cheek reporting of an early club event by the Pasadena *Star* in 1891:

"The fruits of the chase were one rabbit, one small hound and several navel oranges found under orange trees and picked up by the more skillful riders. The hound . . . met his fate at the hands (or the heels, rather) of a horse. The one rabbit harvested by the hounds was not the only one seen on the chase. Many fine runs were had after others, and the circumstances that they eluded the dogs did not greatly detract from the exhilaration of the sport."

The Valley Hunt Club did more than run down occasional rabbits. In 1889 it sponsored a New Year's Day tournament competition of field and riding sports plus a series of rather confused and dangerous chariot races. The Club and the local business houses provided prizes like riding boots or spurs; and the competition site was Sportsman's Park, located north of Walnut Street and east of Los Robles Avenue. The winter event was called the Tournament of Roses in order "to convey to the blizzard-bound sons and daughters of the East, one of the sources of enjoyment which we, of the land of perennial sunshine, boast." The tournament was successful, with 250 spectators filling a shaky grandstand, and some of the people who came to the event had decorated their buggies with roses from their gardens. There was a good deal of sentiment in favor of making it an annual affair, if for no other reason than a Miss Ladds' announcement she intended during the next tournament to wear a bifurcated or divided skirt and sit astride the horse rather than riding sidesaddle. The Tournament of Roses Association eventually took over management of the event and the fame of the New Year's Day festival rippled out far beyond southern California.

Fine fees for the artists combined with extravagantly appreciative audiences brought the whole spectrum of the concert stage and show business to California with the opening of the Pacific railroad. Adelina Patti, the famous soprano, asked for and received a minimum of $5000 for each of her half-dozen "farewell" recitals in San Francisco and a much smaller Los Angeles. This would be the equivalent in mid-1970 dollars of much more than $50,000, and in the days of Mme. Patti the income tax did not exist. There were many other premier performers who came to the South Coast. Names like that of Helena Modjeska or John Philip Sousa who strode in front of his band and gave plentiful encores at his concerts. With rich guarantees even the Metropolitan Opera and Enrico Caruso trundled into Los Angeles in the early 1900s. The region's omnivorous interest in recitals, concerts, operas, vaudeville and the Chautauqua lectures undoubtedly reflected a continuing feeling of geographical isolation. Family roots and traditions for most were thousands of miles away connected by three single-track railroads crossing a particularly harsh and lonesome land.

The local ladies guaranteed the high artist fees and the responsive audiences. To a knowing promoter of cultural assemblages the height and width of the female audience's hats was a sure gauge of the local society's rating of the performer or entertainment. If there were enough of them on opening night, the "three-story," flaring hats or bonnets secured with six-inch long hat pins to an intricate hairdo was positive indication of success. Sitting in back of such a headpiece however was a frustrating experience if a view of the stage was of any interest. The local press did wage a continuing "Hats Off" campaign, and this plus vitriolic side remarks of annoyed theater customers had some limited success until finally the hat fashions changed in the 1910s.

Valiant attempts by the ladies to mix concert virtuosos and vaudeville accomplished little. The recently opened Orpheum Theater on Spring Street found this out in 1895. Classical violin and piano selections were intermixed with a bill of jugglers, comedians and acrobats. A reviewer noted that the more sedate selections "were not at all to the taste of the hot Southern blood of the gallery gods, and there was such a thinning out in the quarter of the house they inhabit that it looked as if it had been swept by a volley of grape and canister. . . . When Mr. Scharf failed to play the piano with his nose, his elbows, his feet, and with his eyes blindfolded, the gallery apparently felt imposed upon and began to shoot for the street." Evidently Riverside's Loring Opera House sidestepped this problem. Its 1900 variety bills featured dancers such as Papinta doing a number of solos with mildly provocative titles like Danse La Volcano, followed by a young W. C. Fields and his juggling act. Reflecting the growing opulence of Riverside, the Loring was on the same talent circuit as Lucky Baldwin's theater in San Francisco, Los Angeles' Grand Opera House and Fisher's Opera in San Diego.

Because of tragic theater fires and resulting panic, particularly at Paris' Opera Comique and Chicago's Iroquois where hundreds of people died, the stage of the up-to-date theater like the Loring had a huge fireproof curtain with "Asbestos" painted on the side facing the audience. Steel entry doors and the curtain isolated the stage and its inflammable properties from the audience in the event of a flash fire. The stage was built over its own basement, and trap doors enabled the Devil to make a surprise appearance in the midst of billowing clouds of steam. Even more exciting to the audience, a rectangular tank was mounted in the basement, with a special stage floor opening "so that real boats could be seen sailing in real water." With these facilities and the excellent talent available, the Riverside Theatre could charge what were considered very substantial prices, ranging from $1.50 for boxes to twenty-five cents for gallery seats.

After-theater supper or snacks to the urban turn-of-the-century man very often meant oysters—raw, fried or in a stew. And at fifty cents a dozen, raw oysters were not cheap. Al Levy got his start in the restaurant business by peddling oysters from a pushcart in front of Los Angeles theaters. The availability of edible shellfish dishes in the local restaurants was a sure indication of improved food distribution and cooking in the small cities and towns of southern California.

Until the time of the Boom of the eighties the region's eating houses in the main had nothing to recommend them other than serving large helpings of badly cooked food. The restaurant customer of those days required a strong stomach on a number of counts. A struggling blue-bellied fly not yet fully immersed in a bowl of soup would be removed by the waiter with a judicious thumb and forefinger in full view of a fastidious diner who had had the temerity to complain. Supplemented by hideous side dishes like garlic vegetable hash, beef steaks of noteworthy stringiness, strong-flavored mutton, and fat pork chops were the standard entrees served. These were immersed in heavy and ancient grease which rapidly congealed on the meat and jacketed potatoes. The excellent Californio cooking had been quickly forgotten, cast aside by the waves of newcomers after the Civil War.

The first oasis in this self-made desert of atrocious food was the Commercial Restaurant opened by Victor Dol in Los Angeles' Downey Block during the late 1870s. To a town used to dirt floors and barefoot cooks, the Commercial, reached through an inner court with a fountain in the center, seemed almost unbelievable. A traditional French dinner cost fifty cents, and Dol's banquet rooms were popular for a generation. A few years later Dol had an irksome competitor who first established a small restaurant north of First Street on Main. Jerry Illich demonstrated an unusual ability to be a friend of and confidant to a fair number of the powerful people in the small city while providing fine restaurant food and service. By 1896 he was calling his establishment the Maison Doree and had moved to an expensive location opposite the Bradbury Block.

One meat entree which routinely appeared on Illich's and other local restaurateurs' menus in the nineties was Belgian hare. After local newspaper articles extolled the merits of this rabbit meat, first by the score and then by the thousands, southern California home owners raised Belgian hares for the market. Freshly organized companies solicited investments, and men quit scarce jobs to raise the rabbits for breeding stock and show exhibits. Like the chinchilla fad of another South Coast generation, prices skyrocketed for prime breeding specimens. Only one flaw existed in the idyllic prospects of this young industry—there was really only a limited public taste for rabbit meat. Shortly, as a punster of the times was quick to observe, the hare bubble burst.

Sea-angling with rod and reel was an even later development in southern California than decent restaurant cooking. One of the first locales of this unfamiliar sport was the South Coast, and its leader there was Charles F. Holder, founder of the Tuna Club. Holder, an established naturalist, born organizer and dedicated fisherman, was impressed with the quantities of game fish in Catalina Island waters. During the 1880s he saw "men throwing cast-lines from the [Avalon] beach and landing fishes weighing from seventeen to forty pounds, more or less, fishes [yellowtails] which for strength and game qualities would put the salmon to shame."

The naturalist believed that hand fishing lines in boats or cast-lines from shore was no sport and were simply devices to slaughter game fish. Holder's Tuna Club in Avalon on Catalina Island became a principal center for a time of the sportfishing world. The club rules provided for light rods, an average twenty-one strand cord and Vom Hofe-type reels with 600 feet of line. This rig could handle a swordfish or the 200-pound leaping tuna, not uncommon catches then in the teeming game-fish waters off Catalina. The early 1900s found sea-angling with rod and reel had replaced cast-lines as the standard sport-fishing procedure. Its acceptance was undoubtedly accelerated by exhortations so typical of the Theodore Roosevelt era as "fair play to game fishes," "He fishes like a gentleman," and the "true sporting spirit."

In contrast to Charles F. Holder and his militant disciples, the people who fly- or worm-fished the southern California mountain streams were not educating anybody. They were there for the pure pleasure of catching the trout and eating the fish the same day. The San Gabriel River was one of the prime accessible trout streams in the state, and Henry K. O'Melveny could note in his 1894 journal that he had taken a 14¾-inch trout in the river's low water at the end of the season. It was also O'Melveny, a few years earlier, who was the key mover in the establishment of the Creel Club with a membership of a dozen or so men. Located about ten miles in from the mouth of San Gabriel Canyon, the club built a two-story cabin with a large fireplace. The members and guests who had received the prized invitations initially rented horses from a livery stable in Azusa for the ride up the San Gabriel to the cabin. Later on, Ralph Follows with his stage met them at the Azusa Station of the Santa Fe.

Creel Club members liked to eat and drink as well as fish. The custom was to prepare a huge midday meal supported by quantities of claret or white wine and served on the cabin veranda. Not surprisingly, after a typical dinner as reported by Jackson A. Graves, little activity occurred around the Creel Club and its environs until late afternoon:

"Beginning with homemade soup, there was usually broiled trout, a roasted haunch of venison or loin of beef or lamb; . . . frequently tamales or enchiladas contributed by Billy Cardwell; tagliarini Italiene, rice Spanish, frijoles cooked to a turn; potatoes, roasted in their jackets in the ashes of the fireplace where the meat was cooking; great black olives, a la Jerry Illich, that is, served hot after being cooked in claret; the best of cheese and delicious black coffee with hot cornbread or good biscuits made by [John E.] Jackson. Sometimes, on special occasions, he would make a plum pudding and at other times we used canned foods for dessert."

Many of the trout fishermen were equally avid wild fowl hunters in a land of plentiful birds and fine shots. They still talked about the shooting of young Frederick W. Henshaw shortly before the advent of game limits in the 1890s. Henshaw, later a California judge, made a legendary kill of 400 canvasback ducks, none sitting, with only 420 shotgun shells.

The South Coast was a principal stopover point for migratory game birds because springs bubbled up into ponds in numerous locations on the rolling hills and plains. This was before groundwater was pumped for extensive irrigation, and swamp and delta lands were drained. Typical of these springs on higher ground were parts of Rancho Rodeo de las Aguas (gathering of the waters). Its ponds, covered with teeming flocks of mallards and canvasbacks, were located east a bit from present-day Beverly Hills near the impressive new carbarns of General Sherman's interurban trolleys. Insomniacs visiting Los Angeles were quick to complain of the honking of triangles of Oregon gray geese passing overhead in the quiet of the predawn hours. Weighing up to twenty pounds apiece, these birds had more than adequate honking capacity to substantiate the insomniacs' grumbles. When the lands were irrigated and farmed, the numerous ponds dwindled and disappeared. Then, commencing in the 1890s, a number of duck or gun clubs were formed carrying forgotten or nostalgic names like Recreation and Del Rey, near Venice, and Bolsa Chica, Westminister, and Blue Wing in the Gospel Swamp district of Orange County.

Like their fathers before them, most men were absorbed with horses. Old-timers on the South Coast were convinced that the Californio horses were unequaled for endurance. They still talked of the time Don Jose Andres Sepulveda and his brother, called to Los Angeles by a family illness, covered forty-two miles while fording three rivers in considerably less than three hours. And on any number of occasions a horse was ridden from Los Angeles to Santa Barbara in a single day.

The deluge of incomers during and after the Boom were primarily interested in well-trained buggy horses. A successful horse purchase was ample cause for boasting; a poor buy could be an investment loss or worse. There was agreement that no finer sport existed than moving out in a light rig behind a fast horse, selected and trained for informal buggy racing with handicap betting. During good Los Angeles weather one of the popular racing locales of the 1890s was the stretch along Figueroa between Washington and Jefferson streets, particularly on a late Friday afternoon. The weekly race day had arrived when men like James H. Shankland, a prominent lawyer, would announce at breakfast that he was driving his buggy to his Baker Block office near the Plaza rather than taking the popular electric trolley. By mid-afternoon Shankland had a fair idea who would be assembled at Washington and Figueroa streets for buggy competition. Likely he had already set up a match race. Notified by the effective bush telegraph of those days, spectators were casually scattered along the route, small boys were perched in convenient trees and dogs and stray children had been systematically put on leash. Certainly, the Friday supper at the Shankland residence tended to be more animated if the master of the house was pleased with his race performance.

Horses, hunting and fishing were traditional frontier avocations on the South Coast; organized sports were not. True, with the sizable influx of Germans to southern California in the 1850s, the turnvereins or athletic clubs were popular because of their gymnastic exercises and calisthenics, popular enough that the Concordia Turnverein in San Diego did put on an unusual and well-attended athletic event in 1888. This was the locally publicized Great Jaguarina-Weidermann Fight, a broadsword competition on horseback. Weidermann, in addition to his calisthenics work, was an instructor in fencing and boxing. Jaguarina, a husky, broad and very athletic woman, had defeated "the Navy Champion" in an earlier broadsword contest. In the turnverein promotion both mounted combatants were helmeted and wore breastplates. After bashing at her opponent during eleven "attacks" of three minutes' duration each, this early representative of women's liberation was declared the winner.

A sweaty Great Jaguarina was still several light-years removed from women's general participation in organized sports. Yet some of them along with their men were learning lawn tennis at the early country clubs of the 1890s and May Sutton Bundy would shortly appear on the courts. The tennis rules were sensible, with admonitions like "No playing with high-heeled shoes," "Only one set or thirteen games when members are waiting" and "The last player must pick up the balls." The clubhouses frequented by the tennis, golf, and polo devotees had what were being called "shower baths," destined shortly to become a peculiarly American tradition. Economic revival toward the end of the century plus an excellent railroad network brought routine intercity athletic competition, exemplified by baseball of the young Pacific Coast League. Even the Burlingame Polo Club near San Francisco sent sixteen ponies to the South Coast for a series of 1897 matches.

But for the ordinary man who could not afford polo, golf or tennis there was a fascinating and exhilarating alternative—riding on and owning the world's first personal transportation machine, the bicycle. This excellent vehicle, in mass production by the turn of the century, symbolized for many their generation's good life.

CHAPTER 16

"These opportunities may honestly be called glorious"

If diversity of language was any measure, Los Angeles was a cosmopolitan town into the 1870s. Since the community's population was about equally divided between Californios, Europeans and Americans, a good deal of French and German was spoken along with the dominant Spanish and English. In addition, the babble of Chinese in the old adobes in and around Calle de Los Negros was noticeably increasing. This had replaced the various dialects of the drunken Indian mobs with their yelling and screaming. The Indians had congregated in the Calle de Los Negros district on weekends after receiving their weekly farm labor pay in raw aguardiente (brandy). Now most of them were dead—from alcohol, brawling, casual murder or disease.

A barber and freed slave, Peter Biggs in the 1850s could enjoy his extracurricular activities as a cosmopolitan man-about-town and a popular master of ceremonies at fandangos and bailes. The fact that a man was a black, like Biggs, or a German Jew, like Harris Newmark, was of minimal interest in those South Coast days. A man's race or religion on the southern California frontier was considered his own affair.

The rapid growth of the Chinese ghettos and then the Boom of the eighties changed the easygoing frontier tolerance. The early mutterings of "Yellow Peril" soon consolidated into an unreasoning hatred and fear of the Chinese. And the Boom brought a deluge of incomers from the Midwest and East, primarily native white stock, usually Protestant, and carrying with them their own strong mores and prejudices. The loss of the casual tolerance saddened old settlers like Newmark when in the 1890s he watched the rolls of the local social clubs like the California closed to Jews except those like himself who had joined in earlier years.

The response of the excluded minority was to establish its own Concordia Club which "in later years became the inner sanctum of high Jewish society." Its Jewish atmosphere eventually became so rarefied that the Concordia annually sponsored for its children what was reportedly "the finest Christmas party in town." As usual, the Los Angeles *Times* reflected the prevailing view, in this instance, of the propriety of blackballing an applicant for club membership: "No member should be admitted as a member of the club whom the average member would refuse to admit as a guest in his own house . . ."

In the existing posture of rectitude and decorum which oftentimes could be equated to stuffiness, the prosperous Los Angeles Jewry of the 1890s was embarrassed by the first influx of East European Jews, particularly Russian, who had fled the pogroms. Arriving on the South Coast with no money, decidedly foreign mannerisms, and a substantial language barrier, they struggled to survive as best they could. Many opened second-hand shops and junkyards characterized in some instances by sharp practices and occasionally by the fencing of stolen goods. Naturally, these episodes served to buttress the stereotyped prejudice against Jews by the dominant majority.

The Jews early discovered they were not alone in the focus of South Coast prejudice. Of course there were the Chinese and then the Japanese but also the freshly arrived emigrants (mostly Catholic) from Western Europe. The hordes of bone-poor, smelly immigrants continued to arrive in America during the depression of the 1890s, taking what work was available. Substantial numbers of them straggled into the South Coast which had its own economic problems.

To workers being laid off by factories and shops around the United States, the outlanders appeared like a locust invasion, taking precious manual jobs at any price. Organized as a secret society, the American Protective Association (or A.P.A. as it was generally called) became a surging anti-Catholic force with bastions in the Midwest and East and a forward stronghold in southern California. At the apex of the A.P.A. strength, the Catholic minority on the South Coast found an effective defender in a recently appointed bishop, George Montgomery. Speaking where he could and always through the newspapers, Montgomery lashed out at bigotry and hate just as the Jews did so effectively years later with their Anti-Defamation League. While the main thrust of the American Protective Association largely spent itself with the business revival of the 1900s, its heritage lingered on, as a kind of miasma, in southern California affairs for a long time.

According to some it was difficult to hear oneself think let alone sleep on a Sunday morning in the 1890s, because of the tolling of South Coast steeple bells. The little cities and towns were awash with morality. Most of the congregations were Protestant and a number of their churches were large indeed. The Methodist Simpson's Tabernacle in Los Angeles, used both as a church and concert hall, easily seated 2500 people, half the population of the whole community a quarter of a century earlier.

The first Protestant chapel in Los Angeles, the Episcopal St. Athanasius constructed during the Civil War, was at the foot of Poundcake Hill in the present Civic Center and below the neglected nonsectarian burial grounds of the town. Two well-maintained Protestant cemeteries were established during the Boom period—Evergreen in East Los Angeles near the new Catholic cemetery and Rosedale in Pico Heights, both reached by streetcar. At the turn of the century, specially designed funeral trolleys with stained-glass windows were rented out to undertakers. The casket was arranged cross-wise in the front of the car and the rear compartment of the elaborate *Descanso* of the Los Angeles Railway seated two dozen mourners in wickerwork chairs. This was the time when embalming of the dead was receiving early acceptance on the South Coast, with the flourishing undertaker arranging an open-casket display in the home prior to the funeral.

In the brave and novel world of electricity, there was an alternative and fiercely debatable choice to burial of the dead. This was an electric furnace which could reduce the flesh and bones of the corpse to ashes in a matter of a few hours. Built through the efforts of Charlotte L. Wills in 1887, the Rosedale Crematorium was probably the second such installation in the United States, and "was opened by the Los Angeles Crematory Society which brought to the Coast an incinerating expert." The burial vs. cremation debate has continued into the 1970s with an increasing number of cremation proponents arguing against embalming and other mortuary procedures.

Not all of the South Coast newcomers were dedicated Methodists, Presbyterians or belonging to any of the conventional creeds. A number had joyously accepted the faddish and offbeat religions which were growing in popularity in Victorian England and the United States, particularly if the minister was an H. Jesse Shepard.

A handsome thirty-eight-year-old bachelor and concert pianist, Shepard gave piano recitals and rode the developing crest of spiritualism and theosophy. Matrons of the South Coast, and San Diego in particular, could scarcely absorb the rarefied atmosphere of the Englishman's cultural musicales and musical seances, especially the ladies with marriageable daughters. Serving as the medium, Shepard played the piano or organ during the seance. While the program progressed, there were sounds of trumpets, drums and tambourines from around the room, with muted voices issuing from the horns. A few years later, the pianist-spiritualist suddenly joined the Catholic Church, moved to Los Angeles and reportedly confessed his spirit claims were fraudulent.

H. Jesse Shepard was a pale and deceitful ghost in religious charisma compared to Madame Katherine A. Tingley. She arrived with a flourish on the South Coast in 1896 and bought 130 acres of land on Point Loma near San Diego for the site of her Universal Brotherhood & Theosophical Society. The organization's objective was "to revive the Lost Mysteries of Antiquity" emphasizing Hindu and Buddhist doctrines of reincarnation and spiritualism.

Madame Tingley was about fifty years of age when she and southern California encountered each other. The confrontation was short—she forthwith overawed a good portion of the population. Full breasted and substantially corseted, her erect carriage and flowing purple gowns hushed conversation when she entered a room. When riding about the streets, the Leader preferred a landau, with a sort of an imperial dias; she properly was one of the tourist sights of San Diego.

Endowed with a personal magnetism which for some was almost hypnotic, Madame Tingley demonstrated a sustained ability to accumulate disciples and followers, many of them wealthy and prominent in the arts. Building after exotic-looking building, all white, was erected at the Point Loma location which overlooked the Pacific and the entrance to San Diego harbor. Eventually there were about fifty structures on the grounds, including homes of wealthy followers or Tingleyites, as San Diego referred to them.

There was one popular local story about the Leader and how her name caused some specialized confusion. This concerned the crew of a ship, long at sea, which was coming into the harbor. Most of the sailors, unfamiliar with San Diego, were looking forward to a night in the Stingaree, the Tenderloin and whorehouse district of the town. The beautiful white buildings on Point Loma were pointed out to them by an old hand while the ship rounded into the harbor entrance with the comment: "That is Madame Tingley's place." One sailor, after ruminating a bit, admitted he was impressed with the size and affluence of the Madame's sporting house which put the San Francisco establishments to shame, but he still wanted to know "why her place was so far out of town."

Libeling Madame Tingley could be expensive as the Los Angeles *Times* along with its publisher, Harrison Gray Otis, discovered. She was more than capable of defending herself against any canards, or allegations of improper financial controls and psychic suasion, in spite of frothy statements such as one made by the *Times'* lawyers: "No despot that sat in Constantinople ever claimed to exercise such powers over men and women as Mrs. Tingley does." The years passed and Katherine Augusta Tingley continued to manage singlehandedly her society, so much so that the movement only briefly survived her 1929 death.

The prevailing public school distemper and malaise of Los Angeles during the 1960s and extending into the 1970s, evidenced as much as anything by security guards and the students' low-scoring records in reading and writing capabilities, would have been inconceivable to teachers and parents a half-century earlier. Laura G. Smith did not overstate the serene confidence and optimism of that generation during the late 1910s:

"Looking back on its past with its record of achievement, the future measured on the same scale is full of possibilities. . . . These opportunities may honestly be called glorious. Los Angeles has a glowing faith in its own possibilities and . . . a certain fearless approach to the new ideas of education."

In the years around the Civil War there was ample room for improvement in Los Angeles education. Relatively few of the population could read, which was scarcely surprising because the first public school of the town was not opened until 1855. Another two decades passed before a public high school class of a half-dozen was graduated. But in the succeeding two generations the growing city developed a brilliantly successful educational system. A number of three-year secondary and intermediate schools were opened and the original Los Angeles High, in 1919, was transferred from Poundcake Hill to a large campus surrounded by vacant lands on Tenth Street (Olympic), its present location.

The relocated high school was designed to be a major secondary school plant, having four stories of classrooms in the principal sprawling brick building. By the end of the 1920s there were well over three thousand students at L. A. High, drawn from a wide geographical area and a range of economic and ethnic groupings. The writer recalls with considerable managerial admiration one important aspect of the viable educational system at that high school. This was the extent of enforcement of school regulations by the students themselves, probably best represented by a Senior Board, elected by the male senior class members.

The student board could and did, after a hearing, award momentous demerits to a student for a variety of reasons including fighting or cigarette smoking on the school grounds. Accumulation of an established number of demerits by a student during a semester meant expulsion from his home high school for a time and relegation to classes at a special school. In those days that was a traumatic sentence, and, being so, the Administration used the ultimate penalty carefully and reluctantly. It depended on major checkpoints like the Senior Board to hold down the demerit offenses by warnings and suasion.

Even the bravado of the most sanguine first-time offender was stretched to the maximum when he faced an appearance before the weekly meeting of the Senior Board. Substantial psychological pressure was felt immediately. The infraction citation slip of a distinctive color had been rather ostentatiously hand-delivered to his homeroom, preferably well in advance of his scheduled appearance at the three o'clock afternoon meeting of the Board.

In theory at least, the offender could readily report in "sick" the day of the weekly meeting. With a vague nausea he certainly felt ill enough. But absenteeism meant parental explanation plus the accused's firm conviction that the implacable system would force his appearance sooner rather than later, perhaps with heavier penalties. He attended school the day of his ordeal, arriving on time and thoroughly aware that his friends and classmates regarded him with the speculative interest of an audience watching a man with a popgun preparing to meet a hungry tiger.

The citation notice, wilted from much handling, was the

defendant's unwelcome and conspicuous authorization to leave a physical education or late study class for his appearance before the Board. Dragging his feet, the offender finally arrived at the anteroom where he stayed in miserable and supervised silence, together with a number of other defendants, while one by one, they were escorted down an aisle to the Board chamber. Eventually, and what for a nervous teenager was an interminable time, it was his turn to be taken into the Board room where he was left standing alone on rubbery legs several paces inside the door. His first impression was a visual blur of blue sweaters, swimming in a dangerous, enveloping silence.

Seated about the perimeter of the Senior Board room were twenty or so seniors, much of the male power structure of the high school, each wearing the distinctive sweater with an insignia. The group's faculty advisor might or might not be in attendance. After an appropriate period of silence, during which the lonely figure stood clasping and reclasping his clammy hands behind his back, the secretary deliberately read the defendant's name, the citation with the demerits or warning to be considered, and the cumulative number of demerits given to the offender during the current semester. The presiding officer then asked whether the facts as cited were correct.

Most defendants found that answering such a query even by a monosyllable was much like talking with a mouthful of viscous taffy. Usually, another question from one of the other members would help the sweating accused progress beyond the mumbling stage into telling his side of the story, if there was one. The accuracy of the citations was always surprising to the writer who had had the dubious distinction of both standing alone there facing his inquisitors and later leisurely sitting during other sessions. Notwithstanding the size of the high school the intelligence which reached the Board, even down to the real initiator of a school ground fight, was usually correct. After members' questions were disposed of, demerits, warning, or exoneration were given along with comment that another appearance before the Senior Board was likely to be substantially more painful. A thoroughly wrung-out teenager was then ushered out of the room. He did not recommend his afternoon experience to his friends.

To a later generation, the extent of student management of school affairs would appear incredible, particularly in the huge secondary schools. And in the opinion of some today, such administrative devices as the Senior Board would suggest "a society far more totalitarian than democratic, one in which discipline dominates over learning." The public of the first part of the century and the education system which it supported undoubtedly would have retorted that a school climate of discipline and order was a prerequisite for broad-scale and systematic learning. Surely there was a basic belief in the community then that the opportunities made available in the education of the day were indeed glorious. Perhaps they were.

CHAPTER 17

"You are taking water out faster than it is flowing in"

In the long harbor fight against Collis P. Huntington and the Southern Pacific, Los Angeles civic leaders had become accustomed to national support and praise for their municipal dedication and imagination. When their city needed water, in the early 1900s, these same men set out to build a 250-mile municipal aqueduct to Owens Valley, recognizing full well that the project could place the small city in financial pawn and, indirectly, their own businesses as well. What they did not envisage was being effectively cast as villains by a strident minority for nearly a half-century afterwards. In 1946 Carey McWilliams wrote that their "Owens Valley project was conceived in iniquity" and Morrow Mayo had a vituperative and choleric essay in 1933 concerning the aqueduct program. The clinchpin of his piece was used by the more erudite opposition in subsequent years:

"Los Angeles gets its water by reason of one of the costliest, crookedest, most unscrupulous deals ever perpetrated, plus one of the greatest engineering follies ever heard of. . . . It was an obscene enterprise from beginning to end. . . . *The Federal Government of the United States held Owens Valley while Los Angeles raped it.*"

If a good part of the flat propaganda statements made by the advocates on both sides of the water controversy, including the saccharine comments of some of the aqueduct supporters, are eliminated or discounted, several conclusions are inescapable. The first is that the Owens Valley project was a memorable engineering effort and demonstrated fluid transport feasibility never before believed possible. Morrow Mayo to the contrary, the aqueduct was a story of accomplishment and efficiency; no other conclusion can be reached after reviewing the project's construction controls as the writer did in a 1949 study of the city department which built the aqueduct. And finally, there were a great many eggs broken to make the aqueduct omelet, unfortunately far more than there should have been. This was so not only because of insider speculation in San Fernando Valley lands but, infinitely more important, the obduracy and overreacting by both sides of an active controversy which lasted for a generation.

Preoccupation with water and rainfall statistics was almost a fixation for old-timers on the South Coast. In any year the region's precious rainfall might be concentrated in a few days or weeks, with water rushing down the precipitous mountains, flooding the plains and then being lost in the sea. For a time after the Boom of the eighties the flowing artesian wells and the tapping of the underground rivers in the coastal plains provided ample water. Yet with the voracious demands of young orchards and sprawling crops irrigationists soon recognized that these flows themselves were creatures of the long-term rainfall/drought cycles of the region. An official of the just established Federal Reclamation Service put the case dramatically, after the drought year of 1898 which showed a minute 4.83 inches of rain and a following year of only half-normal rainfall, when he said that "Los Angeles is living on a huge bowl of water. You are taking water out faster than it is flowing in. Some day you will strike bottom. . . . You are headed for the tragedy of the Mesa Grande ruins . . ."

In May of 1901 George Chaffey delivered Colorado River water to Calexico in the Colorado Desert via fifty miles or so of canal; he had demonstrated the technical answer to Los Angeles' water problem. Why not build an aqueduct north from Los Angeles to the base of the towering Sierras whose high flanks consistently carried heavy snowpacks? The Tehachapi Mountains effectively blocked a route to the western slope of the Sierras. But an approach through the narrow trough of Owens Valley to the eastern side below Mount Whitney was difficult yet perhaps possible.

The hydraulics and other engineering criteria of such a project were just within the state of the art at that time. But nowhere else had an aqueduct system been built of comparable size and complexity in such an unfavorable physical environment, overshadowed by a major earthquake concern. The system must traverse one of the world's harshest deserts and a series of mountain ranges. This meant the men and equipment must routinely operate in blowing sand, alkali dust and drifting snow, in ambient temperatures extending from well below zero to plus 135 degrees. Always was the gnawing design concern of an earthquake effect on the aqueduct, its dams and tunnels. Within the previous half-century, both the Owens Trough and the Tehachapi Mountains at different times had had frightful earth shocks of more than Magnitude 8 on the logarithmic Richter scale; the violent quakes there threw people out of bed 200 miles from the epicenters.

Europeans who have seen the eastern side of the Sierra Nevadas wonder why Americans are so impressed with the Alps. The High Sierras are young mountains, a great tilted block of granite rising sharply from the Owens Trough floor. The height of many of the peaks exceeds 11,000 feet and the highest one, Mount Whitney, rises to 14,494 feet, less than fifteen miles from the town of Lone Pine in the valley below. Intense volcanic action was associated with the formation of the young mountains, along with massive earthquakes similar to the one which occurred in 1872 leaving fault scarps as high as twenty-five feet in the Trough.

During recent centuries the people who lived in this high desert land bracketed by the Sierras to the west and the desiccated Inyo and Panamint mountains to the east were Paiutes (many called them Piutes or Monos). These Indians had the tradition of trees and meadows where they only knew sagebrush in the same places; the ancient petroglyphs similarly suggest a much wetter climate. White settlers came into the Owens Valley in the early 1860s when the Indian population of the region at the time was certainly less than 1,500. Conflict between the two alien groups was not long in coming.

A Paiute while rustling a steer was shot and killed in 1862 by a cowboy herding cattle from Nevada into the Bishop Creek meadows of the Owens Trough. In retribution another cowboy was captured by the Paiutes, scalped and lingeringly put to death. These killings initiated a vicious guerrilla war which flickered on and off for years and brought war parties into the valley from the Nevada Paiutes and the Tulares, across the Sierras to the west. Camp Independence was garrisoned spasmodically with U.S. Cavalry units which attempted to stem the fighting, burning and murder.

During the period of conflict J. P. N. Wentworth, Indian Agent for the Southern District of California, set aside "all the good land" according to the settlers as a possible Paiute reservation in Owens Valley from Big Pine Creek on the north to George's Creek on the south. Wentworth's idea lasted only until the local lobbying influences went to work on principals of the Department of the Interior. There was no further planning of Indian reservations in the long, narrow Trough. Eventually, a kind of an exhausted peace brought the guerrilla fighting to an end. Then the Paiute family clusters, living off an erratic Federal bounty, were scattered about the region, surviving and adapting in a similar manner to other rural Indian groups in the Southern District of California.

W. A. Chalfant, a sound regional historian, son of an early Owens Valley settler and a brilliant antagonist of Los Angeles and its water aqueduct, in writing about his beloved area, felt that the white man's domination and his "ability to make use of resources . . . were as inevitable here as they have been elsewhere as civilization advanced." In its search for water, Los Angeles, with about as much justification or as little, felt the same way about Chalfant and the few embattled Trough farmers standing astride the valuable brawling streams from the Sierras which were wantonly being lost in the alkali marshes of Owens Lake.

Peace in the Owens Valley found white settlers who stayed

during the decade of Indian conflict, those who returned after the fighting, and some tenderfeet who had straggled in. They farmed the land, dug some irrigation ditches and then were impressed with the implications of the 1901 Colorado Desert irrigation work of Chaffey. Some of them located water reservoir sites on the Federal lands (which constituted the bulk of the Trough) and filed requests for the necessary reservoir permits. Shortly thereafter a powerful young government agency became interested in the Owens Valley. The U.S. Reclamation Service, created in 1902 and originally staffed by key Geological Survey people, had the responsibility of engineering and constructing irrigation systems with funds obtained from the sale of public lands. The Service began a preliminary irrigation survey of the Trough in the summer of 1903 under the direction of its supervising engineer for California, J. B. Lippincott. In the next immediate months 565,000 acres of Federal lands which conceivably might be encompassed by an irrigation project were routinely and temporarily withdrawn from public entry. This was a standard and sensible procedure to prevent land rights and use speculation. The prospect of a major Federally funded irrigation project covering scores of square miles was not unnaturally greeted with vociferous enthusiasm by the several thousand inhabitants of Owens Valley.

A new municipal water department in Los Angeles flexed its muscles for the first time in 1902 because of a $2,000,000 water bond issue approved by the voters. The bonds provided for the purchase of the privately owned water system, additional distribution equipment and the establishment of a managing Board of Water Commissioners. The System Superintendent and Chief Engineer was William Mulholland, a dedicated believer in the development of a major Los Angeles metropolitan area, held back in his judgment by only two prime deficiencies—inexpensive fuel and a plentiful water supply. Lyman Stewart, Edward L. Doheny and the like, with their southern California oil discoveries were eliminating the former. Mulholland proposed to correct the latter, particularly after long discussions with Frederick Eaton, a former city engineer and just recently a mayor of Los Angeles.

Eaton had become involved in the Owens Trough where he saw opportunity, both for himself and Los Angeles, in the mountain streams rushing down the eastern flanks of the Sierras. He proposed nothing less than bringing Owens water to Los Angeles, 250 miles away over a series of mountain ranges interspersed with deserts. This was exotic technical thinking for Mulholland; whether the concept was within the financial capabilities of a city of 200,000 population was something else again. After spending days and weeks on horseback over alternative routes, Mulholland's engineering estimate was in the $25,000,000 range—in mid-1970 prices well over a quarter of a billion dollars of bonded indebtedness for the smallish city.

His Board of Water Commissioners did not dismiss Mulholland's expansive and expensive water plan as pure fantasy. Further, the Board accepted the chief engineer's recommendation that it follow the San Francisco precedent of secrecy in the early stages of the Owens Valley program.

James Phelan, shortly after his term as mayor of San Francisco, made application in his own name for water and reservoir rights in the Hetch Hetchy Valley of the Yosemite district. Soon thereafter Phelan assigned these applications to the municipality. This was the first official indication that San Francisco intended to build an aqueduct from the western slope of the Sierras. The decision of the Los Angeles water commissioners to emulate the bay city's secrecy during early site acquisition became one of the most controversial and belabored facets of the entire Owens Trough project.

William Mulholland's board quietly discussed their chief engineer's aqueduct proposal with the principal people of Los Angeles, mostly the same individuals who had braved the Southern Pacific in the harbor struggle a few years earlier. The Mulholland cost estimate for the 250-mile aqueduct usually brought a low whistle of amazement because of its size. With harbor, school, sewer and municipal electrical power commit-

ments and demands, bankers like Tomas L. Duque pointed out
that there would be a very tight horserace between the growth
of the city's income base and the required payments of bond
principal and interest. Failure to meet the city's debt repayment
schedules would place stringent limitations on municipal services
and unquestionably would have a deadening effect on commercial and retail growth of the area. This was not a financial decision to be made lightly. Yet, reflecting the optimism of the years,
the heavy consensus was to take the aqueduct risk at least
through the detailed engineering feasibility studies.

In 1904 the Board of Water Commissioners instructed Mulholland and Frederick Eaton to review Los Angeles' interest in
the Owens Trough water with the fledgling U.S. Reclamation
Service. Because of a large plateful of other irrigation projects
the Service readily relinquished its preliminary plan of Federal
water development in the Valley. The Los Angeles water board
then authorized Eaton to take land options in his own name on
strategic Trough locations for ultimate transfer to the board.

Eaton solicited options during the fall of 1904 and into the
next spring, concentrating on riparian lands along the Owens
River and lands which would be flooded by a major reservoir in
Long Valley. Water board funds were first paid to the former
mayor in the winter or spring of 1905 for the city options he had
been taking up in his own name. By this time Los Angeles survey
parties were making contour maps along the route of the proposed aqueduct, and this activity was triggering the first solid
rumors of the city's interest in Sierra water. Eaton completed
the turnover of the city's options to the Board of Water Commissioners in May of 1905, while retaining certain Long Valley
acreage rights and granting an easement site to Los Angeles for
a reservoir in back of a hundred-foot-high dam.

The terminal of the proposed aqueduct was to be the northern
perimeter of the San Fernando Valley, a score of miles from Los
Angeles. The empty, semiarid valley could be utilized as a principal irrigation customer and storage area for water in excess of
the city's needs. The location was an eminently sensible engineering decision. Yet in practice the secrecy surrounding the

aqueduct and its terminal properly led to a hornet's nest of legitimate criticism for many years.

Most of the San Fernando Valley in the 1900s consisted of two huge wheat ranches, although a 12,000-acre tract in the present-day North Hollywood district had been subdivided into forty-acre farms during the Boom of the eighties. Obviously, if the Owens project was ever completed, the San Fernando Valley landholders would benefit, not only because of an assured water supply but also water excess to the city needs might be available at bargain rates. The owners of the two big wheat ranches knew about the aqueduct planning; the owners of the small farms in the east end of the valley did not. There was a short frenzy of option offers by insiders before the rumors effectively eliminated any bargains.

Ethics aside, the options, most for a year or less, made only marginal business sense. Even if eventually successful, a monumental project like Mulholland's aqueduct would take many years to complete with the intervening period strewn with mischances, changes in policy and unpleasant surprises such as establishing the terminal adjacent to Los Angeles. This view might have been sensible but it was not shared by many of the insiders. They went ahead with the San Fernando options, placing all the principal aqueduct supporters in the position of being savagely lampooned for a long time as a rapacious and unscrupulous gang.

Rumors in July of 1905 had reached such a stage that the Los Angeles *Times* believed it was forced to break the aqueduct story. Most local people agreed with John Steven McGroarty's assessment that "the announcement sent a wild thrill through the whole population. It was like the time in Canaan when Joseph's brethren came back from Egypt laden with corn to succor their famine-stricken homes."

An extremely vocal minority both in Los Angeles and elsewhere did not share McGroarty's enthusiasm, with or without the biblical embellishment. This group believed that the political fat was in the fire and the burning hot grease was going to splatter over all the participants in the aqueduct planning, including the Reclamation Service for relinquishing its Trough irrigation plans. Owens Valley letters were written to the Secretary of the Interior and President Theodore Roosevelt specifically alleging malfeasance upon the part of J. B. Lippincott, the California supervising engineer, and his superiors in the Reclamation Service. Lippincott became even more controversial, if possible, when he went to work for William Mulholland less than a year later. The chorus of allegations by the Owens Valley adherents expanded in 1907 to include the Forest Services and the Chief Forester, Gifford Pinchot, the President's longtime friend, and then Roosevelt himself with the San Francisco *Call* commenting caustically that "anybody who plays tennis at the White House can have anything he wants . . ."

One of the principal battle cries of Roosevelt's frenetic administration was "Conservation" in which Gifford Pinchot's Forestry Service and the Reclamation Service promoted such slogans as "Save the Forests," "Store the Floods," "Reclaim the Desert" and "Make Homes on the Land." Each of these services had more than its share of the 1900s' version of social engineering projects and both believed Los Angeles should have the Owens Trough water. In this framework, it was perfectly reasonable for Pinchot to take the action he did after the Reclamation Service relinquished its Owens Valley position by making the withdrawn trough lands available again for public entry. Pinchot forthwith termed these barren square miles his Forest Service jurisdiction.

The aqueduct opposition bitterly pointed out that arbitrary action of the Chief Forester was a repetition "of a Nevada 'forest' withdrawal in which rangers had to carry their firewood several miles, and a Nebraska case where not 300 trees grew in 300,000 acres . . ." The 1907 National Irrigation Conference, a powerful organization in its day, refused to support the allegations of official irregularities on the part of the two federal services and their representatives. The furor died down for a while to a smoldering hatred of Los Angeles and Federal reclamation policies.

Meanwhile the people of Los Angeles continued their strong support of the aqueduct project. In 1905 a $1,500,000 bond issue for detailed engineering surveys and selected site purchases was overwhelmingly approved by the voters. There were no second thoughts. In June of 1907 and well after the severe San Francisco earthquake, the monumental sum of $23,000,000 for aqueduct construction was voted by a margin of ten to one. The plan simply had to work. By city charter amendment a full-time Board of Public Works was assigned the responsibility for the construction of the aqueduct. But above all else, the universal feeling in the city was that William Mulholland would make the project a success.

"Well, I did the work, but Mathews kept me out of jail!" William Mulholland was discussing William B. Mathews, Los Angeles City Attorney until 1907 and then for years special counsel on municipal water and power matters. The chief engineer of the city water department was reminiscing about the exciting times when no more than fifty men served as a catalytic force in the transfer of water from one distant watershed to another.

Certainly W. B. Mathews had more than his share of legal problems involving the aqueduct, commencing with purchase of land options. There were no specific city funds to pay $150,-000 for the Owens Trough options to be taken over from Frederick Eaton as well as additional valley options which Mulholland felt were necessary. Even if the $150,000 option payments could somehow be legally rationalized, there would have to be a bond issue almost immediately for moneys to exercise the land options and make detailed engineering studies. The dilemma of William H. Workman, City Treasurer and a respected former mayor of Los Angeles, when Mathews laid the Owens Valley option problem in front of him in 1905 is described by his son, Workman's assistant at the time:

"It may not be exactly legal for you to pay the demands

upon that water fund for such a purpose," he said. "Yet if
you feel that morally you are justified, we shall be taking the
first step toward solving our most critical problem . . .

"My father knew that if he honored the demand for $150,000,
and the bond issue failed, the diversion of funds would have to
be made good by himself. He consulted the men who were on
his indemnity bond of $300,000. They sanctioned his going
ahead, regardless of the liability they might incur."

Reflecting the ever-onward feeling of Los Angeles William
H. Workman authorized what in fact was an illegal payment
of municipal funds. In another set of circumstances or time
period he would have been indicted by the county grand jury
with the city attorney, Mathews, named as coconspirator.

The Los Angeles *Times* broke the aqueduct story in July of
1905. It was about time. A $1,500,000 bond issue would have to be
submitted to the voters within a two-month period or the option
money would have been wasted. Except for the managing group,
few people knew any details of the aqueduct plans. Fortunately
for William H. Workman and the men on his indemnity bond, the
Times' announcement did send a wild thrill through the bulk of
the population. Early in September the bond issue was approved
by a seven-to-one margin.

Now Mulholland had to demonstrate the engineering and
cost feasibility of his improbable aqueduct idea to an outside
board of consultants employed by the city. There was no question that the design and construction would stretch the state of
the art, whether it was in hydraulics and pumping, material such
as reinforced concrete and steel, driving a five-mile tunnel
through a mountain chain noted for its interior fault structure
and underground water, or designing and building a water
course through a well-known earthquake region distinguished by
a foul climate a good part of the year. The consultants agreed
with Mulholland that the task could be done, but emphasized
there was substantial technical risk combined with a very high
project cost. William Mulholland added to this risk when he
settled on $23,000,000, the lowest end of the cost/time estimates
developed by the consultants.

Only two decades earlier Senator William P. Frye of Maine had wondered aloud whether the entire South Coast was worth one-fifth of what Mulholland proposed to spend on constructing an aqueduct. A $23,000,000 bond issue was to be submitted to the Los Angeles voters in June of 1907. This time the opposition was not caught unprepared.

The Owens Trough farmers and merchants had been unusually effective in publicizing their aqueduct objections even though the valley's vote was no more than that of a small city ward. While jabbing at the evolving Los Angeles position, they continued to allege corruption of public officials and the San Fernando option grab. Along the way they had accumulated a coterie of support which included private power interests who saw the potentialities of aqueduct hydroelectric power, and northern California newspapers who already were keeping a wary eye on an expanding Los Angeles and South Coast. While the controversy boiled up to the national political level, the Los Angeles *News* vigorously opposed the aqueduct project. The other local newspapers—the *Examiner, Express, Herald, Record* and *Times* were aggressively supporting it. The people of Los Angeles made their own decision. They voted overwhelmingly in favor of the project.

General Adna R. Chaffee of the public works board was the executive head during the five years of aqueduct construction. Chaffee understood that, unless his forces spent the bond money wisely and frugally while having at least a modest degree of construction luck, Los Angeles would attain the dubious national distinction of having a water aqueduct ending in the Mojave Desert or Antelope Valley. There simply was no immediate way to obtain supplemental funds to cure mistakes. In a day before trucks and massive earth-moving equipment, Chaffee could have been forgiven for considering Mulholland's plans too expensive with the funds available. Preliminary estimates showed that a peak workforce of 6000 men would be required, and a million tons of material would have to be transported along the line of construction. The public works head knew that his two-horse dump carts and Fresno scrapers in combination with steam pumps, shovels and tractor engines, would be required to operate in forbidding terrain miles from the main base. The total length of the proposed aqueduct was to be 226 miles not including reservoirs. The design capacity was 420 second feet, enough to supply water for a city of a million population, irrigate 75,000 acres and still have water left over.

The aqueduct intake was to be at the Owens River above Independence, and the plans called for fifty miles of open canal south to the Haiwee Reservoir of 63,800 acre feet. This would serve as the collection point for other streams coming down the east side of the Sierras and the equilibrium base for controlled aqueduct flow. The route south from Haiwee was planned as a covered conduit to Little Lake and thence by a series of tunnels, conduits, flumes and siphons through Red Rock and Jawbone canyons on to the Mohave Desert at the base of the Tehachapi Mountains. The aqueduct would then turn southwest across to Antelope Valley and the Fairmont Reservoir, ahead of a five-mile tunnel leading into San Francisquito Canyon north of Saugus. Again a series of tunnels, siphons, flumes and conduits would take the water south to the terminal San Fernando (Van Norman) Reservoir. An undertaking of this size necessarily required extensive logistics support including a railroad before actual construction work could commence on the aqueduct itself.

The Southern Pacific had bought the Carson & Colorado narrow-gauge railroad in 1900, just before the growth of Tonopah and Goldfield mining camps in western Nevada gave a much-needed business lift to the Owens Trough. By the summer of 1906 Goldfield had a floating population of 30,000; there were well over a thousand prostitutes; and Tex Rickard's Northern Saloon had twenty-four bartenders on duty. The Carson & Pacific Railroad meandered south from Virginia City and its connections with the Southern Pacific main line at Reno. Southwest of Tonopah Junction the rails snaked through the 7100-foot Montgomery Pass down into Owens Valley and terminated at Keeler below the old Cerro Gordo silver camp. After the Los Angeles voters' approval of the aqueduct project, the Southern Pacific pushed construction on a standard-gauge road north of Mojave paralleling the aqueduct survey line to a junction with its Carson & Colorado near Owens Lake.

Meanwhile, the Los Angeles public works board was buying limestone and clay lands in Kern County and building a 1,000-barrel per day cement plant at Monolith. Hundreds of miles of mountain and desert roads for teaming were constructed along with water, power and telephone lines to fifty-seven construction camps. Los Angeles right-of-way agents were busy acquiring an additional 135,000 acres of trough land as buffer zones for water rights and reservoir sites. Actual aqueduct construction was finally underway in October of 1908.

The preliminary engineering and construction logistics for the aqueduct proved equal to the task at hand. Even in the jumbled "bad lands" of Jawbone Canyon the siphon work progressed well, and within a year the aqueduct was crawling over the mountains and deserts at the rate of seven miles per month. David Howarth's remarks concerning the successful Panama Canal construction underway at the same time appeared to be equally applicable to the Owens Valley project:

"To anyone except an engineer, a successful engineering enterprise is duller than one that fails. In failure, there are conflict, drama and emotion; in success, there are only statistics, and a sense of satisfaction which is largely personal."

However there was one last unknown. If, and it was a big "if," the Elizabeth Tunnel could be accomplished within target cost, just enough funds would be available to complete the aqueduct. With no fiscal margin of safety there was a pervading technical concern on the driving of the 26,870-foot tunnel through to San Francisquito Canyon. The Elizabeth was to be located only a few miles from San Fernando Mountain which had nearly defeated the veteran Southern Pacific tunnel crews, the best in the world at the time.

Sixteen months and $2,000,000 had been required to complete the 7000-foot Southern Pacific bore in 1875-76. The railroad engineers found the rock structure of San Fernando Mountain to be heavily fissured, with the fissures filled with a sticky blue clay and holding a heavy accumulation of water and some oil. The result was a herculean engineering and construction job because of cave-ins and underground water. Despite several tunnel faces, the air in the workings was so humid, foul and hot that ". . . the candles disposed along the side of the tunnel burned but dimly."

The grim problems of the San Fernando haunted William Mulholland; his Elizabeth was to be nearly four times longer than the railroad tunnel. Fortunately, in the intervening generation, improved tools and facilities had become available for difficult bores; Mulholland hoped they would make the difference. Most of the reeking tallow candles had gone. The miners now wore carbide lamps on their caps, and the underground passages were more or less lit by electric light and ventilated by fans between repeated power failures. Steam pumps to cope with the quantities of underground water had larger capacities and were much more reliable. But the most dramatic and risky of the engineering improvements was the use of dynamite for a hard-rock explosive in the tunnel face.

At the time of cost projections for the Elizabeth Tunnel, dynamite in underground work was replacing the traditional black powder and the dangerous igniting flame. Alfred Nobel, a Swedish chemist, had discovered a way to handle unstable nitroglycerin by mixing it with relatively inert materials. Dynamite was the result, and the U.S. Bureau of Mines with considerable misgivings had authorized a type of mining and tunnel dynamite in the early 1900s. The new explosive made for dramatic cost improvement over black powder charges. However, only experience would show how to handle the dreaded "red fumes" of dynamite. A weak detonation of a blasting cap could cause a charge to burn rather than explode. The resultant creeping and then enveloping red fumes brought on "slight choking, nausea, profuse perspiration and headaches in the tunnel crew. The men apparently revived on reaching open air. But they soon began to cough up bloody mucus . . ." The Elizabeth Tunnel had its red fumes episodes as did any tunnel operation using large quantities of the new explosive. Yet all the problems including fissures and underground water were surmounted, and the tunnel set an American record for hard-rock tunnel driving. The Elizabeth was within budget and the miasma of technical foreboding was dissipated. Mulholland proved to be both accurate and lucky in his engineering forecast.

Owens Valley water poured down the spillway into San Fernando Reservoir on November 5, 1913. Pointing to the foaming cascade from the speakers' platform while his voice shook a bit, William Mulholland said: "There it is, take it!" He then sat down. The chief engineer had just finished the best years of his life. Perhaps he recognized this.

The single public figure for more than a generation in which the people of Los Angeles and the South Coast had unswerving confidence was this same Mulholland. Even after the 1928 collapse of the municipal St. Francis Dam in the Santa Clara Valley with the attendant heavy loss of life, his enemies (and there were many) still found a unified community support for the revered chief engineer of the city water department.

Mulholland was put on a pedestal by his supporters, but he certainly did not gain his civic popularity by either tact or diplomacy in dealing with those who disagreed with him. Extensively quoted remarks such as "I'll buy Long Valley three years after Eaton is dead" (because his one-time friend asked a high price for an expanded reservoir site in the Owens Trough) established the water engineer's reputation as a gruff, outspoken individual. When provoked, he had the desire to claw his opponents and the power to do it. Above all else he was a dedicated engineer absorbed in his own vision (his enemies preferred the term "fanaticism") of having an abundant supply of water which would support a large population on the semiarid plains of the South Coast.

A lean and handsome Belfast Irishman, William Mulholland was curly haired, and clean shaven except for a full mustache of the period. He must have titillated his share of young ladies, but he remained a bachelor until his mid-thirties. After a fragmentary secondary education the young Irishman went to sea as a deckhand. Eventually, in his early twenties, he wandered into

Los Angeles during 1877 and found a job as a zanjero or ditch tender for the small local water company. Hydraulics and civil engineering (or surveying as it was still called) became an abiding passion and dedication, and he was chief engineer of the water company by the time of the Boom of the eighties. This was the basic job that Mulholland would hold for more than forty years.

The chief engineer supported his subordinates, probably far too loyally at times. Typical of his race, he had a long memory for wrongs, real or fancied, which impugned his professional integrity and competence. Disinterested in money, but accumulating power to accomplish his duty and tasks as he saw them, William Mulholland was a potent force in his region's generation and times.

In an age where towering engineering achievements were becoming the expected, the Owens Valley aqueduct wrote another technical chapter in the long-distance movement of fluids. Concomitantly and unfortunately, the aqueduct launched in Los Angeles a kind of bureaucratic juggernaut of inflexibility and stubbornness, interspersed with unpredictable periods of indecisiveness in reaching agreement with the Owens Trough people on surface and underground water policy. In turn, the antagonists of the city in the Valley managed to display a continuing and almost uncanny facility for rejecting or not pushing aggressively enough at the appropriate time for a feasible and reasonable agreement with Los Angeles. Then several years later they desperately would wish they had made such an agreement with the city. Leavening all of these matters were the well-hoarded enmities of all the key personalities involved. It was only a matter of time until a crisis would arise.

There was no resolution of the differences between Los Angeles and the Owens Valley farmers, merchants and their outside advocates by the end of World War I. Then Los Angeles, sharply increased in area by annexation, found itself in another people boom: "In the year of our Lord 1920, the population of Los Angeles is quite 600,000, and that in all likelihood it will reach 750,000 in 1925, the time fixed by experts for it to reach 400,000." While the people flocked in, the winter of 1920-21 brought only a light snowpack in the Sierras and markedly reduced water runoff. This pattern continued for several years, and Los Angeles had no massive reserve storage system for such a contingency. Any bureaucracy presented with a city population increase far exceeding plan, and faced with the prospect of light snowpacks in the Sierras, would protect itself, and overreact if necessary, to ensure such protection.

In those times of reduced Sierra runoff, Los Angeles commenced an accelerated program of pumping underground water on its extensive Owens Trough lands, at times substantially and stupidly exceeding reservoir capacity. While the Los Angeles pumps worked day and night pulling water into its aqueduct system, the underground water level in the Owens Valley first dropped sharply, and then adjacent farmers' pumps sucked dry. The valley crops withered and died. Violence was not long in coming.

A small blast of dynamite was exploded against the aqueduct structure near Lone Pine in May of 1924. This was the first of a long list of guerrilla incidents which received broad local support. A principal Owens Valley spokesman, W. A. Chalfant emphasized that these acts were simply an emulation of the city's continuing lawlessness and therefore justified. Late in 1924 the aqueduct flow was cut off and turned back into the Owens River for four days, and the cutoff point "took on the appearance of a large picnic" attended by the Trough residents. Sporadic aqueduct dynamite blasts accompanied by fruitless bickering continued as the years went on and even after Sierra snowpacks returned to normal levels. In June and July of 1927 there were six dynamitings, one of which resulted in the carrying away of 450 feet of the steel aqueduct siphon.

Attempts at outside mediation of the city/valley controversy accomplished nothing as even an egotist like Jackson A. Graves discovered in the mid-1920s. By this time the Owens Trough was dying—some three hundred families had moved out. Finally, even the most adamant on both sides recognized that agreement must be reached on reasonable prices for the city to buy out the merchants' businesses along with the remaining valley lands affected by the aqueduct. Within a few years Los Angeles was the owner of the bulk of the property in most of the towns in addition to thousands of acres of ranch lands destined to lie fallow. The result by the mid-1930s was a monument to inept leadership in both Los Angeles and Owens Valley.

CHAPTER 18

"Let's drill an oil well"

The man who had drilled a gusher or flowing oil well in the booming southern California oil fields of the 1900s could easily cadge more than his share of beers in a saloon. Gushers were spectacular rarities, usually unexpected, and most drilling crews never saw one brought in. A wildcat operation, fancifully called Lake View, alongside the dirt road between Maricopa and Taft in the lower San Joaquin Valley was an improbable location in 1910 for one of the major oil spectaculars of all time.

Union Oil had four unpromising holes, dry as dust, being drilled in this unproven Taft district. A few months earlier the oil company reluctantly had taken a fifty-one percent interest in the Lake View operation, then down to a completely unproductive 1800-foot depth. The agreement was that the Union drilling crews in the area might push the Lake View hole deeper on a casual fill-in work basis. While the months went by, the orphaned wildcat was sporadically drilled to 2200 feet with little promise and less interest on the company's part.

The Union Oil test well nearest the Lake View hole sanded up early in the evening of March 14, 1910. When the graveyard shift reported, the crew was told by the foreman, Charles L. Woods, to do some more drilling on the unwanted wildcat. Woods was more familiarly known to his peers as Dry Hole Charlie because he had brought in one barren test well after another. Following Charlie's routine instructions, the bailer was pulled by the graveyard shift from the bottom of the Lake View hole. To the crew's amazement it was dripping with oil. Successive drops of the bailer during the rest of the night showed oil at higher and higher levels. Then the men heard an increasing rumbling and belching in the hole shortly after dawn. Suddenly there was an accelerating subterranean roar, much like a rapidly approaching locomotive, while the surrounding earth trembled.

The drilling crew members ran for their lives. A massive crater was blasted out of the surface dirt and shale; the drilling rig and equipment simply disappeared or disintegrated. A twenty-foot-wide column of gas and oil geysered hundreds of feet into the air. The gusher seemed to feed on itself while the throbbing gas and oil pressure increased by the hour. By what could only be regarded as a miracle, the gusher neither then nor later caught fire. The question was what to be done with this berserk monster:

"No one knew how to cap such a terrific geyser of oil. Dams were hurriedly thrown up to catch the torrent of crude, which by this time was a greater flood than oil men anywhere had ever seen. . . . Dry Hole Charlie was dancing like an Indian. 'My God, we've cut an artery down there,' he yelled.

"Calling every man in the area to help, Woods and his crew frantically piled up earth to throw a temporary reservoir around the well. It was filled to overflowing in no time. Woods sent out a desperate call for help. Hundreds of men responded. . . . For months the well spouted completely out of control. 'Down below,' according to Woods, 'we scooped out storage for ten million barrels of oil. We had nine million barrels stored up before the gusher calmed down.'"

The Lake View gusher lasted eighteen months, long enough so that "preachers conducted excursions to the spot, exhorting people to pray that the oil might not cover the world and bring flaming destruction." There was good reason for some of the praying—the oil rain shadow was thirty miles across and the gas reek downwind extended well beyond that.

To an astounded Union Oil, the Lake View gusher had been decidedly a mixed blessing. Not only was the company settling an array of damage claims and building emergency facilities because of the gusher, but, much more important, the tremendous quantity of Lake View crude remorsely drove the California price of oil to a low of thirty cents a forty-two-gallon barrel. On the other hand, the 1910-11 market did demonstrate its ability to absorb the large quantities of the gusher's crude, a sure indication of the radical shift to oil as an energy source. Only a half-century had elapsed since Edwin L. Drake brought in the world's first oil well in Pennsylvania.

Petroleum seepages had made a rich man out of Samuel Kier, a Pittsburgh druggist. His Kier's Rock Oil, a patent medicine which was supposed to cure most diseases and Kier's Petroleum Butter for burns and cuts was routine clipper cargo to California during the Gold Rush. Yet Professor Benjamin F. Silliman of Yale was convinced that there was a far more important use for petroleum. He believed a production-refining process could be developed which would produce coal oil (kerosene), an excellent source for both light and heat. Publication of Silliman's findings in 1855 stimulated systematic oil exploration and resulted in Edwin L. Drake's historic well at Titusville, Pennsylvania. Oil was brought in at a depth of seventy feet with the hole lined with stovepipe casing, Drake's own invention. The world's first oil rush took place shortly thereafter. Petroleum was selling for twenty dollars a forty-two-gallon barrel, and everybody was going to be rich.

Some did make money but most did not, despite the oil bonanzas of the Pennsylvania fields in succeeding years. In 1881 the Bradford district was pumping 100,000 barrels daily, four-fifths of the nation's entire production. Unfortunately, the transportation monopoly of the John D. Rockefeller organization, so much like the Big Four's railroad control in California, had a firm grasp on Pennsylvania oil movement to the Eastern seaboard and swung the wellhead market price at will. Faced with this effective monopoly, a number of the oil independents sensibly gave up and went to California, where there were supposed to be extensive but unproved petroleum lands. Two of them, Demetrius G. Scofield and Lyman Stewart, became substantial factors in the development of their adopted state as Scofield's enterprise evolved into Standard Oil of California and Stewart's into Union Oil Company. The genesis of both of these operations was in and around Pico Canyon, near Saugus and the Santa Clara River, in southern California.

Andres Pico, the Californio leader, had utilized the seepages of Pico Canyon (known as the Pico to early Western oil men) in the 1850s for asphaltum, and constructed primitive stills for grease and some very poor coal oil. There was a minor oil boomlet a decade later around the Pico and southern Ventura County. Young Civil War veterans like Thomas R. Bard and Denton C. Scott brought in tiny producing wells of the typical heavy black petroleum of California, and then found they had only a negligible coal oil market in competition with the light Pennsylvania crudes.

By building up to a 500-barrel-a-day rate in the Pico Field by 1880, D. G. Scofield established his Pacific Coast Oil Company as the principal factor at the time in California oil production. Scofield had learned by bitter experience all about the importance of railroads, pipelines and market control from that excellent and harsh teacher in the Pennsylvania oil fields, John D. Rockefeller. When the Pico production continued to grow and the Southern Pacific imperially established prohibitive rail rates for the fifty tank cars the Pacific Coast Oil had just bought, Scofield did not argue or plead. Without fanfare, he commenced construction of an oil pipeline to Ventura where his own vessels could carry the oil to San Francisco for his own refinery and distribution network. Forthwith, railroad freight rates for his company's oil were cut in half and Scofield stopped pipeline construction. The transplanted Pennsylvanian was a rare bird indeed. He had taken on the rail monopoly at the height of its power and beaten it.

Another independent who had been painfully educated by the Rockefeller group in the Pennsylvania fields was a Bible-quoting oil plunger by the name of Lyman Stewart, a schoolmate of Scofield. Son of a part-time Presbyterian pastor, a middle-aged Stewart swung down from a train in Los Angeles shortly before the Boom of the eighties. He had distinguished himself as a "seep geologist" and was envied for his Pennsylvania wildcatting ability, neither of which skills was of much value in the tangled rock strata of southern California. His holes were always dusty even though he induced his old oil partner, Wallace L. Hardison, to join him in California, along with a Pennsylvania contract drilling crew and rig, the best by far in the world. Another one of the Eastern expatriates, Isaac E. Blake, finally gave the desperate partners a hand. He turned over a lease in the Pico which Blake was reasonably sure would prove out. It did at 1600 feet with seventy-five barrels per day in 1884, only enough to keep Hardison and Stewart more or less solvent for additional dry or nearly dry holes interspersed with an occasional fruitful well. Still the partners' wells accounted for 50,000 barrels in 1887, about one-seventh of California's crude production.

By this time the Hardison and Stewart families were living in Santa Paula, the young oil capital of the state, while the two partners continued to address each other as Mr. Stewart and Mr. Hardison, even though either's word was the other's pledge. Lyman Stewart took his hat in hand to talk in Los Angeles to the important regional banker, Isaias W. Hellman, who was mildly interested in the developing oil industry. Stewart received a reluctant loan of $10,000 which "tided us over that period when everything else had failed." A year later Hellman turned Stewart down for additional loans but he did not call the outstanding debt. The banker's reason for refusing an increased loan was easy to understand. The partnership was borrowed to the hilt and beyond; the requirements for capital appeared to be insatiable. A recent associate, Thomas R. Bard, for a time provided equity money to finance additional ventures. Still, like the sorcerer's apprentice, the partners were running faster and faster, barely to stay up with the welling cash requirements.

Typical of the partners' continuing financial dilemma was the cost of transportation for their increasing oil production. The Southern Pacific refused to lower its tank-car rates, evidently convinced Hardison and Stewart could not afford an alternative choice of oil movement as threatened so successfully by D. G. Scofield a few years earlier. The badly pressed operators were forced to complete a four-inch pipeline from the Pico to tidewater at Ventura in 1886 and two years later had constructed "an expensive $40,000 steamer" with a capacity of about 4000 barrels. The pipeline and steamer finally accomplished the purpose of forcing the Southern Pacific to reduce rates. However, the oil men's jubilation did not last long. A few months after the vessel went into operation, either a galley fire or a lantern carelessly let down in an oil tank spread flames throughout the moored ship at Ventura wharf. By dawn the *W. L. Hardison* was a burned-out hulk, sold at public auction by the insurance company on the beach at San Buenaventura.

The personal financial affairs of Lyman Stewart and Wallace L. Hardison matched the serious straits of their enterprises. Again and again they borrowed money from each other, their relatives and their friends. Typical was a letter from Stewart to Hardison a few months after losing the oil tanker and shortly before the Union Oil Company was formed: "I saw Mr. Bixby today and he wants some money from me. . . . Can you help me out to the extent of $750? I am not very well; my head has given out again."

The new associate, Thomas R. Bard, who found himself increasingly involved in raising funds to keep the enterprise afloat, had good reason to wonder whether the game being played by the partners was worth the candle or, in this instance, the indifferent kerosene distilled from Western crude. To Bard there was an evident answer to the soul-exhausting cash drain with the associated desperate risks—leave oil refining, market development and sales distribution to others and concentrate on oil production. Such an approach was an anathema to a Lyman Stewart who would spend his last dollar on an oil lease and then readily place a second chattel mortgage on his properties for a refinery or a new product application. The furious squabbling between the conservative Bard and the oil plunger continued for years, and well after the partnership became the Union Oil Company in 1890. Their quarrels were exacerbated as time went by because Wallace Hardison, always the intermediary between the two, was evidently becoming more involved in California citrus rather than oil.

Union Oil grew because of or despite the wrangling of its principals. The young company surely had a plentitude of competition from a fresh array of southern Californian oil fields of the nineties.

Los Angeles with more than its share of petroleum seepages had enviously watched the early stages of oil excitement on the South Coast. Nothing had come from fragmentary searches for oil in and around the city until a man by the name of Doheny, by sheer chance, literally dug his way to Los Angeles' first oil strike.

Edward L. Doheny was just another itinerant prospector in the Southwest whose sole attribute appeared to be the ability of finding just enough gold and silver by bruising pick-and-shovel work to finance the next small strike. At age thirty-six, this smallish fellow had little to show for a life of hard work except a reputation for cold nerve and being an expert shot, thick calluses on his hands, and a friend and partner, Charles A. Canfield. The partners were in Los Angeles during the autumn of 1892 where a good bit of the saloon gossip was about petroleum and its seepages in and around the city. Only professional oil men like Lyman Stewart had learned expensively that an active oil exude was usually only a superficial indication of a shallow oil pool in the fractured rock strata of southern California. Not knowing any better, Doheny listened to the gossip and carefully examined seepages and brea (asphaltum) deposits in and around Los Angeles, and finally selected a seepage site for his and Canfield's oil-prospecting venture near Lake Shore and Patton streets, a few blocks south of present-day Echo Park.

Instead of using a cable tool or spring-pole rig, the partners disappeared like moles into the ground and did what they knew best—driving a pick-and-shovel mine shaft down vertically, hand-windlassing up the debris, and timbering as they went. There was encouragement below the forty-foot level when a heavy oil commenced exuding from the walls of the vertical shaft. At the 165-foot level the bottom of the hole began to fill with petroleum, and the neophyte oil men laboriously hand-pumped seven barrels a day to the tiny eye of blue sky at the surface.

The miners' production of a few barrels of oil a day in 1893 caused a gold-strike type of excitement in Los Angeles. Everybody and anybody who could lease or buy a twenty-five-foot city lot on the west side of the town of those days were trafficking in oil. One of the shrewdest operators was Emma A. Summers, a prosperous real estate agent in the district. After her first oil well on Court Street near Temple was a success, she neatly stitched together a pattern of strategically located city lots. Oil was brought in on many of these parcels, and for years Mrs. Summers was pointed out on the streets as the Oil Queen of Los Angeles. But the Queen was far more sensible than the bulk of sudden South Coast oil millionaires then or later. She saved her money, rode the local oil crest for a time and then calmly diversified into land along with apartments and commercial buildings.

The Los Angeles wells were shallow and cheap to drill—perhaps $1500 including a pump and storage tank. "Let's drill an oil well" was a password around town. And drill they did. Over a period of several years the proliferation of stumpy wooden derricks was extraordinary, fanning out over a narrow, curving four-mile strip of land. When the noise, confusion and stench of hundreds and hundreds of oil wells in a slim crescent had appalled even a case-hardened city council dedicated to civic boosterism during the economic depression, further oil drilling within Los Angeles city limits was declared a public nuisance. The local ordinance, however laudable, accomplished little.

Coincident with the City Council's petroleum drilling prohibition, domestic water suddenly came into acute short supply for a number of perspicacious citizens in and around the oil crescent. An evident cure to a parcel owner's desperate water scarcity was to drill a well. If fate or circumstance meant that oil was brought in rather than water, this of course was an official disappointment, but could be borne with equanimity.

Eventually the home-grown oil wells broke the price of petroleum when the Los Angeles field production in 1895 substantially exceeded all the other California oil fields combined. The

South Coast oil price finally bottomed out at twenty-five cents for a forty-two-gallon barrel, even a few cents lower than the market saturation price precipitated by the great gusher of 1910. The outpouring of crude from the shallow Los Angeles field soon tapered off, although it was more than a half-century later that the last of these old wells was finally sealed up.

After the city flurry, the principal search for petroleum moved north to the San Joaquin Valley around Bakersfield. Yet the biggest oil pool in the West would remain undiscovered for a while. This bonanza was the Greater Los Angeles Basin including much of the sea approaches to the harbor, two miles below the surface, and covering an area of more than a thousand square miles.

Paraphrasing an old Pat and Mike joke, oil exploration in southern California (and anywhere else in the world for that matter) was like sex in Ireland—it was and continued to be in its infancy. About all that was understood after a generation of southern California wildcatting was that the tangled, fractured rock strata of the district's rolling hills and plains had widely distributed oil sands, relics of geologic-age seas with their assorted vegetation and marine life. Other than the empirical petroleum knowledge a crew might have, the principal accouterments of any oil survey party of the day were extra sides of bacon, bags of fresh coffee and several canteens of whiskey. These were for campfire bartering with Basque sheepherders and range riders, for locations of oil seepages in the South Coast back country where the sheep and cattle grazed. The need for a more scientific approach to oil exploration was being recognized by men like H. M. Storey who wrote in a 1907 survey report of the Fort Tejon district of the Tehachapis:

"I feel convinced that an engineer with some idea of rocks and . . . the ability to discern between igneous, sedimentary and altered rock could do much toward producing the results desired. I do not claim that the application of scientific principles to surface structures will develop oil, but I do claim that careful study by the means suggested will reduce the percentage of failures . . .

I feel . . . that the condemning of miles of territory by hurried glances at the country is absurd."

Once the importance was recognized, petroleum geology developed rapidly bringing with it a special breed of young men possessing the inquiring minds of the technically trained. One by-product was the scientific curiosity of geologist William W. Orcutt and G. Allan Hancock, the owner of La Brea Ranch west of Los Angeles. They probed the bubbling asphaltum of the Brea tar pits and hauled out huge animal bones of another era. Overnight the asphaltum deposits became an international rendezvous for paleontologists. Hancock made a thirty-five-acre gift of the tar pits and surrounding land to Los Angeles County in 1916.

Most of California petroleum was heavy and viscous. Oil men muttered that "a barrel of Kern River crude would take a week to ooze down a flight of stairs, and a fly could trod over the surface without wetting its feet." The heavy California oil contained considerable carbon, almost no paraffin, and had a substantial asphalt residue. In the early 1900s while the South Coast was moving into first place as the leading producer of petroleum, a continuing series of matched races evolved between the swelling production tide of heavy oil and the development of additional applications for its use.

Kerosene, the prime refined petroleum product, was essentially closed to California output because of the type of the crude and the extent of distillation knowledge then available. However South Coast petroleum did make a fine fuel oil. Asphalt was of evident value for paving of streets, and experimentation was underway for asphalt roofing paper. Naphtha and other distillates were developed for cooking and heating stoves, and benzene was a valuable additive for paints and varnishes. There were a dozen different kinds of lubricating oils and greases being marketed. Gasoline was a dangerous nuisance with cans of it sold through hardware stores and a few garages, for clothes cleaning and use in a noisy experimental toy of the rich—a vehicle increasingly being called an automobile. The fuel oil markets offered the most immediate opportunities for profitably moving the swelling petroleum output. The man who saw this most clearly was Lyman Stewart. He was indefatigable in his efforts to develop successful power and heating applications, but the process was discouragingly slow.

There had been considerable experimentation in utilizing petroleum for fuel by the mid-1900s. The Russians were supposed to have varying degrees of success with locomotives powered by oil, and E. A. Edwards of Ventura had a U.S. patent issued for a supposedly improved oil burner. The experimental record of fuel oil for marine propulsion was a mixed bag in California. The *Pasadena*, a coastwise vessel, had to be ingloriously hauled into port by tug on its maiden fuel-oil voyage and the *Julia* had an engine-room explosion killing two people. Yet the Southern Pacific had three of its San Francisco Bay train-ferries converted to oil by the end of the eighties.

Industrial applications such as firing the boilers of the new sugar beet factories and the local utilities were developed, stimulated in part by the thousands of promotional oil barrels given away by the petroleum marketers. But the immediate and major fuel oil potential was the railroads. Yet the Southern Pacific had Utah coal mines and Australian coal, brought as ballast by sailing ships to Port Los Angeles at Santa Monica. The Santa Fe was scarcely more interested, but Lyman Stewart finally induced a subsidiary, the California Southern, to lend a locomotive to the Union Oil shops at Santa Paula.

An elderly locomotive with a towering stack wheezed onto the spur track of the Santa Paula shops in 1894. After weeks of fruitless experimentation by the Union Oil technicians, the engine wheezed out again still coal-powered, and the Southern Pacific enjoyed sending a sixty-dollar-track utilization bill to Union. For a man like Lyman Stewart and the people in his shops, who were convinced they were the best in the world in the oil tool and equipment business, the failure was intolerable. Intense collaboration work continued between Santa Paula and the San Bernardino shops of the Santa Fe. Late in 1894 the same elderly locomotive, now oil-fueled, hauled a string of freight cars up the difficult grade of Cajon Pass to the high desert. A major use for California petroleum had been proven out, and Lyman Stewart was pleased.

The development of a sparkling-clear kerosene with the prime burning characteristics of the Pennsylvania competition and which could sell at a comparable price remained a tantalizing challenge to the refiners of the heavy California oil. Eric Starke, a young chemist from the explosive powder industry, had finally demonstrated in 1896 that his fuming sulphuric acid process removed the aromatic hydrocarbons, the reason why California kerosene smoked. Starke's work remained a laboratory process because of the high price of sulphuric anhydride crystals, until chemical advances in the 1900s made the crystals available at acceptable costs. At long last South Coast kerosene was the equal of Pennsylvania's in quality and price; unfortunately at just about this time kerosene's usage for light and heat was dropping off sharply.

The tilted and faulted rock strata of southern California made oil drilling exasperatingly difficult, particularly when the wells went to greater and greater depths. These kinds of rock formation surely meant crooked holes, caving walls and lost strings of drill tools. The previous method of pounding a hole in the strata at depths over a few hundred feet was replaced with a steam-driven bull wheel and a rocking walking beam. The heavy impact tool at the end of a thick manila line was lifted and dropped by the beam. Around the 2000-foot depth, the rope that jerked the tool string had far too much stretch; lost tools and crooked holes were the result. Then specially designed wire cable was substituted for the rope and the stretch problem was cured.

Rotary drilling (a tool with a cutting edge, attached to a rotating string of pipe) was introduced in the 1900s and led to violent saloon arguments and some brawls between the rotary and cable tool crews on the merits of the two drilling methods. But both sides did agree on one point—neither system could drill a hole a mile or more in depth.

Yet one by one the deep hole problems were solved. Typical was the cumulative plague of underground water when drilling to the greater depths. Water, running from a soaked stratum, would stream down the space between the drill casing and the hole walls and saturate the oil sands below. Frank F. Hill, a veteran South Coast driller, came up with a solution. When a stratum of water-bearing sands was encountered. Hill pumped a concrete slurry down and inside the pipe with the pumping pressure squeezing the slurry back up the outside of the casing, filling up the space between the pipe and the walls of the hole. Oil well cementing was only one of a dozen drilling and refining techniques invented locally to handle the swelling output of southern California crude. Separated by thousands of miles from other oil production districts, the South Coast was forced to have its own petroleum shops and works, providing ample opportunity for brilliant, inventive people to push new developments in a whole array of satellite companies in the oil industry.

Petroleum exploration, production, transport and refining gave the South Coast its first broad and unique base of fresh industrial technology. This was shortly to be followed by fledgling motion pictures and in later years by aircraft, and then aerospace and electronics, each in its expansive days being in the forefront of technology.

Meanwhile the independent oil operator of the 1900s and 1910s on the South Coast had another matter on his mind. He had a feeling he was being watched from afar, and he was right. His increasingly successful wildcatting operations were under the interested surveillance of the saurian eyes of international oil, and particularly the Standard Oil Trust.

In New York City, 26 Broadway was probably a better-known address to the nation's financial community at the century's turn than 1600 Pennsylvania Avenue in Washington, D.C. The famed or notorious New York address, depending upon one's viewpoint, was the headquarters of the Standard Oil Trust and its principal operating companies.

The Trust was only involved in the distribution of petroleum products in the western part of the United States although the wildcatting activities in California were high on the agenda of investigation. The shallow wells of Los Angeles City had been of minimal interest to international oil. But the regular drumbeat of subsequent discoveries in the extreme southern end of the San Joaquin Valley and other South Coast fields by independents like Puente Oil were being heard around the world. Western production and refining was led by Union Oil as a result of Lyman Stewart's frenetic leasing and wildcatting activity, with the Pacific Coast Oil Company a poor second because its proven lands were being worked out. Despite Stewart's profound wariness of the Trust, 26 Broadway and Union Oil had had an uneasy courtship since 1895. Triggered initially by the eternal and driving requirements for cash of the South Coast company, the courtship was furthered by an increasing interest of the Trust in the Western fields.

The tilt toward California by 26 Broadway finally occurred with the successful wildcatting of Coalinga followed by the fantastic McKittrick and Kern River, all in the southern San Joaquin Valley. The Union Oil price asked by Stewart was considered too high, and late in 1900 Standard Oil bought D. G. Scofield's Pacific Coast Oil for $750,000, renaming it the Standard Oil Company of California. After learning of the Trust's acquisition Lyman Stewart wryly told one of his associates that "we cannot help ourselves so far as the situation is concerned and it is much better I think to be *pleased* with it."

The Western independents' fears of the Standard Oil Company of California and its powerful parent proved unwarranted. The 1900s turned out to be an era of trust busting, rapidly expanding oil consumption, and the discovery of light California crudes. The World War I decade brought in the Royal Dutch Shell Group with its American Gasoline (later the Shell Company of California). Associated Oil had blossomed from small beginnings in the early 1900s and there were other regional companies like General Petroleum, Captain William Matson's Honolulu Consolidated and Southern Pacific's Kern Trading and Oil. All of them to a greater or lesser extent had mineral rights or leases covering sections of the extensive U.S. lands in California, the title and lease tar baby of the 1910s.

Oil was a relatively late comer to the pantheon of the national Conservation Movement after the turn of the century. However, early in the Taft Administration large quantities of land were preliminarily withdrawn from public entry, lease or sale for oil exploitation. This action included 170,000 acres in Wyoming's Teapot Dome district and nearly 3,000,000 acres in California which impacted to some extent the Coalinga, Lost Hills, Belridge, McKittrick, Kern River and Olinda fields but particularly affected leasing activity in western Kern County. The government move caused consternation in the California oil industry. Confusion and turmoil over titles and leases reigned for a decade while a national oil policy was hammered out for Federal lands.

The Conservationists received strong support from an unexpected source in the middle stages of the stormy petroleum debate. The first two battleships, the *Oklahoma* and the *Nevada*, to be fueled by oil were under construction in 1912. With expert estimates in hand that domestic oil supplies would be exhausted in a half-century, (the writer's father took a similar position a few years later in testifying before a congressional committee), the Navy urged that petroleum reserves be set aside for Fleet use. President Taft concurred and late that year specifically allocated as a naval oil reserve 68,000 acres of Elk Hills/Buena Vista Hills of the southern San Joaquin Valley.

The battlelines were soon drawn on the Federal oil land issue. The Conservation forces moved aggressively under the leadership of Gifford Pinchot, the former Chief Forester, and a persuasive Josephus Daniels, Secretary of the Navy under Woodrow Wilson. Not for the last time the oil industry was pictured as actively and openly against the public interest. Finally in 1920 a kind of a compromise bill establishing Federal oil land policy was approved by the Congress. The bitter rhetoric of the charges and countercharges were dormant for a time, but then the Teapot Dome controversy several years later would bring it out again in full flower.

The violent disputes over the Federal lands were clear indication of the rapid expansion of the petroleum and the concomitant natural gas markets. By the early 1910s the previously ignored naphthas (gasoline and engine distillates) were receiving primary attention instead of the lordly kerosene of earlier decades. The internal combustion engine certainly had an enormous potential, and the engineering advances of a few years were making a practical vehicle out of the automobile. One company, Standard Oil of California, doubled its 1914 gasoline sales of two years earlier to 1,100,000 barrels. And the vast quantities of natural gas in the Kern County oil fields convinced William G. Kerckhoff that artificial gas in Los Angeles readily could be replaced for commercial and domestic use. A twelve-inch pipe line from the Kern County fields, 120 miles away, to Los Angeles became operational in 1913.

South Coast petroleum was big business, but many of the hard-shell independents were having difficulty in adjusting to their rarefied status as industrial statesmen. Probably leading all the rest in this regard was Lyman Stewart. To him, there was not the least separation between his activist religious and Temperance activities and the corporate affairs of his large Union Oil Company. His bankers and many stockholders did not share his views.

The Board of Directors of the Union Oil Company passed a resolution in 1897 which provided "that hereafter no work shall be carried on on Sundays, except in such cases where the field superintendent shall be of the opinion that the cessation of such work shall seriously affect the life of the well or permanently diminish its production." In a twenty-four-hour, seven-day-a-week industry it was laudable perhaps that Stewart's company was breaking trail in establishing a no-work Sabbath, but this was not happy news to the bankers of the debt-ridden firm.

The same year the Union Board authorized the construction of a chapel and the employment of a minister in the flourishing Torrey Canyon field near Piru. Shortly thereafter the Board allocated money for a "Temperance rendezvous to contain a Temperance bar, library, reading room, gymnasium, etc., for the purpose of giving men and boys a place to spend their evenings and help them out of saloons" and "disapproved the [expense account] charges made against the company for wine and cigars and extravagant hostelry expenditures." The driving force behind these and similar Union Oil activities was Lyman Stewart, a devout Presbyterian with strong evangelical leanings who only had been distracted from a missionary ministry by the infant oil industry of his home Pennsylvania county.

The Bible Institute of Los Angeles, the Presbyterian Church and Union Oil were intimately coupled in Lyman Stewart's mind. In this framework, nothing was more logical for the company founder in 1909 than to sponsor Robert Watchorn as corporate treasurer, over the substantial technical reservations of the rest of his Board of Directors. Watchorn was a prominent Presbyterian who shared Stewart's activist religious views and was so popular, according to his sponsor, that he was greeted at the church's national conventions "with the Chautauqua salute." How this type of popularity meshed with the intricate job of keeping the overextended company financially afloat was difficult for the other board members to comprehend.

To the increasing distress of the principal outside shareholders, the new corporate treasurer continued to exercise a powerful influence over a sporadically ill Stewart during the next several years. The Watchorn matter came to a climax after Lyman Stewart determined to raise money for his immediate personal affairs and church interests. The Union Oil founder had always drawn a minute salary and certainly could use additional funds. Equally important to Stewart (and Watchorn), if the Bible Institute was to carry on its central missionary program and hopefully to "provide a Bible for every Chinaman," large quantities of money were required. Robert Watchorn was more than agreeable to the idea of raising funds for the founder while presumably carrying out his corporate treasurer tasks.

Without informing his Board, Lyman Stewart authorized the Union Oil treasurer to sell a *transferable option* for the purchase at $150 per share of all Stewart's Union holdings. Watchorn readily sold the option for a million dollars, a very large sum. Stewart used half of the option payment for his own estate purposes and turned the other half of the fortune over to the Bible Institute with an equivalent amount of Union Oil securities.

The Union Board of Directors and principal shareholders like William R. Staats and Jared S. Torrance were first stunned and then infuriated when they learned of the unilateral action taken by Stewart and the treasurer. The option sale meant that anybody holding the transferable paper and who chose to exercise the option could, at his pleasure until the option expired years later, gain effective control of perhaps the principal independent oil company in the world. In the interim, long-term financing of Union's debts would be seriously hindered because of the unknowns connected with a new controlling management. A somber delegation called on Lyman Stewart to discuss the Board's alternatives in light of these considerations.

The upshot of the option matter in 1914 was the dismissal of Watchorn as Treasurer and the replacement of the oil plunger, as Chief Executive Officer, by his son, Will. The Board was rightfully convinced that the younger Stewart would have no difficulty in separating his religious activities from corporate affairs while providing a financial balance wheel which the company sorely needed. The famous option, never exercised, remained an ominous overhang on corporate affairs until its expiration.

The more conventional Will Stewart and the likes of him were the ones who carried the South Coast oil industry into the age of automobiles and another era of exciting crude discoveries.

CHAPTER 19

"The Model T was no Silver Ghost"

Inventors had been wrestling for decades with personal transportation contraptions like the two-wheeled "pedestrian hobbyhorse" of the early 1800s through the improved French velocipedes of a half-century later. All of them, made of wood, had a common defect—an exasperatingly low gear ratio for effective pedaling. The high-wheeler bicycle of the 1870s was an engineering fix of sorts to this problem because of a five-foot front wheel and a trailing twenty-inch back wheel. Then, almost miraculously, the ultimate solution appeared. This was the Rover Safety Bicycle of the mid-1880s, English-designed and produced, which incorporated the principal features of all bicycles since the Rover. As happens with most important technical systems, a number of key inventions were proven out at about the same time and made the new bicycle possible—the bush-roller chain, ball bearings in a wheel hub, the pneumatic tire and a light tubular steel frame. For the first time man had the means at hand for efficient and self-propelled travel over considerable distances.

Cycling buffs were initially young people, and imaginative designers and engineers flocked into the exciting industry. Unit prices dropped from a $75 to $100 range to an expensive but manageable $15 to $30 at the turn of the century, with several hundred U.S. factories producing a million bicycles a year. "The riders of the silent steed," which the South Coast newspapers called the cyclists, organized touring, social and racing clubs, and the fad obviously required the selection of proper bicycle costumes. A tank-suit top and short tights for the male cyclist

was soon the accepted mode; the bifurcated skirts of some of the
members of the ladies' spinning clubs remained a subject of
prime male interet and intense female debate.

The Southern California Division of Wheelmen was popular
enough to schedule an 1894 annual meeting at the Sweetwater
Track in San Diego and many members arrived on their own
bicycles. The Wheelmen's races, parades and Grand Ball at the
prestigious Hotel Coronado dramatized the public's new passion
for this personal transportation and racing machine. For the
first time the farmer and the beleaguered horse-and-buggy doctor
had some powerful and understanding support from the urban
areas for better country roads. Horace Dobbins went even
further than that—he proposed to construct a bicycle throughway
between Pasadena and Los Angeles. The Dobbins cycleway was
to be ten feet wide, lighted by electricity, elevated to an average
height of fifteen feet and designed for gentle grades. A mile and
a quarter of this cycleway was actually built in 1900. But the
bicycle, the father of the horseless carriage and a beloved uncle
of the flying machine, was soon shuttled aside by its progeny,
and ventures like Mr. Dobbins' cycleway died aborning.

Other than for a few sporty rich to amuse themselves most
people could see little future for the horseless carriage. Sharing
this feeling, Woodrow Wilson flailed at the automobile fans in a
1906 speech: "Nothing has spread socialistic feeling in the
country more than the automobile; to the countryman they are a
picture of arrogance and wealth, with all of its independence
and carelessness."

There appeared to be even less reason for these noisy and
smelly vehicles on the South Coast. The interurban passenger
and freight network was unequaled in the world and the local
trolleys blanketed the urban areas. The increasing mileage of
paved streets in Los Angeles for bicycles, buggies and wagons
was a continuing source of pleasure to an older generation who
remembered the adobe mud and dust with absolutely no nostalgia. As to rural roads, Governor George C. Pardee in his 1907

message to the California state legislature could only see the need of such roads "for the saving of money in horseflesh, harness, wagons, time and draught power." Some years would elapse before a state highway designed for automobiles would be built in California.

The horseless carriage continued to be both a challenge and a major annoyance into the early 1910s. Social etiquette books sensibly emphasized that "no young lady should go alone with a gentleman on an extended afternoon motoring trip. An automobile often stops without apparent cause and is sometimes in disrepair for hours or even all night." Such official warnings for protection of virtue had particular merit because motor rallys were being scheduled at more distant places by sporty fanatics, as they were unlovingly called by harried drivers of teams. Typical of a big local rally was a Run and Barbecue to May Rindge's Malibu Ranch, in from the seacoast and a dozen or so miles north of Santa Monica. The ranch was only accessible via a rough wagon road built a few feet above the surf and below mountain flanks along the coast.

It was hard on those who might have wanted to sleep late on the day of the Run, a bright April Sunday in 1910. The Automobile Club of Southern California, not yet an adolescent itself, had scheduled the Malibu Ranch rally with the assembly point to be the club's tiny office in Los Angeles. The rocketing engine and booming exhaust noises supplemented by occasional banshee howls caused by erratic gearshifting of nearly 250 horseless carriages converging on the club from all directions sent teams bucking, dogs barking and any number of householders cursing those senseless sporty fanatics.

After much bellowing of instructions and enjoyable horn blowing, the trek to Malibu through Santa Monica was underway over Los Angeles' streets whose speed limit was twenty miles per hour, reduced to a six-mile limit at an intersection. Once outside the city, the line of automobiles accommodated its pace to the potholes of the dirt road and absorbed itself into a moving dust cloud several miles long. The first dropouts from the caravan occurred minutes after the Run was underway, primarily because of flat tires which meant tube patching, casing repair and tire pumping.

Priding themselves on the speed of their repairs, the stragglers hastened to catch up to the group, and to do so was a driver's delight. Having a feeling of positive omnipotence, the operator lightly gripped the tiny, jiggling steering wheel of his vehicle and only took white-knuckled control at the last expert moment, just before the vehicle commenced a spin. All of these maneuvers tended to be somewhat hard on the crew. While delicately sweating during the tire-changing episode and then bouncing with the corkscrew motion of the hard-riding open automobile, the driver's chilled and muffled passengers breathed in and were soon cloaked with succeeding layers of adobe dust. There was little question that to enjoy a run, a passenger had to be a fanatic, hopelessly involved with an automobile zealot, or a damned fool.

A majority of the automobiles and their crews successfully absorbed the dust, forded streams, fought sand and bumped through gullies to reach the blessed relief of the Malibu sycamore grove. The Run's success was assured when the vehicles carrying the food, beer and a twelve-piece band rolled into the rendezvous. While automobile repairs were the first priority, barbecued beef and beans uplifted by beer and shop talk were not far behind. A baseball game for the energetic between the "four-cylinders" and "six-cylinders" competed for attention with the usual picnic exercises of a sack race and a three-legged competition. Most of the automobiles were back in Los Angeles by early evening with the drivers lighting their vehicles' carbide-gas head lamps at early dusk. But a good many of the rally entrants did not make it back; their cars were hauled to city garages by teams the next morning.

The Malibu was a grand Run.

Gas-engined automobiles were outsold by electrics and steamers in the early 1900s. The electric's propulsion evolved from the motors of trolley design and operated off batteries, and the first automobile to cover a mile in less than a minute was an electric. The technical difficulty with this type of vehicle then and later was that there was only one of two choices in using it— go fast for a short time or move sedately for a modest distance. The steamer automobile was a natural heir of the steam age of the nineteenth century and mechanics understood the boiler, engine and pumping systems. The Stanley brothers' name became synonymous with the steamer, and one of their vehicles set an automobile speed record of 128 miles per hour in 1906. In spite of their early promise, steamers faded out by the early 1920s, principally because the gas-engined automobile delivered the same or better performance at less cost and effort.

But in the 1900s a gas-engined vehicle was noisy, cantankerous, bone-shaking, and trailed oily smoke; the thing had little reason for existing at all. The engine ran, if it ran at all, after laborious cranking, and a faulty spin of the crank could mean a sprained or broken forearm. Shifting gears was a new art form. A minor whiplash injury was a potential penalty for failure to practice the procedure precisely and a horrendous noise of metal clashing was often an unwelcome bonus. Controlling the automobile with a tiller or a minute steering wheel could be both exhausting and terrifying because direct coupling with the road movement of the front wheels gave a disconcerting jiggle to the steering column which required expert adjustments by the driver. Otherwise the car went into dismaying oscillations. The two-wheel braking system was unbelievably bad and further hindered by knife-edged tires of three-inch width. Braking accidents only remained at a tolerable level because of low car speeds and traffic density.

The noise of a gasoline engine had no saving graces; it had a gnawing, pneumatic-drill quality calculated to put any pedestrian's teeth on edge. But for the automobile's occupants the worse thing of all was the engine vibration, and not because the passengers were given the mobile version of Saint Vitus' dance. Much more important, at least to the automotive zealots, everything which could possibly shake off the vehicle did with traumatic operating results. This type of phenomena moved one owner to comment wryly: "First, don't believe over one-half you read in the printed catalogue; second, never wear a silk hat, frock coat and white linen on an auto trip; they don't look well after an accident." Of course, none of these problems existed unless the gasoline engine could be induced to start. One doctor made some cogent observations on this subject in the *Horseless Age:*

"I have seen an expert work on a gasoline machine all day, and then after it got to running be unable to tell which of his various adjustments had accomplished the end in view. . . . The usual repair shop would hardly care to tackle the mechanism of the gasoline engine, and if the carriage is purchased from a manufacturer some hundreds of miles away the element of time and expense involved is rather appalling. Another trouble with the gasoline machines is that . . . many of them cannot be pulled by a single horse. . . . If one gets down into a ditch it is practically impossible to do anything without the assistance of quite a gang of men."

The evolution of expensive automobiles from a rich man tinkerer's toy to a trustworthy and reliable vehicle incorporating inventions like the self-starter only took a little more than a decade. The Rolls-Royce Silver Ghost of the 1910s became the embodiment of this change, and its quietness in operation a symbol of automotive excellence. Later generations of the Rolls, including the writer's present day Silver Shadow, would continue in this tradition, and the silence in the passenger compartment while cruising at any speed was and is impressive.

The Model T was no Silver Ghost. And Mr. Ford's famous vehicle was never intended to be that. What Henry Ford accomplished was of far more importance. Oftentimes called a flivver or Tin Lizzie, the Model T transformed world transportation because it was cheap and reliable, beautifully engineered so that much of it could be repaired by a farmer or handyman. For years some of its parts were routinely stocked next to the hardware section in countless variety stores. The T's 22-hp, four-cylinder engine moved the car up to forty miles an hour, fast enough with the body rattling and bouncing on its transverse springs. Henry Ford did not invent mass production, but he was the first to use its economies on a massive scale. A quarter of a million of his cars sold in 1914 and carried a $490 price tag (the T reached its all-time low of $290 in 1924). Flivvers had no batteries prior to the installation of some self-starters in 1919; the T made its own electricity from a magneto built into the flywheel. Hand cranking of the vehicle obviously required agility and patience in the procedure described by Richard R. Mathison for a chilly winter morning in Los Angeles:

"If you have a Model T, you climb in on the right side, as there is no lefthand door. You set the spark and throttle levers like the hands of a clock at ten minutes to three. . . . You slip your left forefinger through a wire loop near the radiator and pull it while you cautiously give the crank a twirl with the right hand. When the motor finally catches, you leap to the shuddering running board and move the spark and throttle to twenty-five minutes to two. If the engine is too cold and dies, you repeat the rite until it starts again . . ."

Nobody had any experience in designing roads for automobiles and trucks. And even if someone had, the vehicles were metamorphosing so quickly, and the number of cars increasing at such a fast rate, that highway design specifications would have been obsolete before they were implemented. The result was technical and design confusion while the surfaced roads crept out of the cities and towns into the countryside of California.

Los Angeles County took the lead in highway construction when the voters approved a 1908 bond issue of $3,500,000 to build and improve a county system, and five years later there were 300 miles of surfaced roads of sorts, while a bustling Los Angeles had nearly 700 miles of paved streets. With a minimum of forethought and planning, California in 1910 had its first highway bond issue of $18,000,000. In an inspirational and optimistic mood Governor Hiram Johnson told his fledgling highway officials: "Gentlemen, you face a tough job! You are expected to build for $18 million a highway system that the best engineers of the country have estimated will cost from $35 million to $50 million . . ." The tough job proved to be insurmountable. The state's roads resulting from the first bond issue ranged from very poor to indifferent.

If widespread boodling, stupidity and extravagance could have been blamed for the road fiascos, the whole subject would have been much more interesting to the taxpayer. The actual reasons made for poor newspaper reading. Four-inch pavements laid on negligible foundations with inadequate subsoil drainage preparation could not stand up to the increased automobile and truck traffic. After a few months the pavements commenced falling apart, and the standard lifetime for many South Coast roads was only a little more than four years.

The roads which survived were obsolete. More vehicles driven at faster speeds with the pitifully inadequate braking systems of the day made for a gruesome carnage at the narrow bridge approaches and the hairpin and poorly banked highway curves. Annual traffic deaths nationally reached the 20,000 mark by the end of the 1910s. This meant that an automobilist then had about six times greater chance of being killed than a motorist a half-century later. These dreadful statistics may have discouraged some drivers but not many. Most could only see the mud holes and the choking dust disappearing with the new pavements, while vehicle reliability was much improved and the improved tires now were on quick demountable rims. Dominating everything for the ordinary man was the feeling of magnificent independence which was worth every uncomfortable mile of the Model T and all its ilk.

The Wright brothers demonstrated the feasibility of manned flight in December of 1903, only to discover their dramatic news generated profound public disinterest. Flying machines were thought to be impossible by a good many; some could see their use at the best limited to a few sportsmen; and, anyway, the bulk of the people believed a flying machine was similar to a dirigible airship. Wilbur Wright had flown for fifty-nine seconds; Santos-Dumont had already cruised his dirigible around the Eiffel Tower for an hour. So what was newsworthy about the 605-pound "whopper flying machine" of the Wrights?

The dirigible airship or steerable balloon was the principal aeronautical interest of the early 1900s. Supposedly, $200,000 in prize money and guarantees were to be offered to participants in the air show at the 1904 St. Louis Fair. And it was there that young A. Roy Knabenshue, competing against Alberto Santos-Dumont of France, became the first man to fly a powered lighter-than-air vehicle in America. Two months later Knabenshue piloted his *Arrow* over Los Angeles—taking off from Chutes Amusement Park, reaching an altitude of 3,000 feet, cruising over the city for an hour and a half, and finally touching down where he started. This, the best airborne flight to that time in the United States, technically impressed the New York *Times* with the potentialities of the dirigible, in contrast with the newspaper's lack of interest in the Wrights' flight a year earlier:

"The airship was maneuvered by Knabenshue in every direction, responding readily to the rudder, circling and turning in any direction, sailing directly in the face of wind at any angle and rising and dipping as the operator directed. . . . Knabenshue regulated the height by shifting his weight [precariously running back and forth on a fragile platform] and raising or lowering the bow of the craft as he desired to ascend or descend."

Meanwhile, the neglected flying machine was rapidly outgrowing its swaddling clothes. In 1909 Louis Bleriot easily flew across the English Channel, with the evident implications of breaching the water defenses of the British Isles by air power. Glenn H. Curtiss, Glenn L. Martin and the Farman brothers along with the pilots of the vastly improved Wright machines were staying in the air an hour or so. Belatedly, the general public became absorbed in the excitement of heavier-than-air flight; the 1909 International Aviation Meet in France at Rheims brought newspaper headlines in both hemispheres. Los Angeles, on the other side of the world, announced it would have another international meet the following January.

Caught up in a rash of civic boosterism, the Los Angeles Merchants and Manufacturers Association optimistically underwrote all the expenses of this proposed world aviation competition, including $80,000 in prize moneys and guarantees. More sober counsel argued that the air show could be an expensive fiasco because of the South Coast's geographical isolation. A worried M & M board asked David A. Hamburger, Perry W. Weidner and Lynden E. Behymer to head a Meet Arrangements Committee to salvage what they could.

After much debate, technical and otherwise, agreement was reached on a site for the Los Angeles aviation competition, and the owners of the land allowed the use of several hundreds of acres without a rental charge. The location was Dominguez Hill, a sort of a small butte/mesa adjacent to the railroad and inter-urban tracks to Long Beach and San Pedro. Picking up the lift of the prevailing westerly wind, the hill stood out from the surrounding plains and was the center of the old Rancho San Pedro, now owned by the daughters of Don Manuel Dominguez.

Having a fine site adjacent to transportation, the Meet Arrangements Committee of the M & M sensed that its task was going to be easier than the worried board expected. The international publicity was well received and the local civic support was excellent. Best of all, now there was every indication that the people would come in droves to the competition. And how right the committee was, even though the succeeding waves of customers continued to complain about the concessionaires' poor "five cent coffee which cost ten cents." The Los Angeles Aviation Meet had 20,000 spectators crowded into a big wooden grand-stand for the opening events on a Monday, January 10, 1910. An astonished M & M board happily counted 176,000 paid spectators for the ten-day air show; after all the bills were paid, the local sponsors received their money back plus a handsome cash dividend.

A good reason for the sustained popularity of the Meet was the lively newspaper reports of the opening day's activities. One of the articles tells of a biplane's takeoff through the eyes of a spectator seeing the wonders of manned flight for the first time:

"Over the grass—before your startled gaze!—while your eyes are popping out!—why, man alive, look at that!—the airship picks up astonishing speed! Like an express train she's flying and hurrah! she leaves the ground!—glides upward—higher! and higher, at one hundred miles an hour, off into the blue—hip, hip-hooray!"

The brave men in their flying machines, dirigibles and balloons dominated conversation on the South Coast, and the number of world headlines was a reflection of the public's absorption in flight. Roy Knabenshue in the *Arrow* precisely circled a captive balloon in front of the Dominguez grandstand at one altitude while Lincoln Beachey maneuvered his airship below the *Arrow* and a number of flying machines buzzed about. Followed by the amazed gasps of the grandstand crowd, Glenn Curtiss whipped his biplane around the pylons of an octagonal mile-and-a-half course in just over two minutes, an international speed record. But Louis Paulhan of France, shortly christened "the little man-bird" by the press, was the lionized daredevil of the Los Angeles Meet. Flying just below the dirigibles, he swooped his flimsy flying machine with its sputtering, cranky engine at the jammed grandstand. Spinning at the last moment, Paulhan then casually landed in the center of the field amid a roar of crowd acclaim.

The little man-bird also won the prizes for altitude and endurance, both world records (4,140 feet and an hour and forty-nine minutes respectively). The excitement caused by the Frenchman's cross-country flights equaled his new records:

"Paulhan flew to San Pedro—over the site of the new fortifications [Fort MacArthur], over the Palos Verdes Hills, out over the sea-swept cliffs of Point Fermin, out toward the breakwater and across the harbor. A sleepy deckhand on a tug looked, hastily rubbed his eyes, and looked again and shouted to the pilot. Then the shrill shriek of the whistle aroused the shipping and in a twinkling the harbor and the town awoke. Bells were rung and the crowd rushed out to see the aviator who had so strangely and silently swept across the sky."

The International Aviation Meet ended on January 20 with a parade: "There were men on horseback, in an oxcart, on bicycles and motorcycles, in automobiles, in a carriage and in an aeroplane." The finish of the air show brought no civic hangover; the South Coast and the performers had relished every day of the well-run competition. Speakers at a celebrative banquet, chaired by Max Meyberg, soon ran out of superlatives. Indeed, the Meet was one of the best aviation parties ever.

CHAPTER 20

"The lunatics have taken charge of the asylum"

For those used to the five-cent flickers of a few years earlier, the 1918 opening of the plush Million Dollar Theater in Los Angeles seemed almost inconceivable. Here was a 2,500-seat movie house, and the center of a twelve-story office building at Third and Broadway streets. The premiere had two excellent motion pictures—a Western of William S. Hart and a Mack Sennett comedy. A double line of patrons several blocks long waited patiently to buy tickets, and the world-famous principals of the young motion picture industry were expected to and did attend the premiere—Charles Chaplin, Mary Pickford, Mack Sennett, William S. Hart and even an obscure Cecil B. DeMille.

Such opulence was a quantum leap from Talley's Electric Theater of the 1900s, only two blocks away at Third and Main streets. Thomas L. Talley, a minor penny-arcade operator, converted the rear part of his arcade into a movie show. He bought a secondhand film projector from a vaudeville theater, gambling that the common man hungered for cheap entertainment which the flickering movies of the day might provide. Talley was right. While the middle class, the media and the well-to-do ignored or scoffed at the ventures, hole-in-the-wall movie shows followed Talley's example and opened around the country.

In an age of scientific miracles, the placement of one-inch-square film images on a sprocketed Celluloid strip which, when turned, gave the illusion of motion did not overly impress its famous inventors, Thomas Edison and George Eastman. After the perfection of this novelty in 1889, about the only use that was made of it commercially was in Kinetoscope parlors or arcades. By dropping a penny in the slot and peering into an aperture, a strip of film in the machine could be cranked in front of a light and a minute of action, risque for the day, would be seen. Provocative titles like "How Bridget Served the Salad Undressed" established the popularity of the arcades if not their reputation for probity.

Projection of the one-inch film images on a larger-than-life screen was finally authorized by Edison, and the Kinetoscope Company gave the first public performance in 1896 at New York's Koster & Bials' Music Hall. The illusion of a train charging from the screen created a profound audience impression for a time, but a few years later motion pictures had become a tag-end filler in vaudeville house performances. Following Talley's lead, secondhand projection machines were bought by other penny-arcade operators who sensed an underlying demand for motion pictures at small admission prices. A typical entrepreneur rented a vacant store, set up a screen of sorts, accumulated a number of broken-down chairs and opened for business; the audience was the workingmen, the young and the bums sleeping off a drunk. Called nickelodeons (the admission price was five cents), the rooms and the clientele often stank and the splintery floors were stained with tobacco juice. Still the customers came and came again.

The sustained nickelodeon demand for movies brought about the development of a fairly good orthochromatic film. But with a speed of only about one-tenth that of the mid-1970s product, the cameraman's prime emphasis was focus and exposure. Unfortunately, nothing could be done with orthochromatics' propensity for making all performers look peculiarly white or pale. On the other hand, camera optics reflected major German advances and were good. Film exposure was determined by judgment and past experience, and the results of expensive location shots were often verified by a portable but cumbersome development unit. Under any circumstances, handling of the film negative was crucial, and the prudent cameraman inspected his negative on the development drum after a day's shooting.

Lighting was the perennial problem. For interior shots a roofless stage was preferred with adjustable cloth baffles strung across the top of the structure to control the amount of natural light. Artificial illumination was unsatisfactory at the best. The Klieg arc lights flickered at the wrong time while the players sweated through their makeup and complained bitterly of "arc-light dust" or "Klieg eyes," an inflammation caused by ultraviolet rays.

When the silent movie told a story, the audience could become deeply involved, interpreting the characters and imagining their voices. Edwin S. Porter was the first to recognize this in 1903 with his *Life of an American Fireman* and *The Great Train Robbery*. But the technical potentialities of the narrative concept were submerged and then forgotten for a time until a D. W. Griffith would recognize the importance of Porter's breakthrough. Meanwhile, the infant industry was controlled by a trust who saw only a limited future for motion pictures.

A pear-shaped little man by the name of Carl Laemmle, a nickelodeon owner who expanded into the wholesaling of films, was the unwitting central force which propelled the movies into a major new art form with broad-base appeal. The interlocked Motion Pictures Patents and General Film companies apparently had the patent position, money and monopoly power to control the nickelodeon industry. There was to be no place for a brash and noisy Laemmle and other independent film wholesalers. Laemmle appeared to be either foolhardy or stupid when he refused to quit or sell out. It turned out he was neither. Understanding the violent antipathy the nickelodeon operators felt toward the Trust by the early 1910s, the film wholesaler moved to the attack with an inspired series of cartoon advertisements which attracted national attention in a trust-busting era. Forming his own producing firm, the Independent Motion-Picture Company, Laemmle and others like him were the first to sense that nickelodeon customers, contemptuously disposed of as an assortment of "immigrants, children, chambermaids and street car conductors" could and would pay somewhat more for better and longer movies. The question was where and how to make these new types of motion pictures.

An optimistic claim of 350 sunny days a year by the Los Angeles Chamber of Commerce brought two unnoticed and unusual manufacturing firms to the South Coast in 1906 and 1907, the Biograph Company and a contingent of the Selig Company from Chicago. William N. Selig had sent a one-reeler (ten minutes of screen time) troupe on location around the country and the director, Francis Boggs, and a retread stage actor by the name of Hobart Bosworth made a nickelodeon film, the first in the West, called *The Power of the Sultan*. The movie was shot on a vacant lot in a residential district near Seventh and Olive streets.

Selig's traveling troupe managed to convince the Chicago movie maker as to the natural stage lighting possibilities of the South Coast. The result was a tiny studio on Los Angeles' Allessandro Street near Echo Park and present-day Glendale Boulevard. Shortly thereafter Kessel & Baumann built an open stage a block down the street. The K & B operation was subsequently the Edendale headquarters of the legendary Keystone Company of Mack Sennett.

The crossroads village of Hollywood toddled into history in 1911 merely because Al Christie won a coin toss, and his Nestor film company came to California instead of Florida as a result. Rejecting sensible locations in Edendale (a lyrical subdivision name), Christie went miles into the country, northwest of central Los Angeles. He bought acreage around a moribund Blondeau's Saloon on a dusty lane, later to be called Sunset Boulevard; and still later, Christie's old studio would become the site of a major CBS installation. Behind the saloon Christie and Charles Rosher "made one-reel pictures like *Indian Raiders,* directed by Tom Ricketts, with real Indians brought in from New Mexico by Jack Parson, who later started the Western Costume Company."

Other film companies drifted into the South Coast not only because their shooting schedules had fewer delays due to bad weather but also for the solid legal reason of putting the maximum distance possible between themselves and the patent infringement tentacles of the Trust. In the 1910s Los Angeles, by a combination of several unlikely chances, found itself to be the center of production in the most glamorous new industry of the world. True there were dissidents to the nearly uniform praise for the South Coast. Francis X. Bushman was unequivocal in stating his preference for New York and artificial lighting. He despised southern California's haze, the morning low clouds and occasional outright fog. Whatever Bushman's opinions and those of others like him, eighty percent of the world's motion pictures were being produced on the South Coast by the end of World War I. The result was a pool of technical skills unequaled anywhere else and epitomized best by the directing genius of David W. Griffith and his cameraman, G. W. Bitzer.

A one-reeler, *The Adventures of Dolly,* brought a freshman director to Los Angeles in 1908. A stage actor with strong Southern attachments, D. W. Griffith told his wife shortly after he took the directing job in the disreputable industry that "we can't go on forever and not tell our friends and relatives how we are earning our living."

Fortunately for Griffith and the technical progress of the movies G. W. "Billy" Bitzer, a cameraman, was assigned by the Biograph Company to indoctrinate the new director. For years the two of them went a long way toward creating a fresh medium of artistic expression. In fifteen months, Griffith directed a hundred or so one-reel movies. During this period the new director almost casually added to the technical repertoire of film making the "long shot-mid shot-close shot" sequential combinations, the technical building blocks of any present-day movie. Then with the combinations of shots available the highly creative function of film editing and composition was shortly introduced. All the basic tools were now at hand to make a fine motion picture.

While the Trust was limiting movie directors like Griffith to two-reelers (twenty minutes of screen time), the independents and some Italian and French producers were experimenting with four- and five-reel pictures. A frustrated Griffith finally was in a position with his new employer, Mutual Film, to produce a major feature movie. His choice was controversial—*The Clansman,* a white Southerner's view of the Civil War and the painful reconstruction years following the conflict. Released as *The Birth of a Nation* in 1915 and premiered in Los Angeles' Philharmonic Auditorium, it was then shown around the nation. The film story and treatment brought accolades, virulent headlines and editorial comments, and a huge box office. Oftentimes overlooked because of the controversy was a fluid narrative equivalent to any excellent picture a half-century later.

The indomitable Billy Bitzer was the sole cameraman throughout Griffith's masterpiece even for Civil War scenes involving many hundreds of extras. Lying flat on the ground while a cavalry troop jumped over him in the thickening dust was one of the expected hazards. However, Bitzer did feel that the battle sequences became most realistic for him when Griffith became absorbed in the action:

"The fireworks men shooting smoke bombs over the camera—most of them exploding outside camera range—and D. W. shouting, 'Lower, lower, can't you shoot those damn bombs lower?' 'We'll hit the cameraman if we do,' answered the fireworks brigade, and bang! one of them whizzed past my ear. The next one may have gone between my legs for all I knew. But the bombs were coming into the camera field so it was okay. As I write this, looking at my hand, it still shows the blue powder specks from the battlefield . . ."

The Birth of a Nation was a difficult act to follow even for its creator. D. W. Griffith went on to *Intolerance,* a costly technical success and a serious money loser. The movie's sets of Babylon, which towered over the raw subdivisions of California bungalows on Sunset Boulevard, would only be topped in film history by the 1922 *Robin Hood.* Not surprisingly, Billy Bitzer took his camera up in a captive balloon on the Belshazzar palace set. In the days before camera cranes, Bitzer was slowly raised or lowered while he was expected to compensate for a lurching balloon reacting to errant wind currents, moving around and through the huge plaster structures.

While the master of the motion picture was developing the narrative feature film, Hollywood (as it was increasingly being called) was moving into other forms of the art—the serial, the Western and the comedy. Los Angeles and its environs soon became used to seeing both actors and actresses swing from trees to ledges and trains, stunt on newfangled aeroplanes and automobiles, and make incredible jumps on horses. Doubles were occasionally used in these sequences, but in the main the actual physical feats were done by the performers themselves. Action piled on action was the keystone of what became known as a serial. Every serial episode (usually shown weekly) ended on a pinnacle of disaster from which the heroine must somehow be extricated. The publicity advance on the ninth episode of *The Perils of Pauline* gives an idea of serial tension and suspense which would quiet any young matinee audience of that day:

"Pauline [Pearl White] flees to the shore, persuades a hydroplane pilot to take her to safety. As they soar aloft, he lights a cigarette, flicks away the match, which lights on one of the wings, and in a few mintues the machine is in flames. Coward that he is, he grabs the only parachute and leaves Pauline to her fate . . ."

The artificial one-reel Westerns made in the early days of the flickers had little to recommend them other than filling a screen for ten minutes, and then only in the nickelodeon's heyday. A Wild West show in winter quarters near Santa Monica and a young director, Thomas H. Ince, combined to change the unpromising outlook for Westerns. Early in 1912 Ince rented the entire touring show and commenced shooting horse action film with the backdrop of the rugged Coast Mountains. The resulting two-reelers were good, and the films became superior when Ince and actor William S. Hart joined forces two years later. Raised in the frontier environment of the northern plains, Hart even had some understanding of the Sioux language, learned as a boy, and more than enough knowledge of the itinerant cowhand. He convinced Ince that authenticity and realism in the exterior and interior scenes of the Westerns were imperative; horse falls and saloon brawls would be bloody and painful with no doubles.

Hart then created a sweet-and-sour kind of an outlaw character which had sustained international public appeal. Reviewing the French showing of *The Narrow Trail,* Jean Cocteau in 1917 wrote that "M. Ince may be proud of himself, for a spectacle such as this seems in recollection to equal the world's greatest literature." Even an M. Hart and an M. Ince might have considered this review a bit of exaggeration.

While scarcely equivalent to the world's greatest literature, one of the best things that happened for the world in the early 1910s and a long time thereafter was Mack Sennett. After carefully auditing the new techniques of D. W. Griffith, young Sennett established his Keystone Company in the old K & B facilities near Los Angeles' Echo Park. Then he proceeded to invent a kind of screen comedy which defied duplication, while an array of talents bloomed under his direction. Nobody could complain that life at Keystone was dull—140 films were shot in the first full year of operation and Los Angeles, particularly its police, found the Keystone field units a nuisance. At this hectic production pace, Sennett had crews and actors scattered around the city slowing up traffic with location shots or filming special events like a Knabenshue dirigible ascension with actors getting in the way of the action.

A nuisance the Keystone Company may have been to the local police but to the rest of the public Sennett and his talented corps had the easy ability "of creating satire sharp as a needle while simultaneously extracting the sting. Policemen all over the world guffawed as heartily as their neighbors at the Keystone Kops. . . . Nothing was sacred to Sennett. . . . Frenzied beatings caused the pain of a pinprick, hundreds of bullets produced no fatalities. In Sennett's world all lawyers were shysters, all pious people hypocrites, all sheriffs stupid and venal, and in that world everybody was caught with his pants down."

For these or better reasons most people found they had a common denominator with each other while viewing the flood of one- and two-reel comedies coming from Los Angeles. They laughed and laughed.

The tramp of Charlie Chaplin and Mary Pickford's grown child/little woman role created the star system in Hollywood with its attendant fantastic rewards and public adulation. Chaplin developed the tramp figure at Sennett's studio in 1914. The powerful character projection of a bewildered, pathetic little man possessing a doltish obstinacy shortly had Chaplin earning an unheard-of $10,000 a week (in mid-1970s purchasing power, about $50,000) from Mutual Film Corporation. And this was in the day of only a minute income tax.

Mary Pickford's films were also proving immensely popular, and she asked for and got from Paramount earnings equivalent to those of Chaplin's. Finally, Adolph Zukor felt Paramount had reached the absolute limit that the studio could pay its well-publicized "America's Sweetheart." The movie executive came up with a strategy to put "Little Mary" in check. William C. de Mille, a fascinated spectator, loved to tell about the resulting conference between the producer and his famous star:

"With compassionate eye and throbbing voice, Mr. Zukor told Mary that she was tired, that she had been working much too hard for many years and needed a long rest. . . . So, just for friendship and *auld lang syne*, he would give her one thousand dollars every week for five years on condition that she would take a complete rest during that period and not bother her pretty little head about pictures at all.

"Mary's large, soulful and expressive eyes opened wide as she regarded her generous benefactor with feeling. She was much touched and deeply moved. If the thought occurred to her that, from Paramount's point of view, it was well worth $260,000 to eliminate her for five years as a competitor, she brushed it aside as unworthy. She, too, knew what friendship meant, and her affection for dear considerate Mr. Zukor was fully as deep as his for her. . . . Tempting as his offer was, she would rather work for $675,000 per annum than rest for $52,000. . . . The poor child could say no more; she was a young artist and they kept forcing her to talk about money."

The salary demands of a Pickford or Chaplin were becoming

so high that no producer could afford to meet them. The actor with the best management talent of all, Douglas Fairbanks, recognized this clearly. He became the prime mover in the formation of United Artists in 1919 to produce and distribute the movies of its owners—Chaplin, Pickford, D. W. Griffith and Fairbanks. Comments from the established studios were predictable; Richard Rowland of Metro snapped, "The lunatics have taken charge of the asylum." He and the rest of the critics seriously underestimated Fairbanks' organizing and managerial capabilities.

Douglas Fairbanks, a minor stage actor and a superior gymnast, arrived in Los Angeles in 1915. A compulsive worker with an inexhaustible reservoir of energy and enthusiasm, he found his acting metier in the next few years with the scripts of Anita Loos. Fairbanks was cast repeatedly as an idealistic optimist who conquered adversity largely through his athletic ability. The actor's marriage to Mary Pickford in the same year he formed United Artists accelerated the popularity of his movies. Then Fairbanks produced a very profitable series of costume films in which he played the swashbuckling and supremely active hero. The money lavished on these costume pictures was perhaps best typified by the 1922 sets of *Robin Hood,* which could be seen for miles across the vacant plains to the south and west. Robert Florey tells of Douglas Fairbanks' planning for this film spectacular:

"Mary and I are going to buy a new studio where we can all work together. I am thinking of the old Jesse Hampton Studios on Santa Monica [Boulevard]. There's nothing but fields around there, and we can put up some really big sets—Nottingham in the twelfth century, Richard the Lion Heart's castle, a town in Palestine, Sherwood Forest and the outlaws' lair. There's a big field to the south where we can set up the Crusaders' camp in France. We'll have several thousand costumes designed from contemporary documents, we'll order shields, lances and swords by the thousands, we'll stage a tournament, we'll—"

"And how much is all that going to cost?" asked John Fairbanks, Douglas' brother, who was company treasurer.

"That's not the point," replied Douglas. "These things have to be done properly or not at all."

Both the movies and its camp followers sort of oozed into Los Angeles, now one of the country's prime Temperance and morality centers. The skyrocketing box-office receipts of the movies and the well-publicized star system reeked of money and immediate fame for aspiring bit actors, shop girls, and trade apprentices if they were fortunate. In the mid-1910s, the first teenage crusade of star-struck young women and exhibitionists of all types straggled off the trains, pathetically anxious to work in motion pictures. The gambling sharks, con men, blackmailers and dope peddlers were not far behind. Overviewing all of this was a muckraking media searching for stories.

Unpleasant gossip about Hollywood increasingly circulated about the country, and places like the Sunset Club in Santa Monica and the Vernon Country Club were publicized as locales of motion picture colony revels. With a considerable basis in fact, riotous living and flagrant scandals, buoyed by extravagant sex and quantities of alcohol, were daily reported to a Temperance country. A real and continuing problem was the corps of thousands of young women, drawn by the movie craze to Los Angeles. They all faced poverty, a few committed suicide, and a fair number drifted into professional prostitution. To avoid the local vagrancy ordinances, the latter habitually listed their occupation as movie "extra" or "player" and were associated in the daily press with motion pictures when their names showed up on police blotters. The movie industry and its people were prime news and magazine correspondents and newspapermen seemed to be everywhere, all more than willing to write about Hollywood as sort of ". . . a delightful trip through a sewer in a glass-bottomed boat."

The brawling young industry was surely headed for major

trouble, and it arrived there in the late 1910s with the murder of William Desmond Taylor, an established movie director.

The Taylor murder was never solved, but the well-leaked investigations of the homicide cast a pall over a number of movie careers, including two of the industry's major names, Mabel Normand and Mary Miles Minter. Normand was recognized as a fine comedienne and considered by many the equal of Charlie Chaplin. A former model, she had grown up professionally under Mack Sennett's tutelage and with Ford Sterling, Chester Conklin and Roscoe "Fatty" Arbuckle formed the nucleus of the Keystone comedies. Meanwhile Paramount had been carefully grooming Mary Miles Minter as a replacement for Mary Pickford, and the young actress was already the closest rival of the famous star at the time of the director's murder. The lurid details surrounding the Taylor relationship with Minter and Normand had scarcely been absorbed by a righteous but palpitating public when Mabel Normand's chauffeur shot a fellow guest during an exuberant and alcoholic party at the home of Edna Purviance, the female lead in a number of Chaplin movies. The titillating reports of that affair, featuring Normand's attendance at the party, again made front-page news.

Shortly thereafter Roscoe Arbuckle managed to solidify public opinion against the wild young industry with one of his prolonged drinking parties (later to be called orgies by the press). At an Arbuckle party in San Francisco, Virginia Rappe, featured in two-reel comedies, became ill and later died. The famous comedian stood trial for rape. The case dragged on interminably with blazing publicity. Arbuckle was eventually acquitted but the damage was done. Mabel Normand, Mary Miles Minter and Arbuckle were blacklisted by the producers and their movies were withdrawn from distribution.

The subsequent headlines from Hollywood had a kind of inevitability. Wallace Reid, a popular and likable leading man, died at the age of thirty. Disclosure that he and others were drug addicts brought a cascade of reform demands on the entrepreneurial studio managers. Following the practice of organized baseball after a major scandal, the industry looked for its own morals czar. Will H. Hays, a prominent Presbyterian and Postmaster-General in Harding's Administration, agreed to take the job in 1922. Hays quickly installed morality contract clauses for the players, a Central Casting Agency for movie extras, and a systematic industry public relations and self-censor program. While recognizing it was no panacea from any viewpoint, the industry and its people supported the Hays Office. The rawness and increasing violence in the motion picture colony had begun to frighten even the inmates.

Los Angeles always had its tenderloin and sporting side, with or without Hollywood, and despite Temperance ideals. One of the legitimate heirs to the Calle de Los Negros of the Californios was nearby Vernon, the tiny sin city of the 1910s. With ease, the town assimilated portions of the seamy side of Hollywood and a good many other things including some first-class boxing pro-motions.

Perhaps it was John B. Leonis who had the idea of incor-porating a wide-open town of about four square miles southeast a bit from prosperous and fiercely moral Los Angeles. By the 1900s, lovely Vernon of the Boom of the eighties had become a district of hog farms and the disposal point for Los Angeles garbage. Then, shortly after incorporation, Vernon evolved into a rendezvous for the sports and dudes of the South Coast and, later on, a roosting place for some of the fringe Hollywood gentry. Sports, gambling, and saloons, along with their camp followers, made a prosperous living next to a straitlaced Los Angeles. That city's newspapers were soon reporting in sancti-monious horror that "drunken men and women of dissolute class roamed the streets and were frolicking in a carnival of vice day and night. . . . Sunday the town is wide open and drunken men stagger on the streets, toughs shout ribald remarks at passing women, and crap games are played."

There were plenty of drunks on the Vernon streets, but Jack Doyle policed his own Central Saloon which he opened in 1907 on the southwest corner of Vernon's Santa Fe Avenue and Thirty-Eighth Street. Known as a man who never took a drink, nor bought one for that matter, Doyle and Vernon prospered together. Business became even better when he became a tenderloin boxing promoter along with a young Baron Long and James J. Jeffries, recently retired as an undefeated heavyweight champion.

Boxing had been a shadow sport in the United States for years. In many areas it was either illegal or heavily frowned upon, with the bouts being held in out-of-the-way spots. The professionals finally adopted the Queensberry rules which called for gloved contests; the last bare knuckle championship fight was in 1889 and John L. Sullivan won it in seventy-five rounds. Thereafter the respectability and popularity of the sport increased markedly. After Jeffries retired as champion he was still absorbed in boxing. In conjunction with Jack Doyle, Baron Long and he built the 15,000-seat Vernon Arena on Santa Fe Avenue. Because of the Arena and Jeffries' reputation the famous boxers of the day congregated at Vernon, particularly after Jack Doyle built a ring with training quarters adjacent to the Central Saloon and constructed the Stag Hotel across the street. Along with other assorted characters, the hotel became a favorite rooming place for the boxers and noted for the "hot foot" practical joke— insertion of a kitchen match into the welt of a shoe of an unsuspecting victim and then lighting the protruding match head.

Vernon boxing was topflight, due in good part to a generation of West Coast boxers who trained under De Witt Van Court at the Olympic Club in San Francisco and then at the Los Angeles Athletic Club. Nearly all established Van Court boxers appeared under the promotion of Thomas McCary (or Uncle Tom as he was universally called) first at the converted railroad station at Naud Junction and then at the Vernon Arena. The list of fighters who worked out at Doyle's training quarters and lived at the Stag Hotel covered the great ones of the period—Stanley Ketchell, Adolph Wolgast and Billy Papke.

The sporting complex at Vernon received a major addition in 1909 when Fred Maier of the Maier Brewing Company bought a baseball franchise of the Pacific Coast League. Maier built a stadium next to Doyle's Central Saloon and his brother, Eddie, operated the Vernon Tiger franchise until it was moved to San Francisco after national liquor prohibition. Baseball was at a peak of popularity in the 1910s, and the Vernon club in its amiable surroundings was an immediate favorite. On a Sunday morning before the ball game as many as 15,000 men who had arrived by trolley would be milling about the Central Saloon, the stadium and roped-off streets while they argued, bet, boasted and drank whiskey and Maier beer.

Vernon was where the action was, and the town's customers were dressed to the blood. A real sport or dude wore a pleated silk shirt in a primary color offset by armbands of a violent contrast and supplemented by ornate cufflinks, heavy enough to stand alone. Over the shirt was a fancy vest, hung with a thick gold watch chain festooned with twenty-dollar gold pieces and a gold toothpick. Many of the swell dressers still liked high-button, kid-top shoes having what were called "high military heels." A derby was preferred, and the suit coat was loosely cut, hitting well below the hips. A stickpin in a four-and-hand tie was a minimum requirement. Much better, a horseshoe pin carrying a number of small diamonds and escorted by a gold-headed cane made for the acme of sporting gentry attire in the jostling crowd in and around the Central Saloon.

Jack Doyle's establishment employed up to thirty-five bartenders a shift, each with his own cash register; and the bar operations were kept under surveillance from upstairs peepholes. Mounted animal heads in the saloon stared glassily through the billowing cigar smoke at hundreds of pictures of boxers and racehorses and larger-than-life oil portraits of James J. Corbett, the first gloved champion, and James Jeffries. Along with spittoons scattered at strategic spots were slot machines, played with the same fervor as their Las Vegas counterparts several generations later. The doors of the Central Saloon swung wide at 7:00 A.M. and followed the South Coast tradition of giving any customer a free drink just before the bar officially opened. With the clanging of a bell, the saloon closed at midnight except on Sunday when the lockup time was 7:00 P.M., presumably so that the patrons would have a few more hours to sober up before the Monday workday.

The bouncers handled the policing of Doyle's saloon, and they collected the day's receipts in heavy leather bags for deposit in a vault in Doyle's upstairs office. The previous-day receipts were counted the following morning after the contents of the leather bags were dumped on the office floor. Most of the money was silver and gold; the South Coast was still very much of a hard-money society. If there was a substantial number of paper bills in the receipts, this was a sure sign of Eastern tourists visiting Vernon. The only time Doyle was robbed, two men carrying shotguns rode their horses into the saloon. The outlaws lined the bouncers, customers and bartenders against one of the walls and instructed the crowd to strip themselves and the cash registers of money. The vaunted security system of the Central Saloon proved to be worthless, and the unscathed gunmen galloped out of town.

The people of Los Angeles and Baron Long combined to cinch down Vernon's "sin city" title. In 1910 Los Angeles began passing its local option liquor laws which were designed to limit liquor consumption to restaurants and prohibited liquor where there was dancing. Two years later Baron Long helped to cure this regrettable aberration by opening his Vernon Country Club (a night club, not a golf links) and urging his customers to dine, dance and romance, naturally with all the liquor they cared to drink. Business boomed and Long continued to expand his Vernon facility. Probably the Hawaiian Village addition with its six-piece orchestra from the Islands was best remembered; Long's was one of the first places on the Mainland to feature Island music for dancing. Shortly before the national prohibition of liquor, the Vernon Country Club's receipts were at the $100,000 a month level—this with thirty-five-cent cocktails and a New Year's Eve party costing about eight dollars a couple including liquor, food and wine. The place was considered a den of iniquity by the stewards of Los Angeles morals and was featured in newspaper reports on Hollywood; no respectable woman should have been seen there. The definition of "respectable" must have had some latitude of interpretation in light of the packed dance floor on Saturday nights.

Still Los Angeles was right. Vernon was a tough little town. The gambling and liquor supported an entourage of camp followers, whores, bully boys and the shadowy hard-drug peddlers. Evident pests and serious nuisances were the pickpockets operating in the dense sporting crowds. The Central Saloon had a plumbing firm on a weekly retainer to clean out the toilet and sewer pipes clogged with wallets and coin purses stripped and torn up by the pickpockets and then flushed down the drains. Another productive area for the thieves was the packed trolleys including athletic souls happily waving to pedestrians from the trolley roofs during the trips from Vernon to East Seventh Street in Los Angeles. Many an expansive weekend ended with the borrowing of a five-cent fare back to reality.

The brassy reputation of being the sporting and sin capital of southern California lasted less than fifteen years because of nation-wide liquor prohibition. In the 1920s Vernon represented only solid civic progress. The honky-tonk town symbolized by Doyle's saloon with its several dozen bartenders and the dudes and sports lined up three deep at the bar slipped quickly out of memory.

CHAPTER 21

"The Los Angeles Times building was dynamited at 1:07 A.M."

The Los Angeles *Times* building was dynamited at 1:07 A.M. on October 1, 1910. In several minutes the entire structure was aflame as ruptured gas mains became lines of fire throughout the three floors. A hundred people were caught in the inferno. Contorted faces with gasping, shrieking mouths appeared and reappeared at the upper story windows of the editorial and city rooms, while the ladders and fire equipment were buffeted away from the smoking walls by the lashing flames. Then the trapped men and women jumped, their bodies slamming into the cobble-stones below. Twenty people died; most of the remainder were badly injured and burned, some crippled for life.

The tragedy's spinning vortex not only engulfed the victims and their families. With the McNamara brothers' confession of guilt fourteen months after the bombing, the cause of organized labor was forced back nationally a decade or so and, in southern California, more than a generation. The dramatic progress of the local Socialist Party was stopped dead in its tracks. And the popular reputation of liberal folk heroes, Clarence Darrow and Lincoln Steffens, was badly marred by the vitriolic bitterness of their former supporters.

The *Times'* bombing had its tap root of hatred in the nation's rapid industrialization after the Civil War and the accompanying rise of organized labor.

The severe economic depression of the 1890s forged a brand of militant industrial unionism, intertwined with left-oriented political organizations like the Socialist Labor Party. Even when economic conditions improved, membership in the militant sector of organized labor continued to rise paralleling the growth of the more conservative craft unions of the American Federation of Labor. The angry Western Federation of Miners, the Bridge and Structural Iron Workers and the just-formed Industrial Workers of the World met stiff employer resistance in a series of brutal, head-on clashes. But the more traditional unions were not standing idly by in the drive for employer recognition and better wages, hours and working conditions. On the South Coast the local Typographical Union No. 174 felt strong enough in 1901 to mount an attack on a dangerous long-time enemy—Harrison Gray Otis and his Los Angeles *Times*.

There had been a rancorous standoff between the newspaper and the local union for a decade until the printers' national headquarters sent Arthur A. Hay to organize a fresh labor offensive. His primary move was to set up a boycott against A. Hamburger and Sons, owners of the People's Store and the *Times'* largest advertiser. The Hamburgers were told that the price for ending the union action was the termination of all People's advertisements in the *Times*. The department store owners refused to comply and the boycott continued. Union members and anybody else who could be influenced were urged not to buy from Hamburger's. An aspect of the boycott which seemed particularly clever to its organizers at the time was implemented during the store's peak selling period. Through the hectic sales days before Christmas and particularly during Saturday evenings, members of the Union Label League scattered themselves through the store. Having no intention of buying, they kept the clerks showing merchandise while legitimate customers impatiently shifted from foot to foot and finally left the store to do their Christmas shopping elsewhere.

The Typographical Union's fight against the *Times*, and the associated Hamburger boycott, continued through 1903 while still another major weapon was being readied against H. G. Otis and his newspaper. This was nothing less than bringing the flamboyant and powerful William Randolph Hearst to Los

Angeles. If Hearst could be induced to establish a newspaper there, organized labor expected to have a strong friend, and the *Times'* circulation and advertising position would be seriously weakened. Hearst accepted the proposal with alacrity—he could see a ready-made entry into a rapidly expanding market area. Carrying no Hamburger advertising, the first issue of the Los Angeles *Examiner* was printed on December 12, 1903.

In the following months members of the local union movement were ecstatic with the progress of the war on the hated *Times;* the management of Hearst's young journal was surely not because of the paucity of advertising in the newspaper and resultant financial losses. Nor was the union organizer, Arthur Hay, already concerned about the ultimate success of the boycott and who now watched the union fervor in the *Examiner's* editorial and union bias in its news stories diminish. Finally, neither were the members of the local labor movement after the Typographical Union reported the Hearst newspaper's position:

"Mr. Henry Loewenthal, business manager of the *Examiner,* requested a conference with Hay. . . . Mr. Hearst's representative [said] that the policy of the *Examiner* relative to Hamburger's [advertising] was absolutely to the liking of the *Times* and detrimental to the *Examiner.* . . . Only one inference could be drawn from Mr. Lowenthal's statement. Hay did the manly thing. With full knowledge that he was abandoning a fight upon the eve of victory, he said that the Typographical Union, rather than impede the progress of the *Examiner,* would endeavor to have the Council of Labor lift the boycott against Hamburger's."

The union's report to its members was nonsense. The Hamburger boycott including the pre-Christmas antics of the Union Label League was ineffective; more important, the community had been irritated. And Hearst had simply used the opportunity to move out from his subservience to organized labor in Los Angeles. Another dismaying side effect for the unions was the use that their wily enemy, H. G. Otis, and his *Times* had made of the People's Store boycott to influence the local Merchants and Manufacturers Association. Otis pointed out to the larger business firms of the city that they, like Hamburger's, could be singled out for a united union attack. His arguments were to bring a harvest of bitter, wrathful fruit.

Formed to bring industry to Los Angeles under its secretary, Felix J. Zeehandelaar, the Merchants and Manufacturers Association had not been involved in the squabbling and then the bitter infighting between Otis and the unions. However, the Hamburger boycott effectively consolidated the local employers against labor, and the M & M under Zeehandelaar became the rallying point, particularly when Henry E. Huntington, the Trolley Man, threw in his support. Naturally, General Otis was more than happy to have himself and his *Times* serve as the mouthpiece of the anti-union forces. And what a mouthpiece, if some of Otis' more eloquent enemies were to be believed.

Strong words found a lodestone in the person of the *Times'* owner and publisher. Hiram W. Johnson served up an array of them in a 1910 campaign speech:

"We have nothing so vile, nothing so debased, nothing so infamous in San Francisco, nor did we ever have, as Harrison Gray Otis. He sits there in senile dementia, with gangrened heart and rotting brain, grimacing at every reform, chattering impotently at all things that are decent; frothing, fuming, violently gibbering. . . . This man Otis is the one blot on the banner of Southern California . . ."

Hiram Johnson's oratory ran away with the facts. Otis, aged seventy-three at the time, emphatically did not have senile dementia. What he did have was an assortment of strong prejudices combined with the intelligence, power, and a fierce determination to sway the South Coast to his views. The *Times'* publisher was a deadly antagonist, and his foes soon learned that this was so.

Somehow Lieutenant Colonel Harrison G. Otis survived four years of Civil War combat and wounds, returning to the printing trade. In 1882 he became a part owner of an anemic Los Angeles *Times* which shortly began to prosper with the town's growth. Colonel Otis was called back to active duty in the Spanish-American War as a brigadier general, and chance put his brigade in the center of the bloody insurrection in the Philippines.

After coming back from war a second time and resuming management of his beloved newspaper, the General was nearly white-haired with a goatee and full mustache. His associates found him brilliant as ever but more inflexible in his economic and political outlook. Long noted for his firm convictions, now Otis' views seemed cast in bronze; he was right, those who disagreed with him were certainly wrong and probably venal. Always combative and irascible when aroused, now he "had all of the predatory spirit and something of the nature of a Sierra grizzly. Equally violent in his likes and dislikes, he was true to his limited number of loyalties and profanely and vitriolically opposed in his boundless hates."

Hugging General Otis to one's bosom obviously was a thorny and contentious process, but the publisher's supporters could and did defend him with the same fervor, if not the picturesque language, of Hiram Johnson. And with the advantage of perspective, the recognized South Coast historian of another generation, Robert G. Cleland, would note that Los Angeles owed more to the *Times* and its publisher for the city's development than any other comparable influence. Still, after having been slapped about almost at will by a truculent Otis, the local labor movement, badly mauled and outmaneuvered, took little interest in the publisher's accomplishments.

Times were good on the South Coast after the turn of the century. Despite or because of the wide-open shop advocacy by General Otis, working conditions were improving and wages increasing. By 1904 employers like Arthur Letts and his Broadway Department Store had personnel policies of overtime pay for employees working more than nine hours a day, a week's paid vacation, and a sickness and death benefits plan. The local labor struggle increasingly came to center on the closed shop (wherein an employer only hired union members) rather than on wages.

Organized labor in San Francisco, probably the most unionized city in the nation at the time, was increasingly concerned about robust, errant Los Angeles. The southern community was a potential threat to all the principles and power for which the citadel of California unionism stood. San Francisco employers might be seduced by the casual freedom of General Otis and his cohorts; the pleasurable justification would be the serious competitive threat in the future from the smaller city.

Union funds and key organizers were sent to Los Angeles. To the dismay of the San Francisco labor leaders, and the American Federation of Labor as well, little was accomplished. Hated Otisism was rampant. After the blunder of the Hamburger boycott and the *Examiner* fiasco, the outside organizers found hostile, fearful employer organizations in Los Angeles which did not hesitate to use "black lists [of persons not to be employed], advertisements for 'independent' workingmen, replacement of union by non-union employees, lockouts, open-shop declarations, importation of strikebreakers, use of Mexican and Negro labor, non-union employment bureaus and cancellation of union contracts."

Probably more depressing to the outside union organizers was local labor's own internecine warfare, spawned in the years of failure. Certainly most galling of all was daily to open up the prosperous *Times* and read the vituperative comments of the self-appointed nemesis of the South Coast labor movement.

In the prevailing labor gloom there was a glimmer of hope. This was the occasional and recent success of a few radical candidates in municipal elections around the United States. Organized labor in the main was still convinced that its political posture was to elect its friends to public office and defeat its enemies. This meant little interest in political dogma; labor's thrust was immediate economic improvement for its people. Yet there had always been a strong minority in the labor movement who believed in coordinated political party action, whether it be with the populists in the 1890s or the socialists in the 1900s.

Although given little recognition at the time, the prolonged depression of the 1890s had provided the basis in Los Angeles for a closely knit combination of organized labor and socialism. Job Harriman, then in his late thirties, became the political rallying point for union activists at the turn of the century. Plagued with tuberculosis throughout most of his adult life, Harriman arrived in Los Angeles, like so many other health seekers, after practicing law in Indiana and becoming a lifelong advocate of radical causes. Almost singlehandedly, the lawyer made the Socialist Party a small but viable element in California.

A dedicated organizer and an excellent speaker, Harriman was convinced that the socialists and the labor movement must form a partnership if anything was to be accomplished politically at the local government level. He flirted with the far-out International Workers of the World (called the Wobblies or IWW) but his real courtship was with the local craft unions. After 1907 the Central Labor Council of Los Angeles and the Socialist Party grew more and more close, with the effective organizing ability of the lawyer becoming apparent in the local union membership drives during the late 1900s. Now the two groups had an impossible dream in the land of Otis, the *Times* and the employer associations—a socialist-labor victory in the Los Angeles mayoralty elections of 1911. Job Harriman was the coalition's choice to run against the established candidates, and the keystone of his campaign was the repeal of the local antipicketing ordinance, so detested by organized labor.

The underlying political ferment generated by the radical coalition and the charisma of Harriman had gone largely unnoticed by the press. The only newspaper to come out for the labor-socialist ticket was the Los Angeles *Record,* a minor sheet started in 1895 by the E. W. Scripps chain. The important Good Government League was supporting the reelection of Mayor George Alexander, and the League expected him to win easily over the Republican and Socialist candidates in the primary of October 31, 1911. Instead the Socialist Party won a sensational municipal victory. While not receiving a majority of votes, Job Harriman ran well ahead of the incumbent mayor. This meant a runoff election on December 5 between the two, and the socialist was the heavy favorite to win.

For many in a city boiling with rumors and raw fears of continued terrorism, the primary victory of the Socialist Party appeared to be confirmation of the spread of anarchy on the South Coast.

While the search for bodies continued in the smoking ruins of the *Times* building, another time bomb was discovered shortly after noon just outside a window at the home of F. J. Zeehandelaar, the aggressive secretary of the Merchants and Manufacturers Association. Fifteen sticks of ultra-grade dynamite, strong enough to wreck the house and surrounding structures, were electrically wired to an alarm clock set to go off at 1:00 P.M. Wound too tightly, the clock had stopped. Hasty telephone calls brought a search of the H. G. Otis grounds and residence, and a suitcase with the muffled sound of a ticking clock was found by the house. Just after the police had gingerly moved the case away, it blew up, shattering windows around the neighborhood. Miraculously, nobody was killed or injured.

The dynamite blasts of October 1 represented a peak of violence and fear of violence which had stalked the streets of Los Angeles during the summer of 1910. Local organized labor was on the move, strongly supported by union forces from San Francisco who at last sensed a final victory. Employers were equally disciplined and militant. The number and length of strikes and lockouts were increasing, stringent enforcement of the antipicketing ordinance brought numerous arrests, and physical confrontations between police and strikers were becoming routine.

Continued hit-and-run terrorism with the frightful threat of dynamite clutched in its fist could provide the fillip which would lead to hysteria and vigilante activity. Industrial plants hired security guards after the *Times* explosion, the police force was increased by a hundred men, and there were mass meetings calling for the addition of many more patrolmen. On Christmas morning a tremendous dynamite blast, heard in distant beach cities, destroyed a good portion of Llewellyn Iron Works, a prominent antiunion company. No one was killed but the maintenance staff on the premises was injured. Organized labor vehemently proclaimed it was not involved in the Llewellyn blast just as it did in the *Times* and other bombings. Unfortunately for the national labor movement, these assertions were untrue.

The Bridge and Structural Iron Workers Union turned to terrorism in 1905 under the new president, Frank M. Ryan, and secretary-treasurer, John J. McNamara. During the next five years, from the union headquarters in Indianapolis, McNamara directed nearly a hundred bombings resulting in scores of casualties. An efficient explosive team he frequently utilized consisted of two terrorists—his brother, James B. McNamara, and Ortie McManigal. A team's target might be a steel mill one month and a railroad bridge the next.

Detectives had been on a tenuous and disappointing trail of the terrorists for years; William J. Burns and his agency were the most persistent and knowledgeable. When Los Angeles Mayor George Alexander hired Burns to investigate the *Times* bombing, he could not have made a better choice. The detective was quick to recognize that the dud bomb at the Zeehandelaar home bore a strong resemblance to a dud found at a Peoria, Illinois, factory and which Burns' agency had previously examined.

The major break in the *Times* case occurred when Ortie McManigal was identified as one of the Peoria terrorists. Soon after his arrest McManigal made a detailed confession on April 13, 1911, covering both the Peoria and *Times* bombings. He directly implicated not only his terrorist partner, James B. McNamara, but the national union secretary, John J. McNamara, and an array of other union officials. After an abbreviated extradition hearing, the Burns agency hustled McManigal and the union secretary out of Indianapolis in a special railway car to Kansas City and a Los Angeles-bound Santa Fe train. Meanwhile James B. McNamara had been arrested in Kansas and was put aboard the prisoner car at Dodge City. The trio was booked into Los Angeles County Jail on April 26, a few days short of seven months after the *Times* building burst into flames.

The summary arrest and extradition of the McNamaras and McManigal, to Los Angeles, created a national furor, not only in the ranks of organized labor but in a broad spectrum of civil rights supporters and reform workers. Hundreds of thousands of buttons reading "McNamara Brothers Not Guilty" were proudly worn throughout the country and committees were hastily formed to raise funds for the brothers' defense. Organized labor chose Clarence Darrow, considered by many to be the foremost criminal and courtroom lawyer in the United States and certainly a devoted labor supporter, to head the defense.

Normally dressed with the same neatness as an unmade bed, Clarence Darrow was a moody, humorless man whose spirits tended to fluctuate from complete pessimism to less than moderate optimism while he coped with an array of actual and psychosomatic ailments. After months of investigation the famous criminal lawyer found little in the McNamaras' case to enhance his naturally lugubrious outlook. Despite the brothers' heartfelt protestations of innocence he now was convinced they were guilty as charged and probably would receive the death penalty, a sentence the lawyer abhorred.

Clarence Darrow had an additional heavy burden. He recognized that the American labor movement was going to be judged at the bar of public opinion over the *Times* bombing. Organized labor continued to be happily convinced of the McNamaras' innocence, and another emotional solicitation of funds for the brothers' defense was being sponsored by Samuel Gompers, the beloved president of the American Federation of Labor. Still Clarence Darrow vacillated.

The McNamaras defense had taken over an entire floor of a downtown office building. In addition to associate counsel, Darrow had put together an investigative team under John Harrington of Chicago and Bert Franklin, a former deputy sheriff and U.S. marshal in Los Angeles. Time dragged on during trial preparation, and it was October of 1911 before jury selection was underway, the same month that an associate defense counsel, Job Harriman, won his unexpected victory as the Socialist Party candidate in the mayoralty primary. Impanelment of the McNamara jury moved at a dull crawl until a sudden development brought national headlines. Bert Franklin, a chief investigator for Darrow, was arrested on November 28 for a McNamara jury bribery attempt. For allegedly masterminding Franklin's effort the famous criminal lawyer himself eventually would be tried on two indictments; the first trial resulted in acquittal, the second in a hung jury with two-thirds of the jury for conviction.

For a harassed if not desperate Clarence Darrow, the Franklin arrest must have been the catalytic agent in arriving at a decision he had been moodily mulling for days. In exchange for guilty pleas by the two McNamara brothers, he would accept a plea-bargaining offer of life imprisonment rather than hanging for James and a long prison term for John, the union official.

The unwitting plea-bargaining intermediary between Clarence Darrow and the prosecution along with the local business community was Lincoln Steffens—reformer, writer, egotist and professional busybody. When given his choice Steffens would unfailingly select the simplistic approach to the solution of any social problem (his personal affairs he found much more complicated).

In Los Angeles as a reporter of the McNamara trial for a number of newspapers, Steffens believed that social conditions in the city represented a priceless opportunity for application of the Golden Rule of Forgiveness. And obviously there was no better man than himself to bring such a program to fruition. Steffens proposed that the McNamaras be freed and the investigations, which would likely lead to additional labor leader indictments, be ended. Further, in this mood of forgiveness which would pave the way in Los Angeles for the elimination of class war and strife, the business community was to transform itself from a union-hating to a union-loving group. Nothing remotely worked out as Lincoln Steffens envisaged through his utopian efforts other than becoming a conduit for Darrow's successful plea bargaining.

Organized labor and those who supported social reform had placed their hearts, honor and money in the hands of the McNamaras' stout professions of innocence. And Clarence Darrow had done nothing to dampen the fervor of the brothers' supporters during a half-year of investigation of the bombing.

On December 1, 1911, and fourteen months after the *Times* bombing, the McNamara defense suddenly announced that the defendants wished to change their plea to "guilty." Pandemonium literally broke loose. Reporters sprinted for telephones and the wire services spread the story across the nation. The news was first received by the legion of McNamara supporters with astonished disbelief followed by a wrenching gut fury against their own leaders, and then against Clarence Darrow. The "Not Guilty" buttons were ripped off and stamped viciously in the mud. Job Harriman, an associate defense counsel, knew nothing of the change of plea until it was announced in court. Yet he faced a mayoralty run-off election only four days later. The special cup of bitterness of the joint labor-socialist movement ran over when Harriman, the leading Los Angeles mayoralty candidate prior to the change of plea, was soundly defeated. The national labor movement reeled under successive hammer blows of criminal indictments against some fifty union officials.

Even as the unions and the radical political parties fell back in disorder, some of their long-advocated reforms were being implemented by a fresh political group which called itself the Progressive Party. But the first mission of this new party was to strike at railroad political domination in California.

The Southern Pacific still ran the South Coast on transportation and allied matters in the 1900s, albeit shakily at times. The failure to obtain Federal funds for its Port Los Angeles project at Santa Monica, because of an effective and organized opposition, had made no changes in the railroad's power politics. Nor did the direct public action devices so optimistically adopted by the California voters in 1903—the initiative, referendum and recall.

Doing business as usual in March of 1906 and while the mayor was out of town, the Los Angeles City Council gave a free franchise for a railroad right-of-way along the Los Angeles River to the Pacific Electric, owned jointly by the Southern Pacific and Henry E. Huntington. There was a newspaper uproar when an incensed Edward P. Ripley, President of the Santa Fe, told reporters the grant was worth more than a million dollars. After an intramural brawl, the franchise action was rescinded but the episode stoked up a long-smoldering fire of resentment of the flagrant Southern Pacific domination. Four young men in Los Angeles, all about aged thirty, determined to attack the railroad's inner political fortress first at the city and then at the state level. Their destiny was to spearhead the Progressive Movement in the nation.

The first part of the twentieth century found the makings at the grass-roots level of a major reform movement which, then and later, confused observers as to its origins. No neat party, class or political tags could be placed on it. The Progressives, as they called themselves, cut across established political lines; the constituency and leaders were middle class and even wealthy. Yet their program of reforms contained much that had been considered socialistic when put forward earlier by the William Jennings Bryan camp of Democrats and the agrarian populists.

Chance brought the young Progressive Four—Dickson, Avery, Lissner and Stimson—together in 1906. Edward A. Dickson had just been hired by Edwin T. Earl to be the associate editor of the Los Angeles *Express* with the new editor's stipulation that he be allowed to attack the Southern Pacific. After making a fortune in real estate and citrus, Earl had bought the *Express* in 1901, and, according to some, he acquired the newspaper so that he could carry on more effectively a long personal feud with General Otis, his next-door neighbor. At any event the *Express* publisher introduced Dickson, the new editor, to Russ Avery, an attorney already involved in civic causes and the friend of two other lawyers, Meyer Lissner and Marshall Stimson. The four young men were congenial and their political views harmonious and activist, particularly on matters affecting the Southern Pacific. A series of luncheon meetings at the University Club resulted in the decision to enter a third-party list of "Good Government" candidates in the 1906 municipal election. The Progressive Four also agreed that none of them would run for office, a policy which was followed during the years they moved to national prominence.

Two unlikely bedfellows—the *Times* and organized labor— opposed the Good Government Party in the Los Angeles municipal election. Even so, the new party only lost the mayoralty race by a small margin and elected a majority of its people to the other municipal positions. Three years later after successfully pushing through a charter amendment making municipal election nonpartisan, the Good Government group forced the resignation of the incumbent mayor and elected its candidate. Again this was in spite of the ferocious editorial attacks of General Otis. The Progressive Four now were accused by the *Times* of maneuvering for public power to gain personal real estate profits, and Meyer Lissner was singled out as sort of a Fagan-type pawnbroker.

The limited 1906 municipal election success in Los Angeles convinced the Progressive Four, and Dickson in particular, that the fight against the Southern Pacific could now begin at the state level. He sensed a vigorous grass-roots resentment against a rather stupid hammerlock put on the Republican state convention that year by the railroad, combined with a patronage spree by the 1907 state legislature. Among a good many other employees, the legislature that year had on its payroll ten doorkeepers for four entry ways, fifty-six meeting clerks and, most impressive of all, thirty-six sergeants-at-arms. Nevertheless, Governor James N. Gillett thought this legislature would be judged "one of the best that ever met in the state capitol."

The governor's sentiment was emphatically not shared by men like Chester Rowell of Fresno's *Morning Republican* and Fremont Older, publisher of the San Francisco *Bulletin*. They and a half-dozen other publishers accepted a Progressive Four invitation to a 1907 dinner meeting in Los Angeles at Al Levy's Restaurant. The result was the formation of a Lincoln Republican Club (later Lincoln-Roosevelt League). In addition to supporting Theodore Roosevelt's policies in the forthcoming election, the primary objective of the new club was to be "the emancipation of the Republican Party in California from domination by the Political Bureau of the Southern Pacific Railroad Company . . ." In six months' time more than thirty newspapers had taken up the Progressive cause, and 1910 became the target

year for takeover of the governorship and control of the legislature.

The most electable man for the Progressives increasingly
appeared to be Hiram Johnson, due in no small part to the career
of his father. Grover Johnson owed his entire political life to the
Southern Pacific, and his power and influence in the California
state legislature at the time was unequaled. Grover's two sons,
both lawyers, broke with their father over the railroad political
machine issue and their estrangement and bitterness increased
with time. The brothers became active in Sacramento municipal
reform, giving speeches for the reelection of a reform mayor,
while their father energetically stumped for the opposition. One
night at the peak of the campaign when a scheduled meeting of
Grover Johnson was only a block or so apart from one being
conducted by his two sons, the father pointed wrathfully from
the platform and assured the fascinated audience that his "two
chief enemies [were] down the street, one Hiram, full of
egotism, and the other, Albert, full of booze."

The father knew the weaknesses of his sons. Albert Johnson
eventually died an alcoholic. Hiram, soon to become a national
political figure, had a core of willful egotism which made him
a dangerous competitor and ensured himself a substantial roster
of enemies. Hiram Johnson had the absolute conviction that,
once he made a political decision, it was right, irrespective of
later facts which might surface. When crossed, he reacted with
the fervor and single-mindedness of a biblical prophet. As deadly
in the use of an epithet as Harrison G. Otis, Johnson was never
known to regret a bitter remark at his leisure. Yet these very
characteristics helped to make the reformer the man for the time
and hour.

Not only was there a vital reform force abroad in the land,
the Political Bureau of the Southern Pacific was creaking with
age and malaise in 1909. Like an old tiger turned man-eater, the
Bureau tended now to choose easier prey. Unfortunately for
those who felt its teeth and claws, the results could be just as
painful or fatal.

The South Coast base of the Lincoln-Roosevelt League picked Hiram Johnson of San Francisco to head a full state and congressional ticket in the 1910 election. To nobody's surprise Johnson was an effective campaigner in an election year when the reformers could smell success. By early morning after the polls closed Dickson, Avery, Lissner and Stimson of Los Angeles knew they had fashioned a major victory after four years of effort. The entire state ticket was elected, there were substantial majorities in both houses of the legislature and seven out of eight of the party's candidates for congress were voted in.

Thus ended nearly four decades of domination of California state and local government on matters of Southern Pacific interest. Only a few old settlers like Harris Newmark could remember back to the 1870s when Charles Crocker of the Big Four monopoly thundered: "If this be the spirit in which Los Angeles proposes to deal with the railroad on which the town's very vitality must depend, I will make grass grow in the streets of your city."

CHAPTER 22

"It's a Grand Old Flag"

The South Coast newspapers soberly reiterated to their readers that the new century would not begin until 1901. It was mathematically evident that the first century A.D. ended with the year 100. So the nineteenth must surely finish with 1900.

Purists and logic to the contrary, for most the splendiferous century ended on December 31, 1899. To write "1900" on a letter or check was evidence enough of that. With the accomplishments of the past several generations, oratorical eloquence about the future was easy. Admittedly, there was a gnawing concern, albeit a minor one—an inexplicable and bloody insurrection against American forces in the Philippines, a country the United States had liberated so proudly from an old-world tyranny.

The 1898 war with Spain had been exciting, educational and even profitable. Over in a little more than three months, the conflict was a watershed in the international policy of the United States and brought the brawny young nation into international councils including the central Pacific with the annexation of the Hawaiian Islands after five years of debate. Fueled by inflammatory newspaper reports of revolts in Spanish Cuba, the Spanish-American War got underway with a maximum of U.S. popular support. To the tune of *There'll Be a Hot Time in the Old Town Tonight* the baby war developed into sort of a fine and glorious Fourth of July picnic which lasted several months, with few soldiers or sailors killed or wounded. However, meaningful casualty statistics were not kept on the numbers of troops which died of malaria, typhoid and yellow fever in the swamps and disorganized staging areas of the Caribbean.

Halfway around the world Commodore George Dewey won

a decisive fleet action in Manila Bay and again with broad popular support the Philippines were acquired from a defeated Spain for a token $20,000,000. This moved Speaker Thomas B. Reed of the House of Representatives to comment acidly: "We have bought ten million Malays at two dollars a head unpicked and nobody knows what it will cost to pick them." The insurrection led by a former U.S. ally, Emilio Aguinaldo, soon demonstrated the picking cost would be very high. Ten full regiments in bitter and brutal guerrilla engagements with heavy casualties finally put down the Aguinaldo uprising in early 1901. But the McKinley Administration easily weathered the criticism aroused by men dying during dubious battles in a distant land. The economic weather was good, going to be better, and the President had the ability to identify with the voters.

A pleasant and indecisive man, William McKinley had defeated William Jennings Bryan for the second time in 1900. McKinley liked to shake hands—sometimes at the almost inconceivable rate of fifty a minute—and the people loved him for it. His penchant for handshaking in a reception line was the death of him—he was gunned down in Buffalo, the third President to be assassinated in thirty-six years. The death caused Mark Hanna, a long-time sponsor and friend, to fret about McKinley's successor: "Now look, that damned cowboy is President of the United States!"

"That damned cowboy," a shrewd politician and dedicated advocate of the strenuous life and worthy causes, was Theodore Roosevelt. Because of the determination to sell his array of pet reforms and do-good prejudices, there was soon recognition that "when Teddy Roosevelt was for you, he was *for* you. When he was after you, he was after you." The new president traveled the broad nation and by no means neglected the West.

The flourishing South Coast first saw President Roosevelt in May of 1903. Among other political tasks, he planted with appropriate ceremonies one of the two original Washington Navel orange trees in the courtyard of the recently opened Mission Inn at Riverside. Mr. Roosevelt's overnight stay in the citrus city probably was neither better nor worse than his traveling experiences elsewhere in the country. But to do these routines day after day required nearly the strength of a horse and the stomach of a goat. Riverside clearly was no exception.

The President stoically surveyed his suite at the Mission Inn which had been lovingly embowered by the local ladies into their version of a sylvan dell, decorated with symbols of Roosevelt's interest in sports. Guns and athletic equipment were strategically distributed among many pine boughs, roses and oranges. An elk's head, suitably antlered, peered myopically from the wall through a screen of spruce branches, and a fern canopy was precariously hung over a too-short, Napoleonic bed. The assorted smells in the suite were strong, and miscellaneous debris and a few insects were already dropping to the floor and bed.

All stops were pulled for the presidential dinner that evening at the Inn. In the Temperance jargon of the day, this was to be a cold-water banquet, neither wine nor liquor was to be served. The sponsors attempted to make up for this omission by the sheer volume and weight of the dinner courses—well beyond even the typical hearty servings of the period. And the President, astute politician that he was, knew the risks of merely toying with the food. Eventually the heavy meal and the endless speeches were over, and the guest of honor now could retire to his suite, hopefully to get some sleep in that sylvan dell. This was not to be. Esther Klotz describes the next incident:

"When President Roosevelt accompanied by his bodyguards entered his decorated private rooms, the lights suddenly went out. Fearing that an assassin might be in the room, Roosevelt threw himself flat on the floor, expecting an attack. When the lights flashed on after the short electrical failure they revealed all Roosevelt's bodyguards sitting on him with their pistols drawn and pointed."

Riverside's distinguished guest soon discovered there was still another force at work to keep him from sleeping. The local unit of the National Guard was determined to protect the country's Commander-in-Chief during the night. In full uniform including clanking swords, the unit mustered itself in and around the perimeter of the Mission Inn. Loud challenges, exchange of passwords and stentorian "all is well" reports were guaranteed to keep Mr. Roosevelt and the surrounding neighborhood awake most of the night.

"That damned cowboy" was planning another one of his wild tricks. In the summer of 1907 Theodore Roosevelt ordered the nucleus of the United States Fleet to prepare for a cruise around South America to the Pacific Coast (Panama Canal construction was just underway), no innocuous decision for a variety of reasons. Shortly before, Japan had launched a surprise attack and then easily defeated Russia in a Pacific war. Suppose Japanese torpedo boats ambushed and sank the Fleet? But there were more immediate public concerns. Naval defense of the East Coast, the nation's heart, would be denuded while the dangerous currents and winds of the Straits of Magellan, feared for centuries, might wreck the vessels on unknown rocks. During discussion in the Senate Appropriation Committee about a possible refusal to fund the Fleet's trip, word came from the White House as to the President's position. He had the funds to send the Fleet to the Pacific Coast—let the Congress worry about getting it back. However, even a cocky Roosevelt did not have the temerity to tell the Congress and the public that he hoped to send the Fleet across the Pacific and thence around the world.

Reflecting the surging tide of confident nationalism, both Theodore Roosevelt and the nation were proud indeed of their first line of battleships. All sixteen of the vessels had been built during the previous decade. Coal-burning, they steamed at nine knots with more than fifteen-knot flank speeds. Now repeatedly referred to as the country's first line of defense, the Fleet was an affirmation of the United States' new and major position in the world's power structure. The term "Great White Fleet" (white hulls and superstructures, buff funnels) entered the language on December 16, 1907, at Norfolk, when the line of battleships and their auxiliaries passed in review before a proud president and headed south toward the Straits of Magellan and then north to California.

The Great White Fleet made goodwill visits to a number of South American ports, and the cruise became a rolling crescendo of success for the President. There was no taint of battleship diplomacy; instead every country wanted to be included on the visitation schedule. Still, at home, worry persisted over the Straits of Magellan passage and possible shipwreck and cannibalism. The Sacramento *Union* made the point: "We don't want any of our jackies eaten by the terrible Tierra del Fuegans."

Those awful things did not occur to the ships and the blue-jackets. And the Fleet continued its triumphal course along the west coast of South America while the U.S. newspapers were bursting with prideful articles. Now Roosevelt felt he could announce that the Fleet after visiting San Francisco, ravaged two years earlier by a violent earthquake, would go to Asia and return to Norfolk via the Suez Canal. By this time San Diego was in a tizzy. Ulysses S. Grant, Jr., urged the President to bring the Fleet into the city's beautiful bay. An overly cautious Navy refused because of channel depth, and San Diego had to settle for the ships anchoring at sea off the Hotel Coronado. This meant that the small city's fine natural harbor would receive no world-wide publicity while a ubiquitous Los Angeles was luxuriating in an expensive government-paid breakwater at San Pedro. No wonder again that San Diego felt bitterly "like a starved dwarf, wandering among trees laden with fruit beyond his reach."

Most memorable to a South Coast generation all too familiar with coal oil lamps and gas jets were the Fleet lighting displays at anchor while at San Diego and San Pedro. Each evening "for three hours every vessel was outlined in fire. Thousands of incandescent bulbs were strung along deck lines, up military masts, far out on the signal yards, down the huge funnels, to water's edge from stem to stern. . . . During a half-hour period . . . a searchlight display [added] infinitely to the wonderful effect. The flashing shafts of light were sent dancing over the waves."

After the gala receptions at Los Angeles and San Diego, the crews of the ships ever afterward referred to the famous cruise as their tour of "Flower battle duty." Innumerable ladies' com-

mittees pelted unwary sailors with bouquets of flowers and
swamped them with orange juice and unwanted attention. Despite these occupational hazards, the fourteen-month world
cruise demonstrated again Theodore Roosevelt's sense of timing
and showmanship. For the nation and for the world the long
voyage was a dramatic synthesis of technical achievement and
a show of power and goodwill. When the American people
hummed or sang the new George M. Cohan hit *It's a Grand Old
Flag,* they thought of their own Great White Fleet steaming to
Asia from a vibrant and proud San Francisco, arising again from
its earthquake and fire ruins.

In the *World Almanac* tabulation of major earthquakes
around the globe since the year A.D. 1000, the only one showing
no deaths is the New Madrid, Missouri, series of shocks which
began in late 1811. Yet this was perhaps the greatest earthquake
recorded in United States history. The explanation of course is
that the epicenter was in a vast, vacant wilderness area with
minimal communications—more than a hundred miles south-
southeast of a severely shaken trading village of St. Louis.
Astonishing reports were received there that the Mississippi
River for a period actually reversed its flow. California and its
San Andreas Fault have been attempting to top Missouri's
quake record; fortunately to date this has not been accomplished.
Nor have there yet been major tsunamis (erroneously called tidal
waves) caused by underwater quake displacements on the
nearby continental shelf.

Newcomers to the Los Angeles area after the Gold Rush
received a major introduction to the South Coast's propensity for
earthquakes during the evening of July 11, 1855. The shock was
more than Magnitude 6 on the Richter scale, about the same
rating as the quake of February 9, 1971, in the general San
Fernando Valley area. The 1855 epicenter was located between
the San Gabriel and Los Angeles rivers, just a few miles from the
Plaza, and ". . . almost every structure in Los Angeles was

damaged, and some of the walls left with large cracks. Near San Gabriel, the adobe in which Hugo Reid's Indian wife dwelt was wrecked, notwithstanding that it had walls four feet thick with great beams of timber. . . . In certain spots the ground rose; in others it fell; and with the rising and falling, down came chimneys . . . and even parts of roofs, while water in barrels, and also in several of the zanjas, bubbled and splashed and overflowed." Aftershocks continued for months.

The populated areas of the South Coast were fortunate on the morning of January 9, 1857. A great earthquake of more than Magnitude 8 (nearly a hundred times more intense than the Los Angeles shock) occurred on the San Andreas Fault, with its epicenter in the Tehachapi Mountains near Fort Tejon. The first shock was relatively light, but the succeeding ones grew rapidly in strength for a three-minute period. In Los Angeles, about a hundred miles away, the population rushed into the streets and "horses and cattle broke loose in wild alarm." The second great earthquake of the nineteenth century in California again was in its southern part, along the Owens Valley Fault on March 26, 1872. And again the shock was more than Magnitude 8 on the Richter Scale. Two hundred miles away in Los Angeles, the force was violent enough to throw people out of bed.

A strong earthquake is like a severe back strain accompanied by a pinched nerve; until you have experienced one, you have only a nodding acquaintance with the reality of the phenomenon. The writer still vividly recalls his own rapid indoctrination in the first thirty seconds of the 1933 Long Beach tremors. The influx of newcomers with the Boom of the eighties knew nothing about earthquakes, and the subsequent California quakes were usually in isolated places like the major 1899 earth movement near Hemet on the San Jacinto Fault. For many Californians of that generation the induction into earthquake reality occurred just at daybreak on April 18, 1906. The third great series of shocks in a half-century of more than Magnitude 8 had its epicenter in the San Francisco Bay area, the most populous region in the West. In the city itself the quake initiated a kind of a crown fire which ravenously fed on the central districts of the metropolis. The arrival of the news in Los Angeles about the awful calamity befalling San Francisco brought immediate reaction:

"With lightning rapidity, the report spread throughout the city. Newspapers and telegraph offices were besieged for particulars as to the earthquake, which, strange to say, while it also affected even San Diego, was scarcely felt here; and within a couple of hours, more than a thousand telegrams were filed at one office, although not a single message was dispatched. A throng of agitated tourists and even residents hastened to the railroad stations, fearing further seismic disturbances and danger, and bent on leaving the Coast; and soon the stations and trains were so congested that little or nothing could be done with the panic-stricken crowds. Meanwhile, more and more details of the widespread disaster poured in. . . . Soon refugees from the North commenced flocking into the city; and these thousands, none with complete and few with decent attire, each pleading pathetically for assistance . . ."

After a fine response to San Francisco's tragedy, the people of California commenced soberly to evaluate the earthquake environment and associated tsunami potential in which they lived. The quiet comment of Charles F. Richter, an eminent seismologist and South Coast resident of the present-day period, applied then as it did to later generations: "Just as some people have a fixed neurotic fear of cats, others have an excessive and unreasonable fear of an earthquake. They should not try to live in California." For months after the San Francisco catastrophe, the trains to the East were full of people who had made their decision.

Every generation or so, the South Coast goes on a commercial building spree which lasts for about a decade. The 1910s constituted one of those periods of frenetic activity. John D. Spreckels brought San Diego to life when he commenced the construction of a direct railroad line to Yuma, Arizona, and connection with the Southern Pacific. The U. S. Grant Hotel, the equal of any

California hostelry, opened in 1910 and advertised two swimming pools and a ninth-floor ballroom, locally asserted to be the finest in the West. Certainly the 1912 Spreckels Theatre with a six-story stage loft and surrounding office building was impressive for a community of 40,000 population. But no matter what San Diego accomplished, the southern city appeared destined to live in the shadow of Los Angeles.

After Herman W. Hellman broke with his brother, I. W., over Farmers & Merchants Bank affairs, he constructed a fine Los Angeles office building at Fourth and Spring streets, the first of many at the maximum 150-feet height then allowed by law. This was the beginning of the central financial district which eventually would extend south along Spring beyond the Van Nuys Building at Seventh Street. The rows of height-limit, thirteen-story structures put up during the 1910s became the standard photograph of a bustling Los Angeles, rapidly overtaking San Francisco as the West's principal city. Meanwhile, Hamburger's (later the May Company) and Bullock's ventured south on Broadway to Eighth and Seventh streets respectively. In 1914, J. W. Robinson's took the advice of Shirley P. Ward and risked going south and west to Seventh and Grand streets, then "but the merest shadow of a business center." Ward, a lawyer cum real estate investor, was generally given credit for turning the central business district west.

A principal factor in the making of the World War I skyline of downtown Los Angeles was Robert A. Rowan. Forming his own real estate firm while still in his twenties, Rowan soon recognized the advantages of raising capital by a financial technique new for the South Coast. This involved establishing a separate corporate vehicle for each of his major building ventures and transferring the construction site to the new corporation in exchange for the capital stock. Then that company sold long-term mortgage bonds to pay for the construction of the building. The first structure to be built under this plan was the 1905 Alexandria Hotel at Fifth and Spring streets, and Rowan repeated the formula any number of times until his early death in 1918.

"A gem set in tile, steel and marble." This was a 1906 *Times* appraisal of the Alexandria, the premier Los Angeles hotel until the Biltmore opened many years later. Forthwith, the Alexandria was the city's social and banquet center. "Peacock Alley" in the hotel was soon to become the meeting place of the newly acceptable movie powers, both talent and producers: "It was here around the magic carpet that graced the center of the main hotel lobby, that all deals were signed by the picture moguls. One had to belong to be permitted to lounge around there. The common 'lounge lizard' was soon spotted and told in a polite way to move on."

The affluent Alexandria was only an example of a flourishing Los Angeles which, almost as an afterthought, welcomed the 1905 arrival of the San Pedro, Los Angeles & Salt Lake Railroad. This connection brought the Union Pacific to the South Coast. Population growth was exceeding the local boosters' fondest dreams but, as always, the land boomers quickly adjusted to pleasurable reality. Now William May Garland was putting up signs forecasting a million people in the city by 1920, and nobody laughed that much anymore. Continued real estate appreciation was soon taken for granted except by a few oldsters who remembered the Boom of the eighties and its aftermath. In the forefront of the solid optimists were the principals of the Los Angeles Investment Company (or LAIC as it was known locally). Incorporated as a "cooperative building company" in 1899, LAIC had been organized by Charles A. Elder, a musician at the Orpheum Theater, who early recognized the potential in the revival of South Coast real estate values.

The Los Angeles Investment Company prospered mightily under the musician's leadership and by 1913 was one of the largest and most celebrated enterprises in southern California with nearly 20,000 stockholders. Elder's company was by far the best known land subdivider, had sold many hundreds of new homes on easy installment plans and owned thousands of acres of land along with central city parcels and buildings. An overdue testimonial banquet was held in June of 1913 for the LAIC founder, and he was hailed as a major benefactor to the common man by Mayor George Alexander and other community leaders.

Less than two years after the community honors, George A. Elder and his two principal associates were serving terms for mail fraud in Federal prison. The striking feature of this turn of events was that then and later Elder and his board members of LAIC had broad-scale public support. The people viewed the jury verdicts and penitentiary sentences as a tragic miscarriage of justice. After all, as the *Times* commented, the growth of LAIC "not only kept pace with that of Los Angeles but exceeded it. Its momentum was so great that it could not be promptly checked when the times called for more conservative policies." In this kind of an environment a well-meaning and competent group of civic-minded LAIC salvagers found that the new board of directors spent a fair amount of time dodging verbal brickbats and worrying about bodily injury threats.

The Los Angeles Investment Company foundered because of poor management, whether most people recognized this fact or not. Charles A. Elder and his associates assumed that local property values would climb to perpetuity without interruption. In this framework, optimistic land commitments were made which subsequent events would show to be absurd. But so long as there was a reasonable, upward spiral of land prices stoked by a continued influx of investment cash, the enterprise could pay very substantial dividends and ignore high repossession costs on installment-sale homes. Unexpectedly, housing sales fell off sharply in the last half of 1913, real estate prices declined precipitously for a time, and the entire LAIC board of directors was indicted by a Federal grand jury on mail fraud charges. Unless immediate community action was taken, the investment company would shortly be liquidated on a piecemeal basis—corporate reorganization under Section 77B of the National Bankruptcy Act was still a score of years away. In a community of 450,000, already shocked by the drop in real estate prices and far over-committed on municipal debt, little imagination was required to visualize a domino effect occurring which could lead to regional business panic.

A strong community board of directors for LAIC was designated in late 1913—Stoddard Jess, J. E. Fishburn, D. A. Hamburger, Henry O'Melveny (shortly replaced by Joseph Scott), William H. Allen Jr., Harry Chandler and Robert Rowan—all serving without compensation and all ill-prepared for the insults they and their immediate successors would receive. While serving as LAIC counsel Henry W. O'Melveny made notes in his daily journal on the feverish excitement pervading the first two annual stockholder meetings in which the new management was involved. Both of these meetings went on for nearly a fortnight, being adjourned from day to day.

On January 10, 1914, after the annual meeting was transferred to a hastily rented skating rink to accommodate some 2,000 milling people—"I directed the doors to be thrown open and all allowed to enter. I mounted a table and explained to the stockholders that we desired . . . a roll call to determine whether a quorum was present."

On January 13, 1915—"I have had threats of violence, of vitriol throwing. . . . It's a pleasant situation, this working for poor unfortunates."

On January 23, 1915—"At [the stockholders' meeting] conclusion Joe Scott read his minority report. Loud cries immediately on its conclusion. Shouts of Mr. Chairman—yells, derisive shouts. General confusion prevailed from this time, and not a meeting but a mob."

The Los Angeles Investment Company did survive albeit with tears, wrath and no cooperation from two heirs of Elias J. (Lucky) Baldwin—Clara, his much married daughter by his first wife, and Anita, the daughter of his third marriage. The original LAIC management had made an atrocious business contract with Clara and Anita for the installment purchase of Baldwin Hills (the hill portions of Rancho Ciengas). The new board of directors pleaded with the multimillionaire half-sisters for readjustment of the contract. In the iron-fisted tradition of their father, who had acquired his vast South Coast land holdings primarily by systematic foreclosure after the 1875 bank panic, the sisters' answer to the LAIC board was an unequivocal "no."

When the *Titanic* in 1912 collided with a north Atlantic iceberg, foundered and sank with heavy loss of life, the sinking made headlines on the South Coast, not only because the tragedy was a first-rate news story but also because several local people aboard the ship were lost. Yet when Archduke Franz Ferdinand was assassinated during a June 1914 visit to Sarajevo, someplace in a squabbling central Europe, there was absolutely no interest, let alone concern in southern California. And why should there have been? Public interest in national and world affairs were minimal. Days could go by in the Los Angeles newspapers without a story from Washington because the Federal government as the all-powerful nucleus of all things had yet to be invented. Bolstered by a minute income tax first levied in 1913, annual Federal expenditures (expressed in the dollars of the 1970s) were about one-thirtieth of today's yearly budget for about half the population.

Three transcontinental railroads, all single track, were the sole bridges from the South Coast to the rest of the nation. Effective use of the Panama Canal was delayed by landslides in the Gaillard Cut through 1916 which meant ocean freight continued to move around the tip of South America. A long-distance telephone call was a production, a cross-country call had just become a possibility with the completion of a few trunk lines to California. Sensibly, no telegram delivered at home was opened until a family member or friend was mustered to provide support. Of course there was neither radio nor TV, and the mass movie audience was just aborning. Sales of sheet music and records for the bulky windup phonographs were significant, confirmation if any was needed that people on the South Coast spent a good deal of time at home.

In late July of 1914 and a month after Franz Ferdinand's assassination, all of the nation stirred and then awoke from the dog days of summer somnolence and ice-cream socials. European news spewed over the front pages, and the New York *Times* on July 28 felt it necessary to point out that "a general European war is unthinkable." A week later World War I had begun. Southern California was a microcosm of the rest of the country in its intense absorption in the conflict. The root stock of the population was drawn chiefly from those nations now at war—the particular side an American chose was determined as much by emotion as a comprehension of the basic causes of the massive conflict.

For a time the U.S. tradition of noninvolvement in European affairs appeared to be firmly established. But as time went on and bitter episodes like the sinking of the *Lusitania* were piled upon effective propaganda songs and slogans, the posture of neutrality gradually weakened. The Civil War and its frightful casualty lists were already a forgotten half-century away. Wrapped up in a comfort blanket of Manifest Destiny and do-goodism, the recent Spanish-American War and even Emilio Aguinaldo's insurrection were pleasant storybook affairs. By early 1917, the United States was emotionally ready for war with Germany.

The House of Representatives followed the Senate in giving a 373-to-50 vote for war on April 6, 1917, after seventeen hours of debate featured by "unemotional acquiescence" spiced with an unexpectedly vocal opposition. The following winter found the embarkation ports jammed with soldiers. A hundred thousand and more of American troops were put ashore in France monthly, and shortly the battle lists of those killed and wounded lengthened dramatically. During the Meuse-Argonne series of engagements in which almost 1,200,000 U.S. soldiers, most inexperienced, were eventually committed, one man out of every ten was a casualty; for the first 400,000 troops which moved into position, the ratio was much higher than that. But these gloomy numbers were still over the immediate horizon for the American people as they settled into feverish war preparations following the congressional action.

After much bickering between Los Angeles and San Diego proponents, the War Department designated San Diego as the location for one of the sixteen cantonments sites around the nation. Called Camp Kearny, the base would become the Army training center for recruits from California, Arizona, Nevada, New Mexico and Utah, as well as the staging area for the 40th

Division. A 10,000-acre site was purchased on Linda Vista Mesa and shortly stretches of hastily built wooden barracks and rows of tents replaced jackrabbits and dry brush on the windswept mesa. As facilities became available, the volunteers and the draftees, in irregular files behind marching bands, paraded down the streets of their home towns to board the railroad coaches for Camp Kearny.

The wives, sweethearts and parents of the new citizen soldiers living in and around Los Angeles were fortunate. They usually saw their tanned young men on a final home leave, because Los Angeles was the regional railroad center. Here the troop trains, some cars dating back to the Boom of the eighties, were assembled for the long trip to one of the Atlantic ports and then ship embarkation.

Clattering over the switching points and crossover frogs of the Los Angeles yards, the troop trains carried the young men to a vast, bloody war. Unrecognized then, those departing cars full of soldiers constituted the last scene of a grand era on the South Coast, and the rest of the country as well.

In the very nature of things there is always an end and then a beginning. While born out of the past, this particular future was far from twice blessed. The turbulent war would lead to years of cynicism, then frustration and finally almost despair, a stark and sad contrast to the wonderful period of confidence and ebullience only a generation or so before.

Source Notes on Quotations

CHAPTER 1

Page

17 "At the start the cars are rude but," From *Harper's Weekly* (1883), *American West*, May 1975, 64.
19 "were in cahoots with train," Marshall, *Santa Fe, the Railroad That Built an Empire*, 98.
20 "one of the family," Lindley and Widney, *California of the South*, 71.
20 "elderly ladies and children," Ibid., 71-72.
20 "crying in childish glee," Ibid., 71.
22 "a magnificent railroad station," Newmark, *Sixty Years in Southern California*, 562.
23 "Hell! We're giving away the land," Glasscock, *Lucky Baldwin*, 222.
23 "to be a success you've got to," Ibid., 118.
25 "through his left arm," San Francisco *Call*, Jan. 5, 1883.
26 "Baldwin looked the agent over coldly," Glasscock, *Lucky Baldwin*, 250.
27 "After all, the climate was wonderful," Willard, *A History of the Chamber of Commerce*, 41.

CHAPTER 2

28 "A brass band of some," Van Dyke, *Millionaires of a Day*, 57-58.
30 "Bargains in Real Estate," Los Angeles *Times*, Mar. 7, 1886.
32 "To call it a craze or bubble," Los Angeles *Tribune*, May 29, 1887.

Page

33   "which a good vaulter could leap," Lindley, *California*, 91.
34   "LET US REASON TOGETHER," Adler, *History of Normandie Program Area*, Plate 3.
35   "buyers stood in line all night," Dumke, *Boom of the Eighties*, 83-84.
35   "the *Times* is worse than a mad dog," Los Angeles *Tribune*, Apr. 4, 1887.
36   "a beach of hard white sand," Lindley, *California*, 145.
37   "Oh, fireman fill the teacup," Hoffman, *Long Beach, From Sand to City*, 29-30.
38   "crawled along for years like a," Dumke, *Boom*, 133.
38   "living largely on faith," Ibid., 134.
39   "In fact, we may say that," San Diego *Union*, Oct. 1, 1887.
39   "Los Angeles is part of our back country," Pourade, *Glory Years*, 194.
39   "It has oranges of finer flavor," Ibid., 179.
40   "Near Santa Barbara, vast quantities," Dumke, *Boom*, 158.
40   "the oleaginous fumes wafted," Tompkins, *Little Giant of Signal Hill*, 73.
40   "These professionals had learned," Guinn, *Historical and Biographical Record of Los Angeles*, 260.
41   "Boom—will it break soon," Newmark, *Sixty Years*, 582.

CHAPTER 3

42   "General Applehead," Van Dyke, *Millionaires*, 175.
43   "As the Boom had arisen," Willard, *History*, 54.
45   "What is to prevent one," Cleland and Putnam, *Isaias W. Hellman and the Farmers and Merchants Bank*, 12.
45   "Mr. Temple's only qualifications," Graves MSS.
46   "Graves, I have to be a better man," Ibid.
46   "I certainly have no objections," Ibid.
47   "crops, which could not be sold," Cleland, *Isaias*, 58.
47   "June 20. The City Bank," O'Melveny MSS.
47   "June 21. The First National," Ibid.

Page

47 "June 22. Excitement still intense," Ibid.
49 "I had considerable money invested," Graves MSS.
50 "the Chinese were the great features," O'Melveny MSS.
51 "the best and most rapid growth," *Land of Sunshine*, June 1894.

CHAPTER 4

52 "the government must have," Willard, *The Free Harbor Contest at Los Angeles*, 36.
53 "and the caskets of some," San Pedro *News Pilot*, Mar. 31, 1928.
54 "Here, take this and buy," MacPhail, *The Story of New San Diego*, 18.
56 "Rattlesnake Island, Dead Man's," Willard, *Free Harbor*, 50-51.
59 "one ocean resort, Terminal Island," Willard, *History*, 272.
59 "who loved the windblown," *Five Year Book of the Los Angeles Yacht Club*, 25.
59 "a damned old fool," Lewis, *The Big Four*, 182.
63 "You people are making," Willard, *Free Harbor*, 106-107.

CHAPTER 5

66 "Viva Los Estados Unidos," Bell, *Reminiscences of a Ranger*, 129.
66 "There were crowds," Warner, Hayes and Widney, *An Historical Sketch of Los Angeles County*, 142.
66 "A fat young steer," Lindley, *California*, 129.
69 "Decay and extermination," Los Angeles *News*, Feb. 2, 1869.
70 "four wool-combers," Cleland, *Cattle*, 74.
70 "The flush times are passed," Los Angeles *Star*, Apr. 26, 1856.
71 "On the assessor's lists," Cleland, *Cattle*, 183.

Page

76 "Here the girls were," Dillon, *Hatchet Men*, 230.
76 "white girls between the ages," Ibid., 66.
77 "A lamp sits on the bed," Ibid., 64.
80 "June 11. I went out," O'Melveny MSS.
81 "the only salvation of our properties," Cleland, *Cattle*, 167.

CHAPTER 6

84 "I would that no person," Furnas, *The Life and Times of the Late Demon Rum*, 80.
86 "of the infuriated nature of men," Ibid., 285.
88 "unless the saloon men have," *Out West*, Oct. 1914.
88 "one shoe or two shoes," Klotz, *The Day the Bank Failed*, 53.
88 "The man who takes the red, red," Covina *Argus*, May 25, 1895.
89 "What, oh, what can I do," Bell, *On the Old West Coast*, 93.

CHAPTER 7

92 "Grand rain—3.57 inches," O'Melveny MSS.
98 "a weakness of George," Alexander, *The Life of George Chaffey*, 191.
98 "A Sahara of hissing hot winds," Ibid., 110.
101 "He acted with such decision," Ibid., 304.

CHAPTER 8

106 "filling all the air with clouds," Hornbeck, *Roubidoux's Ranch in the 70s*, 151.
107 "The old-timers among the men," Ibid., 143.
108 "Cantaloupes, oranges, grapefruit," Ibid., 142.
112 "It was customary for the," Clary, *History of the Law Firm of O'Melveny & Meyers*, 108-109.
115 "disputatious and eccentric," Hornbeck, *Roubidoux's*, 164.

Page

117 "A gleaming white orchard," Pflueger, *Covina*, 165.
118 "no plan can be worse than," Erdman, *The California Fruit Growers Exchange*, 6.
120 "new sort of norther," Riverside *Daily Press*, Jan. 14, 1913.
121 "as though they had been swept," Klotz, *A History of Citrus*, 42.

CHAPTER 9

123 "Mr. Huntington's Santa Monica," New York *World*, June 20, 1894.
124 "At this hour, I have succeeded," Willard, *Free Harbor*, 136.
124 "Well, you are by all odds," Ibid., 140.
125 "the shrewdest, most persistent," Graves MSS.
126 "Oh, it is too paltry to undertake," Willard, *Free Harbor*, Addendum.
129 "worked this afternoon at White's office," O'Melveny MSS.
129 "had been on and off the stand," St. Johns, *Final Verdict*, 93.
129 "Requiescat in pace," O'Melveny MSS.
130 "I will never be remembered," Lewis, *Big Four*, 213.
131 "it is though a community," Willard, *Free Harbor*, 203.
134 "naturally, the mud and silt," Matson, *Building a World Gateway*, 78.

CHAPTER 10

135 "Out on the back platform," Rowsome, Trolley Car Treasury, 19.
138 "the system of the Pacific Railway," Los Angeles *Times*, Nov. 2, 1889.
138 "Heavy rains on the night of," *Interurbans*, Dec. 1951.
142 "best advertisement that Los Angeles," Newmark, *Sixty Years*, 535.

CHAPTER 11

Page

145   "then relax and watch the money," Los Angeles *Times*, Nov. 2, 1889.

148   "he could talk money out of," Hendricks, *M. H. Sherman, A Pioneer Developer*, 16.

148   "Oh, better than that," Ibid., 17.

149   "wore an enormous, below-knee," Ibid., 15.

149   "No better boy than Ed," Lewis, *Big Four*, 192.

151   "I wanted you [Hellman]," Graves MSS.

152   "I waylaid Mr. Huntington," Carr, *Los Angeles, City of Dreams*, 358-359.

154   "Hellman: When we went into this," Graves MSS.

156   "They bought heaps of sand," Newmark, *Sixty Years*, 632.

158   "extraordinary sea-angling," Holder, *The Channel Islands of California*, VII.

158   "the climatic charm of the Riviera," Ibid., VI.

160   "With foot on the heavy brake," Ibid., 114-115.

163   "this tall, erect, portly master," *The Founding of the Henry E. Huntington Library*, 291.

CHAPTER 12

164   "The condition begins with," Fishbein, *Modern Home Medical Adviser*, 241.

164   "No one . . . who has actually seen," Ibid., 241.

165   "anyone with a reasoning mind," Ibid., 231.

167   "He hired a hack and drove," Workman, *The City That Grew*, 245.

169   "When I got to the hospital," Graves MSS.

CHAPTER 13

171   "The unpleasant odor of gas," Newmark, *Sixty Years*, 469.

172   "BEWARE OF QUICKSAND," Ibid., 584.

176   "he delivered himself into," Workman, *City*, 238.

176   "Six dark lanterns," *First Hundred Years, the City of Los Angeles*, 57.

Page

176 "Keep your coat buttoned," Ibid., 57.

177 "Sir: You will use," Santa Barbara *News-Press*, Apr. 7, 1893.

180 "shameless bawds," Los Angeles *Daily News*, May 25, 1870.

181 "a brisk traffic in young," Mason and McKinstry, *The Japanese of Los Angeles*, 8.

184 "there was little excuse for," Lindley, *California*, 95.

185 "standing in the midst of," Adler, *History*, 5.

186 "Every year there were," Workman, *City*, 101.

187 "crude Pavillions," Adler, *History*, 15.

187 "with the dawn, Bowen and," Ibid., 16.

CHAPTER 14

188 "Mr. . . . has been quite," Pasadena *Daily Star*, Feb. 10, 1890.

189 "her long light step," Wharton, *The House of Mirth*, 7.

189 "vigorous and exquisite, strong," Ibid., 7.

190 "Billy Garland and I," Workman, *City*, 213.

191 "Ladies in tights are," Klotz, *The Day*, 21.

192 "4/6 Mrs. X," O'Melveny MSS.

192 "4/16 We called," Ibid.

192 "5/14 We called [Mrs.]," Ibid.

192 "6/26 [Mrs. X's mother]," Ibid.

192 "if a lady got involved," St. Johns, *Final Verdict*, 110.

193 "Men. All of them," Ibid., 466.

194 "The French windows were," Ibid., 136.

194 "the highest moral and ethical," Ostrander, *The Prohibition Movement in California*, 64.

194 "Los Angeles was overrun," Ibid., 65.

CHAPTER 15

195 "one could choose the," Bixby-Smith, *Adobe Days*, 97.

198 "the customary noises around," Newmark, *Sixty Years*, 531.

201 "an aristocratic and," Page, *Pasadena: Its Early Years*, 196.

202 "The fruits of the chase," Pasadena *Star*, Apr. 13, 1891.

Page

202 "to convey to the blizzard," Pasadena *Star*, Dec. 12, 1889.

204 "were not all to the taste," *Performing Arts*, June 1970.

204 "so that real boats could," Riverside *Daily Press*, Jan. 9, 1890.

206 "men throwing cast-lines," Holder, *Channel Islands*, 81.

207 "fair play to game fishes," Ibid., 81.

207 "Beginning with homemade soup," Graves MSS.

CHAPTER 16

212 "in later years became," Vorspan and Gartner, *History of the Jews in Los Angeles*, 94.

212 "No member should be," Ibid., 94.

214 "was opened by the Los," Newmark, *Sixty Years*, 567.

215 "why her place was so," MacPhail, *Story*, 118.

216 "No despot that sat in," Ibid., 118-119.

216 "Looking back on its," McGroarty, *Los Angeles, From the Mountains to the sea*, 262.

219 "a society far more," Hoffman, *The Branding Iron*, Mar. 1976.

CHAPTER 17

220 "Owens Valley project was," McWilliams, *Southern California Country*, 187.

220 "Los Angeles gets its water," Mayo, *Los Angeles*, 245-246.

221 "Los Angeles is living on," Carr, *Los Angeles*, 206-207.

223 "ability to make use of," Chalfant, *The Story of Inyo*, 229.

227 "the announcement sent a," McGroarty, *Los Angeles*, 231.

228 "anybody who plays tennis," Chalfant, *Story*, 326.

228 "of a Nevada 'forest' withdrawal," Ibid., 327.

229 "Well, I did the work," Workman, *City*, 311.

229 "It may not be exactly," Ibid., 307.

233 "To anyone except an," Howarth, *Panama*, 245.

234 "slight choking nausea," Peele, *Mining Engineers' Handbook*, 23-18.

Page

235 "There it is, take it," Workman, *City*, 316.
237 "In the year of our Lord," McGroarty, *Los Angeles*, 229.
237 "took on the elements of," Chalfant, *Story*, 392.

CHAPTER 18

240 "No one knew how to," Welty and Taylor, *The 76 Bonanza*, 152-153.
240 "preachers conducted excursions," Ibid., 153.
244 "an expensive $40,000 steamer," Los Angeles *Times*, Dec. 31, 1888.
244 "I saw Mr. Bixby," Welty, *76 Bonanza*, 93.
246 "Let's drill an oil well," Graves MSS.
247 "I feel convinced that," White, *Formative Years in the Far West*, 336.
248 "A barrel of Kern River crude," Ibid., 239.
252 "we cannot help ourselves," Ibid., 211.
254 "that hereafter no work," Welty, *76 Bonanza*, 118.
254 "Temperance rendezvous," Ibid., 122.
255 "disapproved the [expense account]," Ibid., 142.

CHAPTER 19

258 "Nothing has spread," Mathison, *Three Cars in Every Garage*, 27.
259 "for the saving of money," Ibid., 9.
259 "no young lady should," Ibid., 1.
261 "First, don't believe over," Stein, *The Treasury of the Automobile*, 53.
262 "I have seen an expert," Ibid., 55-56.
263 "If you have a Model T," Mathison, *Three Cars*, 61.
263 "Gentlemen, you face a," Ibid., 47.
264 "whopper flying machine," Lord, *The Good Years*, 86.
265 "The airship was maneuvered," New York *Times*, Dec. 26, 1904.

Page

266 "five cent coffee which cost," Los Angeles *Times*, Jan. 11, 1910.

266 "Over the grass—before," Newmark, *Quarterly of the Historical Society*, Sept. 1946.

267 "Paulham flew to San Pedro," Ibid.

267 "There were men on horseback," Ibid.

CHAPTER 20

271 "made one-reel pictures like," Brownlow, *The Parade's Gone By*, 31.

272 "we can't go on forever," Griffith and Mayer, *The Movies*, 24.

273 "The fireworks men shooting," Ibid., 33.

274 "Pauline [Pearl White] flees," Lord, *Good Years*, 310.

275 "M. Ince may be proud," Griffith, *Movies*, 96.

275 "of creating satire sharp as," Ibid., 74.

276 "With compassionate eye," de Mille, *Hollywood Saga*, 102.

277 "The lunatics have taken," Griffith, *Movies*, 61.

277 "Mary and I are going," Brownlow, *Parade's*, 248.

278 "a delightful trip through," Ibid., 36.

280 "drunken men and women of," Kilty, *Leonis of Vernon*, 23-24.

CHAPTER 21

287 "Mr. Henry Loewenthal," *Mr. Otis and the Los Angeles Times*, 10.

288 "We have nothing so vile," Ibid., 8-9.

289 "had all of the predatory," Mowry, *The California Progressives*, 47-48.

290 "black lists of persons not," Stimson, *Rise of the Labor Movement in Los Angeles*, 289.

298 "one of the best that ever," Mowry, *California*, 65.

298 "the emancipation of the Republican," Ibid., 70.

299 "two chief enemies [were] down," Ibid., 112.

300 "If this be the spirit in," Newmark, *Sixty Years*, 505-506.

CHAPTER 22

Page

302 "We have bought ten million," Tuchman, *The Proud Tower*, 183.

302 "Now look, that damned cowboy," Lord, *Good Years*, 38.

302 "when Teddy Roosevelt was," St. Johns, *Final Verdict*, 308.

303 "When President Roosevelt," Klotz, *Day*, 6.

305 "We don't want any of," Lord, *Good Years*, 197.

305 "like a starved dwarf," Dumke, *Boom*, 133.

305 "for three hours every vessel," Los Angeles *Times*, Apr. 15, 1908.

306 "almost every structure in," Newmark, *Sixty Years*, 165.

307 "horses and cattle broke," Ibid., 204.

308 "With lightning rapidity," Ibid., 633.

308 "Just as some people have," Los Angeles *Times*, Feb. 28, 1971.

309 "but the merest shadow," Newmark, *Sixty Years*, 536.

310 "A gem set in tile, steel," Los Angeles *Times*, Feb. 11, 1906.

310 "It was here around the," Swigart, *Biography of Spring Street in Los Angeles*, 28-29.

311 "not only kept pace with that," Los Angeles *Times*, Jan. 11, 1915.

312 "I directed the doors to be," O'Melveny MSS.

312 "I have had threats of violence," Ibid.

312 "At [the stockholders' meeting]," Ibid.

314 "unemotional acquiescence," Los Angeles *Times*, Apr. 6, 1917.

Bibliography

Adler, Patricia, *The Bunker Hill Story*. Glendale, Calif., La Siesta Press, 1963.

──────, *History of the Normandie Program Area*. Los Angeles, Calif., Community Redevelopment Agency, 1969.

Alexander, J. A., *The Life of George Chaffey*. Melbourne, Australia, MacMillan & Co., Ltd., 1928.

Barry, Iris, *D. W. Griffith: American Film Master*. New York, Museum of Modern Art, 1940.

Beebe, Lucius, *The Overland Limited*. Berkeley, Calif., Howell-North Books, 1963.

──────, and Clegg, Charles, *U.S. West*. New York, Bonanza Books, 1969.

Bell, Major Horace, *On the Old West Coast*. New York, Grosset & Dunlap, 1930.

──────, *Reminiscences of a Ranger*. Santa Barbara, Calif., Walter Hebberd, 1927.

Bennett, Martin, *Rolls-Royce: The History of the Car*, New York, Arco Publishing Co., 1974.

Bigger, Richard, and Kitchen, James D., *How the Cities Grew*. Los Angeles, University of California Press, 1952.

Bixby-Smith, Sarah, *Adobe Days*. Cedar Rapids, Iowa, Torch Press, 1926.

Bowman, Lynn, *Los Angeles: Epic of a City*. Berkeley, Calif., Howell-North Books, 1974.

Brownlow, Kevin, *The Parade's Gone By*. New York, Alfred A. Knopf, 1968.

Bruckman, John D., *The City Librarians of Los Angeles*. Los Angeles, Los Angeles Library Association, 1973.

329

Bryant, Keith L., Jr., *History of the Atchison, Topeka and Santa Fe Railway*. New York, MacMillan Publishing Company, 1974.

Butterfield, Harry M., *A History of Subtropical Fruits and Nuts in California*. Berkeley, Calif., University of California Press, 1963.

Carr, Harry, *Los Angeles, City of Dreams*. New York, Grosset & Dunlap, 1935.

Carse, Robert, *The Twilight of Sailing Ships*. New York, Grosset & Dunlap, 1965.

Caughey, John and Laree, *Los Angeles, Biography of a City*. Berkeley, Calif., University of California Press, 1976.

Chalfant, W. A., *The Story of Inyo*. Bishop, Calif., W. A. Chalfant, 1933.

Chinn, Thomas W., *A History of the Chinese in California—A Syllabus*. San Francisco, Chinese Historical Society of America, 1969.

Clary, William W., *History of the Law Firm of O'Melveny & Meyers*. Pasadena, Calif., Castle Press, 1966.

Cleland, Robert Glass, *The Cattle on a Thousand Hills*. San Marino, Calif., Huntington Library, 1941.

————, *From Wilderness to Empire*. New York, Alfred A. Knopf, 1959.

————, *The Irvine Ranch of Orange County*. San Marino, Calif., Huntington Library, 1952.

————, and Putnam, Frank B., *Isaias W. Hellman and the Farmers and Merchants Bank*. San Marino, Calif., Huntington Library, 1965.

Cotton, Oscar W., *The Good Old Days*. New York, Exposition Press, 1962.

Cowan, Robert G., *A Backward Glance—Los Angeles 1901-1915*. Los Angeles, Torrez Press, 1969.

————, *On the Rails of Los Angeles*. Historical Society of Southern California, 1971.

Cramer, Esther R., *La Habra, The Pass Through the Hills*. Fullerton, Calif., Sultana Press, 1969.

Crocker, Donald W., *Within the Vale of Annandale*. Pasadena, Calif., Donald W. Crocker, 1968.

Crump, Spencer, *Henry Huntington and the Pacific Electric.* Los Angeles, Trans-Anglo Books, 1972.

Darrow, Clarence, *The Story of My Life.* New York, Grosset & Dunlap, 1932.

Davis, J. Allen, *The Friend to All Motorists.* Los Angeles, Anderson, Ritchie & Simon, 1967.

de Mille, William C., *Hollywood Saga.* New York, Dutton, 1939.

Dillon, Richard H., *Hatchet Men.* New York, Coward Co., 1962

Doig, Leroy L., *The Town of Garden Grove.* Santa Ana, Calif., Pioneer Press, 1966.

————, *The Village of Garden Grove—1870-1905.* Santa Ana, Calif., Pioneer Press, 1962.

Doran, Adelaide LeMert, *The Ranch That Was Robbins.* Glendale, Calif., Arthur H. Clark Company, 1963.

Duke, Donald, *Pacific Electric Railway.* San Marino, Calif., Golden West Books, 1967.

Dumke, Glenn S., *The Boom of the Eighties in Southern California.* San Marino, Calif., Huntington Library, 1944.

Erdman, H. E., *The California Fruit Growers Exchange.* New York, American Council Institute of Pacific Relations, 1933.

Fishbein, Morris M., *Modern Home Medical Adviser.* New York, Garden City Co., 1937.

Fitzell, Lincoln, *County Lines.* New York, William Morrow & Company, 1947.

Fogelson, Robert M., *The Fragmented Metropolis.* Cambridge, Mass., Harvard University, 1967.

Forbes, Jack D., *Native Americans of California and Nevada.* Healdsburg, Calif., Naturegraph Publishers, 1969.

Fried, John F., *Life Along the San Andreas Fault.* New York, Saturday Review Press, 1973.

Furnas, J. C., *The Life and Times of the Late Demon Rum.* New York, G. P. Putnam's Sons, 1965.

Gillingham, Robert Cameron, *The Rancho San Pedro.* Los Angeles, Cole-Holmquist Press, 1961.

Glasscock, C. B., *Lucky Baldwin.* Indianapolis, Ind., The Bobbs-Merrill Company, 1933.

Gleason, Duncan, *The Islands and Ports of California.* New York, The Devin-Adair Company, 1958.

Goode, Kenneth G., *California Black Pioneers*. Santa Barbara, Calif., McNally & Loften, 1974.

Goodrich, E. P., *Report to Harbor Commissioners of Los Angeles Concerning the Development and Construction of an Ocean Harbor, 1913*. Los Angeles, Los Angeles *Examiner*, 1922.

Gordon, Dudley, *Charles F. Lummis: Crusader in Corduroy*. Los Angeles, Cultural Assets Press, 1972.

Graves, Jackson A., *California Memories*. Los Angeles, Times-Mirror Press, 1930.

————, *My Seventy Years in California*. Los Angeles, Times-Mirror Press, 1928.

Grey, Zane, *Tales of Swordfish and Tuna*. London, Hodder & Stoughton Ltd., 1927.

Griffith, Richard, and Mayer, Arthur, *The Movies*. New York, Bonanza Books, 1960.

Guinn, James M., *Historical and Biographical Record of Los Angeles and Vicinity*. Chicago, Chapman Publishing Company, 1902.

Hall, William H., *Irrigation in California [Southern]*. Sacramento, Calif., State Printing Office, 1888.

Hammond, Robert, and Lewing, C. J., *The Panama Canal*. London, Frederick Muller, 1966.

Harlan, Hugh, *The Story of the Negro in Los Angeles County*. Federal Writers Project, U.S. Works Progress Administration, 1936.

Haywood, William D., *The Autobiography of William D. Haywood*. New York, International Publishers, 1929.

Hendricks, William O., *M. H. Sherman, A Pioneer Developer of the Pacific Southwest*. Corona del Mar, Calif., The Sherman Foundation, 1971.

Hill, Laurance L., *La Reina—Los Angeles in Three Centuries*. Los Angeles, Security Pacific National Bank, 1929.

Hilton, George W., *The Night Boat*. Berkeley, Calif., Howell-North Books, 1968.

Hoffman, Hortense, *Long Beach from Sand to City*. Long Beach, Calif., The Bookmark, 1957.

Holder, Charles Frederick, *The Channel Islands of California*. London, Holder & Stoughton Ltd., 1910.

————, *An Isle of Summer, Santa Catalina.* Los Angeles, Calif., R. Y. McBride, 1901.

Hornbeck, Robert, *Roubidoux's Ranch in the 70s.* Riverside, Calif., Press Printing Company, 1913.

Howarth, David, *Panama—Four Hundred Years of Dreams and Cruelty.* New York, McGraw-Hill Book Company, 1966.

Kahanek, Richard L., *A History of Norwalk, Los Angeles County, California.* City of Norwalk, 1968.

Kaplan, Justin, *Lincoln Steffens.* New York, Simon and Shuster, 1974.

Kent, William, *Reminiscences of Outdoor Life.* San Francisco, A. M. Robertson, 1929.

Kilty, James, *Leonis of Vernon.* New York, Carlton Press, 1963.

Kirsch, Robert, and Murphy, William S., *West of the West.* New York, E. P. Dutton & Co., 1967.

Klotz, Esther H., *A History of Citrus in the Riverside Area.* Riverside, Calif., Riverside Museum Press, 1969.

————, *Riverside and the Day the Bank Broke.* Riverside, Roubidoux, 1972.

Kneiss, Gilbert H., *Redwood Railways.* Berkeley, Calif., Howell-North Books, 1956.

LaFuze, Pauliena B., *Saga of the San Bernardinos.* San Bernardino, Calif., County Museum Association, 1971.

Lavender, David, *The Great Persuader.* New York, Doubleday & Company, 1970.

Lecouvreur, Frank, *From East Prussia to the Golden Gate.* Los Angeles, Angelina Book Concern, 1906.

Lewis, Oscar, *The Big Four.* New York, Alfred A. Knopf, 1938.

Lindley, Walter, and Widney, J. P., *California of the South.* New York, D. Appleton and Company, 1896.

Loose, Warren, *Bodie Bonanza.* New York, Exposition Press, 1971.

Lord, Walter, *The Good Years,* New York, Bantam Books, 1962.

Ludwig, Ella A., *History of the Harbor District of Los Angeles.* Los Angeles, Historic Record Co., 1927.

McFie, Maynard, *The Gay Nineties.* Los Angeles, Sunset Club, 1945.

McGroarty, John Steven, *History of Los Angeles County.* Chicago, The American Historical Society, 1923.

———, *Los Angeles, From the Mountains to the Sea.* Chicago, Amer. Hist. Soc., 1921.

McWilliams, Carey, *Southern California Country.* New York, Duell, Sloan & Pearce, 1946.

MacArthur, Mildred Yorba, *Anaheim "The Mother Colony."* Los Angeles, The Ward Ritchie Press, 1959.

MacPhail, Elizabeth C., *The Story of New San Diego.* San Diego, Pioneer Printers, 1969.

Marshall, James, *Santa Fe, the Railroad That Built an Empire.* New York, Random House, Inc., 1945.

Mason, William M., and McKinstry, John A., *The Japanese of Los Angeles.* Los Angeles, County Museum of Los Angeles, 1969.

Mathison, Richard R., *Three Cars in Every Garage.* New York, Doubleday & Company, Inc., 1968.

Matson, Clarence H., *Building a World Gateway.* Los Angeles, Pacific Era Publishers, 1945.

Mayo, Morrow, *Los Angeles.* New York, Alfred A. Knopf, 1932.

Meadows, Dan, *Orange County.* Los Angeles, Dawson's Book Shop, 1966.

Moreau, Jeffrey, *The Mount Lowe Pictorial.* Los Angeles, Pacific Bookwork, 1964.

——— and Walker, James, *Glendale & Montrose.* Los Angeles, Pacific Bookwork, 1966.

Morgan, Neil, and Blair, Tom, *Yesterday's San Diego,* Miami, E. A. Seeman Publishing, Inc., 1976.

Mowry, George E., *The California Progressives.* Chicago, Quadrangle Books, Inc., 1963.

Muir, John, *Picturesque California and the Regions West of the Rocky Mountains.* New York, J. Dewing Publishing, 1888.

Murphy, Bill, *A Pictorial History of California.* San Francisco, Fearon Publishers, 1958.

Nadeau, Remi, *City-Makers.* Los Angeles, Trans-Anglo Press, 1965.

————, *Los Angeles from Mission to Modern City.* New York, Longmans, Green and Co., 1960.

Newell, Gordon, and Williamson, Joe, *Pacific Coastal Liners.* Seattle, Superior Publishing Company, 1959.

Newmark, Harris, *Sixty Years in Southern California.* Boston, Houghton Mifflin Company, 1930.

Newmark, Marco R., *Jottings in Southern California History.* Los Angeles, The Ward Ritchie Press, 1955.

Nordhoff, Charles, *California: For Health, Pleasure and Residence.* New York, Harper & Brothers, 1872.

O'Connor, Richard, *The Oil Barons, Men of Greed and Grandeur.* Boston, Little, Brown and Company, 1971.

O'Flaherty, Joseph S., *An End and a Beginning.* New York, Exposition Press, 1972.

O'Melveny, Stuart, *It's Best to Divide with Our Friends.* Los Angeles, Anderson, Ritchie & Simon, 1955.

Ostrander, Gilman M., *The Prohibition Movement in California.* Berkeley, Calif., University of California Publications in History, 1957.

Overholt, Alma, *The Catalina Story.* Avalon, Calif., Catalina Museum Society, 1971.

Page, Henry Markham, *Pasadena: Its Early Years.* Los Angeles, Lorrin L. Morrison, 1964.

Patterson, Tom, *Landmarks of Riverside.* Riverside, Calif., Press-Enterprise Co., 1964.

Peele, Robert, *Mining Engineers' Handbook.* New York, John Wiley & Sons, Inc., 1941.

Perry, Louis B., and Perry, Richard S., *A History of the Los Angeles Labor Movement, 1911-1941.* Berkeley, Calif., University of California Press, 1963.

Pflueger, Donald H., *Covina: Sunflowers, Citrus, Subdivisions.* Pasadena, Calif., The Castle Press, 1964.

Pitt, Leonard, *The Decline of the Californios.* Berkeley, Calif., University of California Press, 1966.

Pomfret, John E., *The Henry E. Huntington Library and Art Gallery from Its Beginnings to 1969.* San Marino, Calif., Huntington Library Publications, 1969.

Pourade, Richard F., *The Glory Years*. San Diego, Calif., Union-Tribune Publishing Company, 1964.

Powell, Ruth and Chuck, *Chester Place*. Los Angeles, Historical Society of Southern California, 1964.

Raitt, Helen, and Wayne, Mary C., *We Three Came West*. San Diego, Calif., Toufa Press, 1974.

Renshaw, Patrick, *The Wobblies*. Garden City, New York, Doubleday & Company, 1967.

Riesenberg, Felix, *The Golden Road*. New York, McGraw-Hill Book Company, 1962.

Ritter, Ema I., *Life at the Old Amphibian Airport*. Santa Ana, Calif., Pioneer Press, 1970.

Robinson, W. W., *Los Angeles from the Days of the Pueblo*. San Francisco, California Historical Society, 1959.

————, *Panorama, a Picture History of Southern California*. Los Angeles, Title Insurance and Trust Company, 1953.

————, *San Pedro and Wilmington*. Los Angeles, Title Insurance and Trust Company, 1942.

————, *The Story of Pershing Square*. Los Angeles, Title Insurance and Trust Company, 1931.

————, *The Story of Riverside County*. Riverside, Calif., Riverside Title Company, 1957.

————, *The Story of San Bernardino County*. San Bernardino, Calif., Pioneer Title Insurance Company, 1958.

————, *The Story of San Fernando Valley*. Los Angeles, Title Insurance and Trust Company, 1961.

————, *The Story of Ventura County*. Los Angeles, Title Insurance and Trust Company, 1956.

————, and Powell, Lawrence Clark, *The Malibu*. Los Angeles, Ward Ritchie Press, 1958.

Rowsome, Frank, *Trolley Car Treasury*. New York, McGraw-Hill Book Company, 1956.

St. Johns, Adela Rogers, *Final Verdict*. Garden City, New York, Doubleday & Company, Inc., 1962.

Stanley, Norman S., *No Little Plans—The Story of the Los Angeles Chamber of Commerce*. Los Angeles, Southern California Business, 1956.

Steere, Collis H., *Imperial and Coachella Valleys*. Stanford, Calif., Stanford University Press, 1953.

Steffens, Lincoln, *The Autobiography of Lincoln Steffens*. New York, Harcourt, Brace & World, Inc., 1931.

Stein, Ralph, *The Treasury of the Automobile*. New York, Golden Press, 1961.

Stewart, Don M., *Frontier Port*. Los Angeles, Ward Ritchie Press, 1966.

Stimson, Grace Heilman, *Rise of the Labor Movement in Los Angeles*. Berkeley, Calif., University of California Press, 1955.

Stone, Irving, *Men to Match My Mountains*. Garden City, New York, Doubleday & Company, Inc., 1956.

Surface, George T., *The Story of Sugar*. New York, D. Appleton, 1910.

Swanner, Charles D., *Santa Ana, A Narrative of Yesterday*. Claremont, Calif., Saunders Press, 1953.

Swigart, William Russell, *Biography of Spring Street in Los Angeles*. Los Angeles, W. R. Swigart, 1945.

Symonds, John, *The Lady with the Magic Eyes*. New York, Thomas Yoseloff, 1960.

Talbert, T. B., *My Sixty Years in California*. Huntington Beach, Calif., *News-Press*, 1952.

Tompkins, Walter A., *Little Giant of Signal Hill*. Englewood Cliffs, New Jersey, Prentice Hall, Inc., 1964.

Tuchman, Barbara W., *The Proud Tower*. New York, Bantam Books, 1967.

Van Dyke, T. S., *Millionaires of a Day*. New York, Fords, Howard & Hulbert, 1890.

Vorspan, Max, and Gartner, Lloyd P., *History of the Jews in Los Angeles*. San Marino, Calif., Huntington Library, 1970.

Walters, L. L., *Steel Rails to Santa Fe*. Lawrence, Kansas, University of Kansas Press, 1950.

Warner, J. J., Hayes, Benjamin, and Widney, J. P., *An Historical Sketch of Los Angeles County*. Los Angeles, O. W. Smith, 1936.

Weaver, John D., *El Pueblo Grande*. Los Angeles, Ward Ritchie Press, 1973.

Welty, Earl M., and Taylor, Frank J., *The Black Bonanza*. New York, McGraw-Hill Book Company, Inc., 1956.

————, *The 76 Bonanza*. Menlo Park, Calif., Lane Magazine & Book Company, 1966.

Wharton, Edith, *The House of Mirth*. New York, Harper and Brothers, 1905.

Wheelok, Walt, *Angels Flight*. Glendale, Calif., La Siesta Press, 1966.

White, Gerald T., *Formative Years in the Far West*. New York, Appleton-Century-Crofts, 1962.

Willard, Charles Dwight, *The Free Harbor Contest at Los Angeles*. Los Angeles, Kingsley-Barner & Neuner, 1899.

————, *The Herald's History of Los Angeles City*. Los Angeles, Kingsley-Barnes & Neuner, 1901.

————, *A History of the Chamber of Commerce of Los Angeles*. Los Angeles, Kingsley-Barnes & Neuner, 1899.

Wilson, Neill C., and Taylor, Frank J., *Southern Pacific*. New York, McGraw-Hill Book Company, Inc., 1952.

Wilton, George, *The Cable Car in America*. Berkeley, Calif., Howell-North Books, 1971.

Workman, Boyle, *The City That Grew*. Los Angeles, The Southland Publishing Co., 1935.

Young, Nellie May, *William Stewart Young*. Glendale, Calif. The Arthur H. Clark Company, 1967.

The First 100 Years, the City of Los Angeles. City of Los Angeles, 1950.

Five Year Book of the Los Angeles Yacht Club. Los Angeles, Los Angeles Yacht Club, 1969.

The Founding of the Henry E. Huntington Library and Art Gallery. San Marino, Calif., Huntington Library, 1969.

History of Hollywood. First Federal Savings and Loan Association of Hollywood, 1970.

An Illustrated History of Los Angeles County. Chicago, The Lewis Publishing Company, 1889.

Los Angeles 1900-1961. Los Angeles, County Museum of Los Angeles, 1961.

Los Angeles Exchange. Los Angeles, Los Angeles Telephone Co., 1882.

Mr. Otis and the Los Angeles Times. Los Angeles, Typographical Union No. 174, 1915.

The Port of Los Angeles. Board of Los Angeles Harbor Commissioners, 1913.

Reports on the Organization of the Department of Public Works, City of Los Angeles. Los Angeles, Griffenhagen & Associates, 1949.

A Southern California Paradise. Pasadena, Calif., R. W. C. Farnsworth, 1883.

MANUSCRIPTS

Graves Manuscripts. A very large collection of letters, business papers and documents originally belonging to Jackson A. Graves, *Huntington Library.*

O'Melveny Manuscripts. The daily professional journals from 1891 to 1941 in annual folio volumes originally belonging to Henry W. O'Melveny, *Huntington Library.*

PERIODICALS

De Graff, Laurence B., "The City of Black Angels: Emergence of the Los Angeles Ghetto, 1890-1930," *Pacific Historical Review,* Feb. 1970.

Fries, Amos A., "San Pedro Harbor," *Out West,* Oct. 1907.

Gleason, Duncan, "The Lost Islands of San Pedro," *Sea Magazine,* June-August, 1951.

Guinn, James M., "The Great Real Estate Boom of 1887," *Annual Publications of the Historical Society of Southern California,* 1890.

Harrigan, Mildred, "Our 75th Year—Cunningham & O'Connor," *Cunningham & O'Connor,* 1973.

Hoffman, Abraham, "Jewish Student Militancy in the Great Depression," *The Branding Iron*, Mar. 1976.

Karson, Burton, "Music in California from Boom to Quake," *Performing Arts*, June 1970.

Loomis, Charles F., "Making of Los Angeles," *Out West*, Apr. 1909.

Mahoney, John C., "Cinema's Women at the Top," *Performing Arts*, Feb. 1974.

Miller, Lucille V., "Edward and Estelle Doheny," *Ventura County Historical Society Quarterly*, Nov. 1960.

Newmark, Marco R., "The Aviation Meet of 1910," *Quarterly of the Historical Society of Southern California*, Sept. 1946.

Osborne, Thomas J., "Claus Spreckels and the Oxnard Brothers," *Quarterly of the Historical Society of Southern California*, Summer, 1972.

Petersen, Eric Falk, "The Adoption of the Direct Primary in California," *Quarterly of the Historical Society of Southern California*, Winter, 1970.

Sievers, Michael A., "Malfeasance or Indirection," *Quarterly of Historical Society of Southern California*, Fall 1974.

"Los Angeles Railway," *Interurbans*, Dec. 1951.

"Our Bank—then and now," *UCB Banker*, June-July 1962.

"Prohibition," *Out West*, Oct. 1914.

"Scenes from Life on Board an Emigrant Train, 1883," from *Harper's Weekly*, *American West*, May 1975.

NEWSPAPERS

Los Angeles—*Examiner, Express, Herald, News (Semi-Weekly Southern News), Record, Star, Times, Tribune*.

New York—*Times*.

Pasadena—*Daily Star*.

Riverside—*Daily Press*.

San Diego—*Union*.

San Francisco—*Call*.

San Pedro—*News Pilot*.

Santa Barbara—*News-Press*.

Index

About the Author

Joseph S. O'Flaherty has been one of the pioneer senior executives of high technology companies (involving such things as transistors and solid state physics) during the last quarter-century in the United States. He was manager of the Hughes Aircraft Semiconductor Division for a number of years in the 1950s and then went on to found the highly successful Continental Device Corporation in 1958, later acquired by Teledyne. Currently, O'Flaherty is chairman of two companies—Matrix Science and Semtech. He serves on the boards of a number of organizations and is a former mayor of Rolling Hills, California. His deep interest in California history stems from the time of his graduate work at Stanford.